SIR CHRIS HOY

SIX-TIME OLYMPIC CHAMPION

HOW TO RIDE A BIKE

For Mum and Dad

An Hachette UK Company
www.hachette.co.uk

First published in Great Britain in 2018 by Hamlyn,
an imprint of Octopus Publishing Group Ltd
Carmelite House
50 Victoria Embankment
London EC4Y 0DZ
www.octopusbooks.co.uk

ISBN 978-0-60063-521-5

A CIP catalogue record for this book is available from the
British Library.

Printed and bound in Italy

10 9 8 7 6 5 4 3 2 1

Publishing Director Trevor Davies
Senior Editor Pauline Bache
Art Director Yasia Williams-Leedham
Special Photography by Chris Terry
Technical Illustrations by Beau and Alan Daniels
Design by Grade Design
Picture Research Manager Giulia Hetherington
Senior Production Manager Peter Hunt

All reasonable care has been taken in the preparation of this
book but the information it contains is not intended to take
the place of treatment by a qualified medical practitioner.

Before making any changes in your health regime, always
consult a doctor. While all the therapies detailed in this
book are completely safe if done correctly, you must seek
professional advice if you are in any doubt about any
medical condition. Any application of the ideas and
information contained in this book is at the reader's sole
discretion and risk.

FROM STARTING OUT TO PEAK PERFORMANCE

SIR CHRIS HOY

SIX-TIME OLYMPIC CHAMPION

HOW TO RIDE A BIKE

with Chris Sidwells

hamlyn

Sir Chris Hoy MBE is Great Britain's joint most successful Olympic athlete of all time, with six gold medals and one silver. Chris has competed across all disciplines of cycling, from BMX to mountain biking, to road, time trial and cyclo-cross, before specializing in track.

He won his first Olympic gold medal in Athens 2004 in the one-kilometre time trial. After this event was dropped from the 2008 programme, he took this in his stride and switched focus to three other track sprint events – the keirin, sprint and team sprint. He went on to win a gold medal in all three, becoming the first British Olympian in one hundred years to win three gold medals at one games.

Chris was voted 2008 BBC Sports Personality of the Year, and he was also awarded a Knighthood in the 2009 New Year Honours list. In 2012 at his home Olympic Games in London, Chris won his fifth and sixth gold medals – in the keirin and team sprint – becoming Great Britain's most successful Olympic athlete ever.

In June 2016 Chris added to his record list of achievements when he finished the world's most demanding motorsport endurance race, the Le Mans 24 Hours, on his debut. Chris was also a key part of the BBC TV's commentary and punditry team for the World Championships and the Commonwealth and Olympic Games.

CONTENTS

INTRODUCTION

In writing this book I want to help you maximize your enjoyment of cycling. The bicycle is a wonderful and adaptable thing. It's an easy to use fitness apparatus, an almost zero environmental impact form of transport, and cycling is a wonderful sport and pastime. The bicycle has also played a crucial role in social history.

Cycling was my career. It brought me Olympic gold medals and world titles, but I always enjoyed riding my bike for its own sake, and I still do. There is nothing so accessible, so invigorating as a bike ride in the countryside. It's the perfect way to sort out your mind and put any troubles in perspective while doing your body a lot of good.

But, like everything in life, there are mistakes you can make in cycling, and things you can do to improve the experience. This book starts by addressing those things. It will guide you through everything from buying a bike to techniques that will help you stay safe on the roads and improve your general cycling efficiency, thus increasing your enjoyment.

But once you are on the right path and have mastered the skills to get the most out of cycling, you will probably find it addictive. I did, most people do. So the next section looks at the world of cycling and the various challenges in it. There will be something there to inspire you, I guarantee it. Even

now, after my competitive cycling career ended in 2013, I have found a couple of cycling challenges that inspire me, and I am determined to do them.

Once you've picked a challenge you'd like to take on, something that excites and inspires you, maybe even scares you a bit, I'll show you how to set goals along the way to achieving it and how to plan for them. I'll show you how to train for them physically and mentally.

My recommended training sessions aren't complicated, even the most advanced ones. Using a power meter and/or heart-rate monitor can be useful but they aren't essential. I recommend training by feel as well as by numbers. It's a vital part of becoming familiar with the sensations of exercising at various intensities that improve your physical capacity.

Finally, the book addresses an area of sport that is so crucial to performance and yet seemingly shrouded in mystery – the power of the mind. How you think will have a

huge bearing on how you perform, not just on the big day of your chosen challenge, but on every session of every single day throughout your journey. I was very lucky to have access to some of the best coaching support in the world throughout the latter part of my career, to grasp the theory and put it into practice. However, it wasn't always the case. In the early years, prior to National Lottery funding and the investment in British sport over the past two decades, I had to find out the answers to my own questions on performance by trial and error. I even completed a degree in sports science in a bid to understand how I could train effectively to become a better cyclist. You may not have the luxury of a coach, but hopefully this book will help you grasp the theory and put it into practice.

Once you have the component parts you can build a path to achieving your first goal in cycling. That goal might be enough for you, or it could be a stepping stone to a greater challenge in the future. There is a whole world of cycling challenges you can pedal toward and, whether it's winning Olympic gold or finishing your first sportive, they are all worth the effort. They all give an extra buzz to riding a bike.

Throughout the book, you'll see QR codes (see right). I've demonstrated some of the less-well-known exercises and have given you some useful advice on areas of your cycling in videos that can be accessed by scanning the QR codes on your phone or tablet.

To access these, you'll need a QR code reader on your device. This can be downloaded through the App Store, Google Play or other app providers. Once the app is downloaded, scan the QR code to unlock exclusive video content.

I hope you enjoy this book. I really hope it is of value to you but, above all, I hope it helps you enjoy riding your bike even more.

TECHNICAL

BIKE FIT, SAFETY & SKILLS

1

1.1 BUYING THE RIGHT BIKE

There are many different types of bike on the market, but buying one need not be confusing. Just tell the sales person what type of cycling you want to do, and get the right size. Sizing is crucial when buying a bike as it affects the bike's weight, comfort, handling and riding position. The following will help you work out what size you need, but do not underestimate the experience and knowledge on offer at good independent cycle retailers. This is by no means a definitive list, it's just a guideline and, if in doubt, ask for help.

Scan this QR code to hear for tips and advice about setting up your bike and cycling kit on a budget.

WHAT KIND OF CYCLING DO YOU WANT TO DO?	RECOMMENDED BIKE
Rough off-road, trail centre, really wild off-road touring and camping.	Hard-tail mountain bike with 26-inch wheels for a closer connection with the terrain. Plus long-travel front suspension or even full suspension if you want to ride rougher terrain.
Downhill mountain bike racing.	Downhill specific, full-suspension mountain bike.
Cross country racing (XC).	Hard-tail or full-suspension XC mountain bike with 700 (or 29-inch) wheels for taller riders, or 650c (or 26-inch) wheels for shorter ones.
Riding trails and bridleways, in woodland or across heaths and moors. Cyclo-cross racing and off-road cyclosportives.	Gravel bike, cyclo-cross bike or mountain bike.
Road touring, bike camping, long-distance riding, Audax and other long-distance challenges.	Touring or Audax bike.
Commuting, general fitness and family riding.	Mountain bike, hybrid bike, fixie bike, basic road bike or an e-bike.
Road cyclosportives and entry-level triathlon.	Sportive bike or medium to high-end road bike.
Road races and circuit races.	Medium to high-end road bike.
Serious about triathlon.	Time trial bike.
Entry-level time trials.	Medium to high-end road bike with aero bars.
Serious about time trials.	Time trial bike.
Track racing.	Track bike.

MOUNTAIN

- Wide, knobbly tyres with durable wheels
- Often comes with suspension
- Wide range of gears for climbing and descending

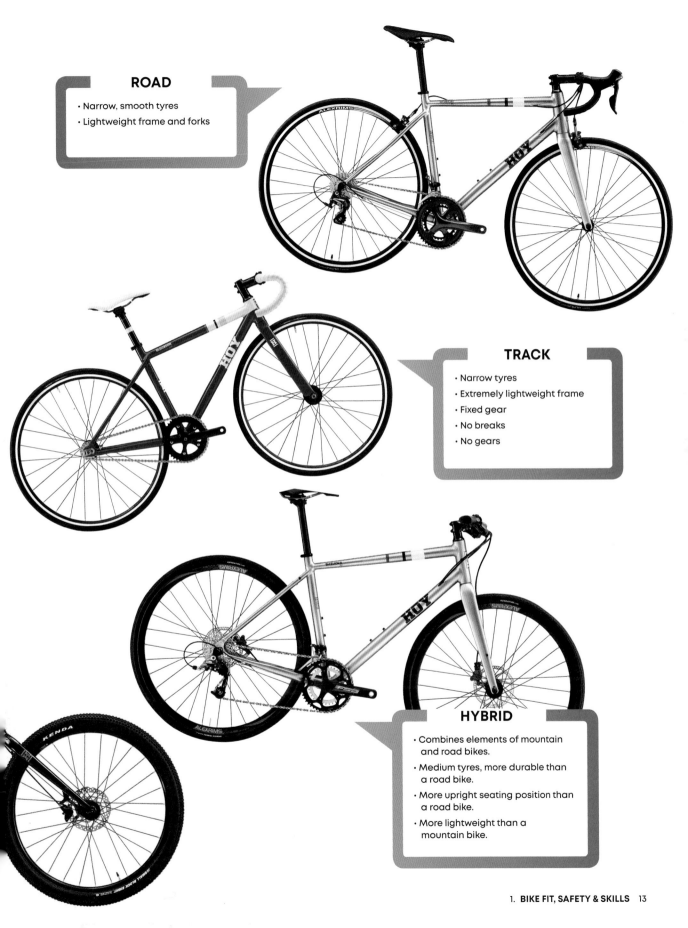

ROAD

- Narrow, smooth tyres
- Lightweight frame and forks

TRACK

- Narrow tyres
- Extremely lightweight frame
- Fixed gear
- No breaks
- No gears

HYBRID

- Combines elements of mountain and road bikes.
- Medium tyres, more durable than a road bike.
- More upright seating position than a road bike.
- More lightweight than a mountain bike.

SIZE MATTERS

When talking about the size of a bike we are referring to the size of its frame, and in particular the frame's vertical and horizontal dimensions, which are part of its geometry. Most adult bikes have standard size wheels, referred to as 700c (29-inch), but there are bikes with smaller wheels called 650c (26-inch), which are well worth considering for shorter cyclists. There are also bikes designed specifically for women, known as Women's Specific Design (WSD), which have 700c and sometimes 650c wheels.

Smaller wheels preserve good handling in smaller bikes because they keep the bike in proportion, so its handling characteristics are the same as a taller rider would experience on a bigger bike. Smaller wheels are safer for a smaller bike because, with a small frame, the pedals can sometimes overlap a 700c front wheel, which can be dangerous.

Once you have chosen the type of bike you need, how do you determine what size to buy? The answer is a sum of your overall height and the length of your inside leg, measured barefoot, from the floor to your crotch.

Take the above measurements – you might need help to do them accurately – and then consult the following tables for standard road bike (meaning the top tube is parallel to the floor), compact road bike (sloping top tube) and mountain bike sizes. For gravel or cyclo-cross bikes choose a size that is 1cm (½ inch) less than you would choose for a standard road bike.

These tables provide a generic set of measurements to help you decide which frame size you need. Always try a bike for size before you purchase it as dimensions can vary from brand to brand. If you are ordering a bike online, ensure you will be able to return it if it does not fit you correctly.

ROAD BIKE STANDARD GEOMETRY		
HEIGHT (CM/FT & IN)	INSIDE LEG (CM/IN)	FRAME SIZE (CM/IN)*
155–60/5'1"–5'3"	69–74/27–29	48/19
160–65/5'3"–5'5"	71–76/28–30	50/19¾
165–70/5'5"–5'7"	74–79/29–31	52/20½
170–75/5'7"–5'9"	76–81/30–32	54/21¼
175–80/5'9"–5'11"	79–84/31–33	56/22
180–85/5'11"–6'1"	81–86/32–34	58/23
185–91/6'1"–6'3"	84–89/33–35	60/23½
191–96/6'3"–6'5"	86–91/34–36	62/24½

* The way a frame is measured will vary between manufacturers so this is only a generic guide to frame size.

ROAD BIKE COMPACT GEOMETRY			ROAD BIKE STANDARD GEOMETRY WSD		
HEIGHT (CM/FT & IN)	INSIDE LEG (CM/IN)	COMPACT FRAME SIZE	HEIGHT (CM/FT & IN)	INSIDE LEG (CM/IN)	COMPACT FRAME SIZE
157–63/5'2"–5'4"	69–74/27–29	XS	152–7/5'0"–5'2"	66–71/26–28	2XS
163–70/5'4"–5'7"	74–79/29–31	S	157–63/5'2"–5'4"	69–74/27–29	XS
170–78/5'7"–5'10"	79–81/31–32	M	163–68/5'4"–5'6"	71–76/28–30	S
178–83/5'10"–6'0"	81–84/32–33	M/L	168–73/5'6"–5'8"	74–79/29–31	M
183–91/6'0"–6'3"	84–86/33–34	L	173–78/5'8"–5'10"	76–81/30–32	L
191–93/6'3"–6'4"	86–91/34–36	XL			

MTB OFF ROAD (HARD-TAIL)			MTB OFF ROAD (FULL SUSPENSION)		
HEIGHT (CM/FT & IN)	INSIDE LEG (CM/IN)	COMPACT FRAME SIZE (CM/IN)	HEIGHT (CM/FT & IN)	INSIDE LEG (CM/IN)	COMPACT FRAME SIZE (CM/IN)
147–52/4'10"–5'0"	66–71/26–28	33/13	163–70/5'4"–5'7"	71–76/28–30	35.5,3 8/14, 15
152–60/5'0"–5'3"	69–74/27–29	35.5, 38/14, 15	171–75/5'8"–5'9"	74–79/29–31	40.5, 45, 45.5/16, 17, 18
161–70/5'4"–5'7"	71–76/28–30	40.5, 43/16,17	176+/5'10"+	76–81/30–32	48, 51, 53.5/19, 20, 21
171–75/5'8"–5'9"	74–79/29–31	45.5, 48/18, 19			
176–80/5'10"–5'11"	76–81/30–32	51/20			
181–88/6'0"–6'2"	81–86/32–34	53.5/21			
189–93/6'3"–6'4"	86–89/34–35	56/22			

USEFUL KIT

I'll talk about cycling-specific clothing and other essentials later in the book, but initially I want to mention a very useful piece of kit that's worth buying early because it's a great training tool. I'm talking about turbo trainers. They help you to stick to your training programme when the weather is bad outside, and they also provide the control you need when doing specific and high-quality training sessions.

There are lots of turbo or static trainers on the market, including all-in-one machines, but although extra features such as a power meter for measuring power output are useful, they aren't essential. A simple turbo trainer that supports your bike and provides resistance to your pedalling is all you really need.

A turbo trainer will help you train during the winter or evenings when it's too dark outside. They're also great when it comes to specific workouts, such as sprint training and intervals.

1.1 BIKE SET-UP

Buying the correct size bike is the first step to enjoying cycling, the next is setting the bike up so it fits you perfectly. This is done by adjusting your three points of contact with the bike:

1. CLEATS
2. SADDLE
3. HANDLEBARS

This enables you to put all your power into the pedals while riding in an aerodynamic position. You might not attain your optimum riding position at first. Shortened muscles and injuries can prevent that, but there are exercises and techniques later in the book that will help you get there. It's best to put your bike on a turbo trainer when setting up your riding position because you have to check adjustments by pedalling. You can lean against a wall and back pedal, but it's not ideal. You also need somebody to act as an observer with some bike set-up steps.

1 FEET FIRST: CLEAT SET-UP

For most cyclists, bike set-up is a work in progress, which should be reviewed regularly until you achieve the perfect riding position. However, some things don't change and can be fixed now. Cleats attach to the soles of cycling shoes and connect with clipless pedals, where they are retained in a way that helps transfer your leg power with minimal loss.

Correct cleat position is the foundation of powerful pedalling. Too far forward and the foot and ankle become a weak link, unable to transfer the power of your legs efficiently. Set the cleat too far back and you lose potential power from the lower leg muscles, as well as flex from your ankle joints helping to spin the pedals quickly and smoothly.

Cleats should be set straight, and unless you know your pedalling is biomechanically perfect you should use a pedal/cleat combination that allows your feet a degree of sideways rotation during each pedal revolution.

Put your cycling shoes on and note where the widest part of each foot is on the outside edge of the uppers. Attach the cleats to the soles so the centre of the cleat lines up with the widest part. Cleats often have lines marking their centre to help with this.

Engage with the pedals and turn the cranks until they are parallel to the floor.

Dismount and move the cleat until the widest part is in the correct position, then fully tighten the cleat fixings.

1.1
Cleats should be fixed so that when engaged with the pedal, the pedal axle is directly under the widest part your foot.

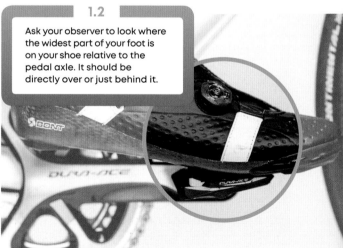

1.2
Ask your observer to look where the widest part of your foot is on your shoe relative to the pedal axle. It should be directly over or just behind it.

Sprinters like me tend to fix their cleats so that the widest part of their foot is just in front of the pedal axles, so less load goes through the ankle joint, which is an advantage when doing standing starts.

2 SADDLE HEIGHT & POSITION

Place your heels on the pedals.

Adjust the saddle up and down until your leg is fully locked with the pedal at the bottom (6 o'clock) position.

Next, ask your observer to stand behind you while you pedal in a very low gear quite slowly, or back pedal slowly, still with your heels on the pedals. The observer watches your hips, which should not rock up and down while you are pedalling. If your hips rock, lower the saddle bit by bit until they are dead level when you are pedalling.

Next up is the saddle position relative to the bottom bracket and the ground. As a starting point, set the saddle up parallel to the ground. Any adjustment either way should only be a degree or two maximum. Pointing the nose of your saddle downward too much to alleviate discomfort is usually a sign that the rest of the set-up is incorrect. »

2.1

The correct saddle height is when your leg is dead straight at the bottom of each pedal revolution, with the heel still on the pedal.

>> When setting up the fore/aft position, it's helpful to think of your thigh as a lever while the saddle acts as its fulcrum. As a rule of thumb, to get the most force from your thigh lever the saddle should be positioned so that your forward kneecap is directly above the forward pedal axle when the cranks are parallel to the floor.

You need a plumb line and an observer to help you set up your saddle position. For a standard riding position, which works for most riders on most bikes, drop the plumb line from the forward kneecap and ask your observer to see where it falls in relation to the pedal axle.

Keep checking until the kneecap and axle line up. When you've finished moving the saddle, check that it's level with a spirit level, first checking that the surface you are on is level too. Once all that's done, tighten the relevant bolts to fix your saddle in position.

2.2

If the kneecap is in front of the pedal axle, move the saddle backward. If your kneecap is behind the axle, move it forward.

Some riders, such as Tom Dumoulin (above), prefer to have their forward knee just in front of the pedal axles because of their pedalling style or the events they do. Aerodynamic time trial bikes and triathlon bikes are set up so their rider's forward knee is well in front of the forward pedal axle, but that is only because the whole geometry of those bikes, and their aerodynamic time trial handlebars, require a forward riding position.

3 HANDLEBARS

Handlebars are next, and the first thing to address is reach. There's a very simple test to see if you are too stretched or hunched up. Either position will compromise your power output.

You can do the test out on the road or on your turbo trainer. Ride enough to warm up and relax your muscles. Then hold your handlebars on the "drops" with straight arms.

If the handlebars obscure the front hub as you look down then your reach is perfect. If you can see the hub in front of the handlebars, the handlebar stem is too short. If the hub is behind the handlebars, the stem is too long.

Correction requires a longer or shorter handlebar stem. Use a tape measure to establish what length stem would see the handlebars cover the front hub, then buy it and have it fitted it to your bike or fit it yourself.

> ### 3.1
> Hold the bottom of the handlebars with your arms straight and look down at the point where the handlebars go through the handlebar stem.

Once you've finished adjusting them, make sure your saddle and handlebar stem are dead straight. That means lining up the saddle's longitudinal axis with your bike's top tube, and the stem's with the front wheel. Take care doing this, ask for a second opinion, and check after any adjustment. You must be millimetre perfect. Check alignment again if you have a crash on your bike, or even if it just falls over. Ensuring everything is in line on your bike is the first level of defence against injury in cycling. If anything is even slightly out of whack, the first you might know about it is a sore shoulder or a painful knee.

> ### i
>
>
>
> One of the keys to reducing drag is to reduce your frontal area when cycling. The main way to do that is by lowering your upper body when you ride, especially in conditions when you want to ride fast, because drag increases exponentially with increasing speed. Try holding the bottom of your handlebars, a riding position referred to as "on the drops".
>
> You might need to increase your core strength and flexibility before you can hold the drops comfortably for long periods. There are exercises in chapter 3 that help you do that, but for now, set your handlebars as low as you can reach comfortably. Then try to go lower as you get stronger and slimmer.

1.1 BIKE CONTROL

Bike control, or bike handling as it's often called, is a function of having the correct bike set-up and distributing your weight over the bike to match different situations and conditions. Good bike control means safer and faster cycling. On a bike with dropped handlebars you should vary your hand position according to conditions and terrain. Subtle shifts in how you distribute your body weight helps with bike control too. And no matter what you are doing, always be aware of what's happening ahead of and around you, so you can anticipate things and react accordingly.

DEFAULT HAND POSITION

Modern brake lever hoods are designed to be held, their ergonomic shape encourages us to ride on the hoods, so for most people that's their default hand position. You can get the power down while riding on the hoods, and can become aerodynamic by crouching down and keeping your elbows tucked in and bent at 90 degrees with your forearms flat.

However, the best position for descending and cornering is holding the bottom of the handlebars, the drops. Doing that lowers your centre of gravity, which helps you corner. But even more, it helps you keep a tight line through corners because holding the drops loads the front wheel, improving front tyre grip.

Watch Moto GP racing on television. That should convince you of the importance of loading the front tyre in corners. A good motor cyclist might control a rear wheel slide in a corner, but they can't control front wheel slides. That's because the rear tyre naturally has more load on it than the front, so more grip.

Holding the bottom of your handlebars has other advantages. You ride lower, so you're more aerodynamic without thinking about it, and holding the bottom of the handlebars is a very secure riding position. You fully grip the handlebars when you hold the drops, so hitting a bump won't knock your hand off the handlebars and cause you to lose control.

BRAKING & SPRINTING

Holding the drops also helps when you brake. Not only can you pull the brake levers with more force when holding the drops, but because the front wheel is loaded the front tyre has more grip.

So, ride on the brake lever hoods on nice flat straight roads, ride on them, too, when climbing, because that helps you breathe deeply and efficiently. However, when you need safe, precise bike control, when cornering, descending and riding over rough surfaces such as wet, slippery cobblestones, you should hold the drops.

It's also best to hold the drops for sprinting and for accelerating out of corners. Not just because you have better control, but because holding the drops gives you greater leverage. Also, your wrist joint is straight, so it transfers power efficiently.

Many riders will train hour after hour on the tops or hoods but find they spend a large proportion of the toughest parts of their races on the drops. It's always good to train as specifically as you can, and this applies to riding position too. If you don't ride a lot on the drops, doing so can feel strange at first. You could also have tight and/or weak hamstring and hip flexor muscles, which makes riding on the drops harder, but the hip flexor and hamstring stretches on pages 65–6 and the Romanian deadlift on page 86 will help you to rectify that.

SHIFTING WEIGHT

I see so many new cyclists just sitting on their bikes, holding the handlebars and pedalling. Effectively, their upper body is being carried by their bike, like static cargo, but you should be active on your bike.

You and your bike should work as one, so try to visualize that and always keep it in mind. Your bike is an extension of you. You can influence how it moves, not just by steering it but by moving your upper body to help you steer or descend, as well as flexing your arms to absorb bumps. Aim to think of yourself and your bike as one, and interact with the way it moves.

Riding on the hoods helps with comfort, but when you are sprinting or taking on corners, riding on the drops is always preferable.

The best bike riders in the world look efficient and graceful. Over years of practice they've mastered the art of how to position their bodies on the bike to match the terrain and environment around them.

1.1 FAST, EFFICIENT PEDALLING

Pedalling transfers the push and pull of your leg muscles into the circular motion of the pedals and cranks. Pedalling efficiently means powering the pedals through as much of each pedal revolution as possible with as little metabolic cost as possible, while doing so quickly and fluidly. You achieve this by having an awareness of which muscles power the phases of each pedal revolution, how your ankles flex through each one, and by being as relaxed as possible no matter how hard you are pushing.

THE PHASES

Imagine your bike's chainset as the face of a clock, and although I'm going to explain pedalling technique by referring to your descending leg and your ascending leg separately, you should always think of them working together.

So, the clock face. When the crank is at 12 o'clock, that's called top dead centre, and when it's at 6 o'clock, that's bottom dead centre. Your legs apply the greatest force from just after top dead centre, so from around 1 o'clock, to just before bottom dead centre, so around 5 o'clock.

Switch to a much lower gear than you need to practice pedalling quickly. This educates your muscles to contract and relax at the right time and improves ankle flexing. You can do it during any ride. Relax your upper body. Think of a swan, still and serene above the water, but pedalling forcefully and smoothly below. Or a good drummer keeping up a fast beat without strain.

i

MOUNTAIN BIKERS

Mountain bikers came top in a study to find out which cyclists put force into the greatest proportion of each pedal revolution. It was thought this was because racing on uneven surfaces means they have to get the most from each pedal revolution. They also become very good at matching the power they put into the pedals to the surfaces beneath their wheels, which smoothes their pedalling by avoiding peaks and troughs of force being applied. Try some off-road riding to vary your routine and improve your pedalling technique.

FIXIE RIDERS

Riding a bike with a fixed gear forces you to complete more pedal revs in a ride than you would on a bike with a freewheel. Pedalling a fixed gear also teaches the muscles of your ascending leg and torso to relax, because the direct drive of a fixed gear provides feedback. If your coordination is poor, you will bounce up and down in the saddle when pedalling a fixed gear quickly. Focus on controlling and eradicating the bounce and it forces your muscles to relax.

1.3

It was once thought that good cyclists pulled upward with their ascending leg, but that only happens at low pedal revs, when climbing out of the saddle or accelerating from low speeds, for example. What really happens is they relax the muscles in their ascending leg so they don't resist the force applied by their descending leg. Pointing your ascending foot downward during the latter part of the power phase helps relax the muscles in your ascending leg, as does visualizing the different leg muscles contracting and relaxing.

1.2

Gradually lifting your heel through the second half of the highest power phase (3 down to 5 o'clock) brings your calf muscles into play. It also puts your foot in position to go through the bottom dead centre and start ascending.

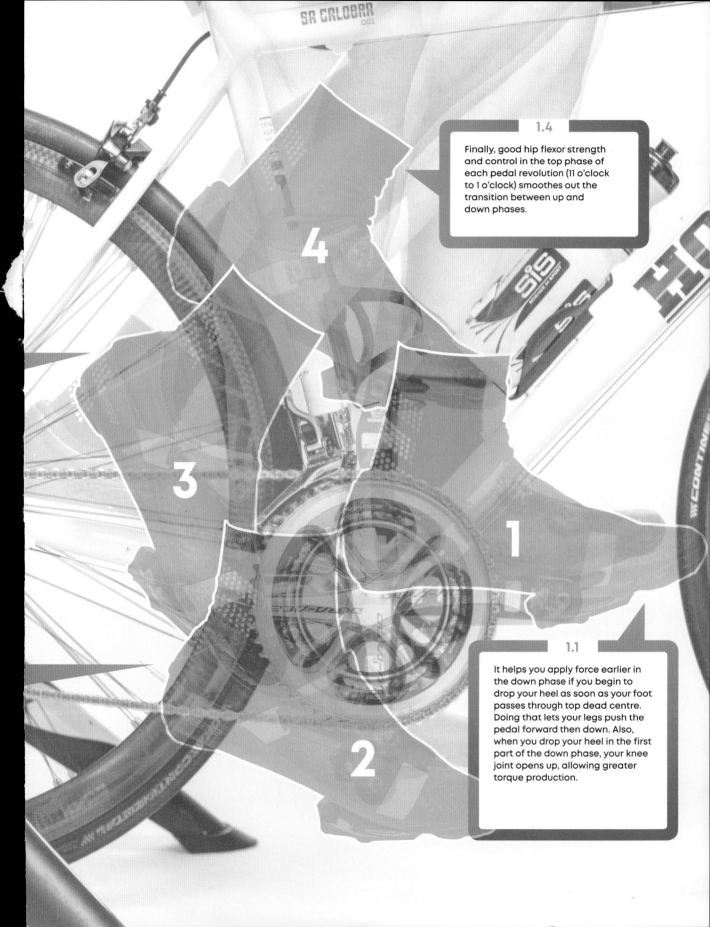

1.4

Finally, good hip flexor strength and control in the top phase of each pedal revolution (11 o'clock to 1 o'clock) smoothes out the transition between up and down phases.

1.1

It helps you apply force earlier in the down phase if you begin to drop your heel as soon as your foot passes through top dead centre. Doing that lets your legs push the pedal forward then down. Also, when you drop your heel in the first part of the down phase, your knee joint opens up, allowing greater torque production.

1.1 SAFE & EFFECTIVE CORNERING

Never take risks when cornering. Cycling performance improves drastically by carrying speed through corners, but that's achieved through skill, not by taking risks. Going faster than you or the laws of physics can handle is inefficient and dangerous. Practice your technique all the time, but stay in your comfort zone when cornering. Over time you will become more skilfull, and that's the safest and surest way to get quicker.

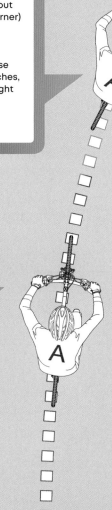

2 ENTRY

Make sure the inside pedal, so the right pedal for a right bend, is up before entering a corner, and you are pressing down on the outside pedal. Keep your body low. This helps you guide your bike around the corner, following the line you choose.

The most efficient way to corner, if traffic allows, is to start a bit out from the corner direction, cut across the apex (the middle of the corner) and come out wide. That's the best way to preserve speed, but conditions, especially on the road, don't always allow that.

If there is traffic behind or in front of you, corner conservatively, keeping well across to your side of the road. Also, the line you choose through any corner should avoid potholes, puddles and damp patches, if possible. Brake to reduce speed while you are travelling in a straight line, and shift to a lower gear to reduce strain on your legs when accelerating out of the corner.

1 SPEED JUDGMENT

The first thing to consider when approaching a corner is your entry speed. Entry speed depends on how tight the corner is and what the surface is like. Tight corners require lower entry speeds, as do corners with loose, wet or muddy surfaces, or corners with adverse cambers, meaning the surface slopes away from the direction you are turning.

You must do your braking before going into a corner because your bike tracks straight under braking. Once in the corner your bike still tries to track straight if you brake, which means you end up taking a wider line around the corner than you otherwise would. You might even end up on the other side of the road, or go off it completely. So, avoid braking in a corner.

And that's not all. Different forces act on your bike when you are cornering, so the chances of a wheel locking if you brake are much higher, as are the chances of crashing when either wheel locks. Get your braking done early and with practice you'll get better at judging when and how much to brake.

3 EXIT

Keep your inside knee up, press down on your outside pedal and lean your bike into the corner, aiming it through the line you've chosen. If you feel your wheels slip, press harder on the outside leg and move your upper body over it too. Do not brake.

Continue freewheeling through the corner and only start pedalling when you are going in a straight line. Shifting to a lower gear before the corner makes accelerating out of it easier. It also helps to get out of the saddle for the first few pedal revs to help you pick up speed quickly.

Practice these techniques through every corner you can, but always within your skill level. In time you'll get a feel for cornering, a feel for how your bike is handling, and you'll soon be able to corner quickly and safely, which has a positive effect on your average speed for rides. Plus, cornering skilfully is a huge advantage in races.

Your pedal position is important when cornering. Here, Chris Froome keeps his inside pedal up and his body arched over the drops in order to retain as much control as possible.

RIDING IN LIVE TRAFFIC

This diagram depicts the ideal trajectory of the rider on a closed road with no other traffic. If you are cycling on a road with oncoming traffic ensure that you only take the apex of the corner on your side of the road, this will be less extreme than that shown on this diagram but will keep you safe from oncoming traffic.

1.1 RIDING IN TRAFFIC

Riding a bike in traffic can be intimidating, but it doesn't have to be, not if you get some basic skills down and follow the advice here. Always know the law as it affects cyclists in your country, and obey it. Other road users can get really wound up when they see cyclists flouting the law, and you just don't need their animosity. Be aware of everything going on around you, and riding with music or a phone in your ears is not a good idea in traffic. Ride confidently, interacting with other road users and always ride defensively.

Scan this QR code to hear for advice on starting to commute by bike.

1 SKILLS

Before riding in heavy traffic, you should be comfortable with the following skills:

- Riding and manoeuvring at very low speeds without wobbling around
- Riding in a straight line with one hand off your handlebars
- Looking around and behind you on either side while still riding in a straight line

Bike control at slow speeds requires practice, so if you are new to cycling, or riding in traffic is a bit of a bogey for you, pick a very quiet stretch of road, or a park, and ride as slowly as you can while doing left and right turns, and even U-turns, without wobbling. Always cover your brake levers when riding in traffic, and it's better to ride in a more upright position than you normally would. The brake lever hoods are the best place to hold the handlebars on a dropped handlebar bike.

Practise riding one-handed while signalling your intentions to other road users with the other arm. Slightly flex and relax the arm holding the handlebars, so if you hit a bump your elbow joint absorbs the shock and it doesn't knock you off course. Finally, looking behind is easier if you take the arm on the side you are looking off the handlebars. Practise all of the above, and once you are comfortable with it, you are ready for traffic.

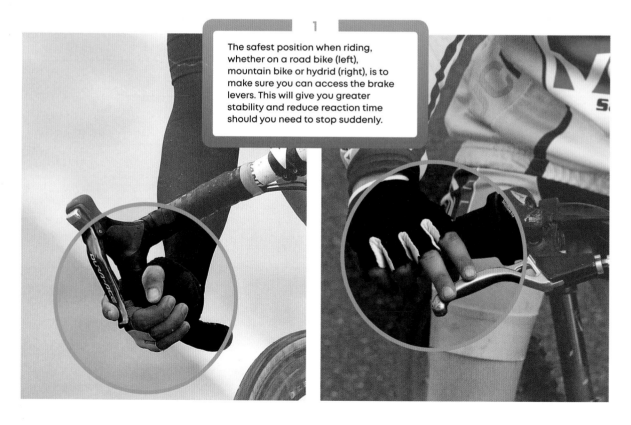

1

The safest position when riding, whether on a road bike (left), mountain bike or hydrid (right), is to make sure you can access the brake levers. This will give you greater stability and reduce reaction time should you need to stop suddenly.

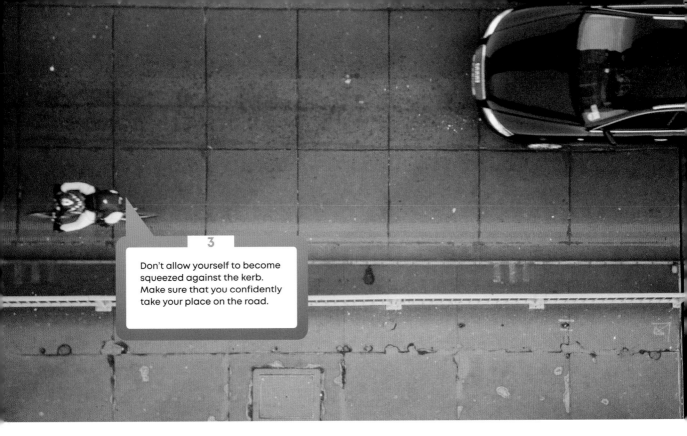

3

Don't allow yourself to become squeezed against the kerb. Make sure that you confidently take your place on the road.

2 MANOEUVRES

Always look behind you before making any manoeuvre, including every time you set off into traffic. It's important to know where other vehicles are around you, and only move when there's enough space in the traffic flow for you to do so. However, don't be timid. If there is space, signal what you are about to do and do it. Letting others know and understand your intentions, then acting on them, if it's safe to do so, is crucial when cycling in traffic.

Turning into a street on the side you are riding is simple. Just signal your intention and keep close to the kerb going around the corner. Never turn inside another turning vehicle. Turning into a street on the opposite side of the carriageway is done in two stages. First, well before the turn, look behind you and, if there is space, signal your intention to move out to the offside of the carriageway, and then move. Continue assessing oncoming and following traffic, then when there's a gap, signal your intention to turn, and then turn.

3 GO WITH THE FLOW

It's often safest to ride near the kerb, and always use cycle lanes if they are there, but don't allow yourself to be squeezed against the kerb. Ride at least 45cm (18in) out from it, and never undertake stationary cars. Somebody could be getting out of the car and hit you with an opening door. Try to keep up with the traffic flow. If other vehicles are moving slower than you, and if it's safe to do so, overtake them on their offside, but signal what you intend to do before doing it.

Be aware of heavy-goods and mass-transport vehicles, such as vans, lorries, trucks and buses. Their driver's view, both front and rear, is restricted. Don't undertake them, don't assume anything and always remember that if you cannot see their mirrors there is no way their driver can see you.

4 EYE CONTACT

This is a crucial thing for all cyclists to develop. Try to make eye contact with other road users all of the time, and especially before you manoeuvre. You need to know they've seen you before you do anything. If in doubt, wait for them to move.

Finally – although you shouldn't have to do this because other road users should be aware of cyclists, and the big emphasis in cycling safety should be on improving driver awareness and road layout – it's best to assume the worst and do everything you can to be as visible as possible. Lights, bright and reflective clothing, and anything else you can wear or put on your bike that increases your visibility is worth doing.

Cyclists take up very little road room compared to other vehicles, which is why cycling is one of the solutions to urban congestion, but until driver awareness and education improves, as well as road layout and construction, you should make yourself as visible as possible against everything else that's going on.

1.1 RIDING IN A GROUP

Group cycling is great. By sharing the pace you can ride faster than you might on your own, so developing group skills is useful for cyclosportives. It's a fundamental part of road and track racing, and it's also good fun, an experience shared and heightened because of it. Group riding helps some people train because they feel committed to the group, while others work harder in a group than they would on their own. There are skills and etiquette for group riding, most of which help the group stay safe.

SIGNALS

Signals are given verbally or manually and they are made to warn the rest of the group about potential hazards. There are three signals you need to know, which vary locally, but are based on the following.

The main hand signal is a quick downward point to the right or the left, to make those following you aware of oncoming road hazards such as potholes or drain covers. Whoever makes the signal will deviate their path to avoid the hazard, so be aware of that too.

"CAR UP" & "CAR BACK"

If somebody shouts "car up" it means a vehicle is coming in the opposite direction. If someone shouts "car back" it means a vehicle is coming up from behind. These warnings are not given all the time, there would be no point on busy wide roads, but they are used on narrow roads or where the group has moved out toward the centre of the road to avoid an obstruction on the inside.

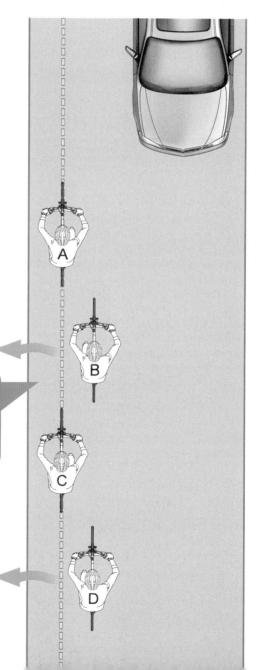

"Car up" indicates a vehicle approaching in the opposite direction. Be aware and move inward if necessary.

"INSIDE"

"Inside" coming from a rider in front of you means there's a parked car or other hazard on the inside of the road, so the group moves out to avoid it. If you hear "inside" from behind it means someone is trying to move forward in the group on your inside. Be wary of that one in races, because experienced riders often shout "inside" as a trick to make you move over and they pinch your place in the line.

FOLLOWING

Don't follow directly behind the rider in front because if the group slows abruptly your front wheel could touch their rear wheel and you might crash. Ride a bit to one side, but don't overlap their rear wheel.

When you first ride in a bunch you inevitably focus on the wheel you are following, but as you grow more confident you should judge the distance you are behind the rider by focussing on their upper body. That makes you more aware of what's happening ahead of you. If you're always looking down you miss a lot, including potential hazards.

And no matter how skilfull you are and how much experience you've had of group riding, always allow more space between you and the rider in front of you if you aren't familiar with how they ride. They might ride erratically or not give signals, and in that case you will need a bit of space to react.

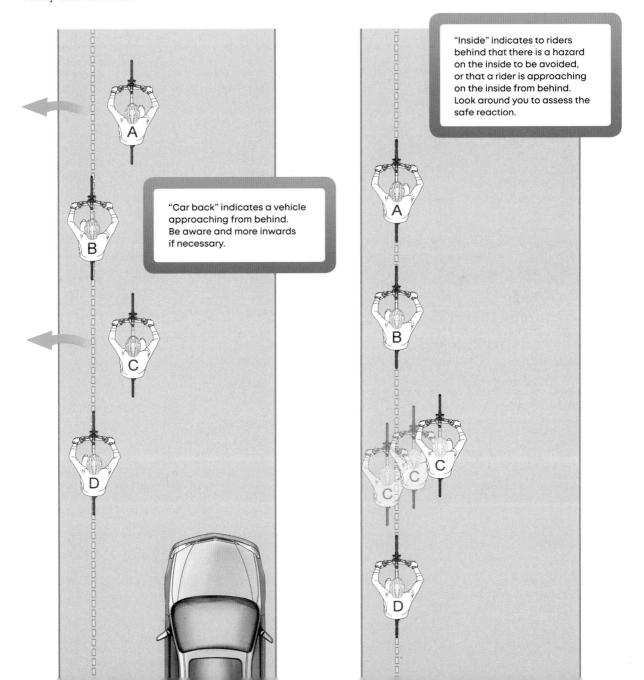

"Car back" indicates a vehicle approaching from behind. Be aware and more inwards if necessary.

"Inside" indicates to riders behind that there is a hazard on the inside to be avoided, or that a rider is approaching on the inside from behind. Look around you to assess the safe reaction.

1.1 AERODYNAMICS IN GROUP RIDING

One of the key skills when riding in groups at competition level is working together as a team to set the pace and be aerodynamically efficient. The rider at the front bears the full brunt of the wind and so it's a position in which you need to take turns with other members of the group. A smooth transition into and out of the front position is crucial to make the most of your group rides and not disrupt the group.

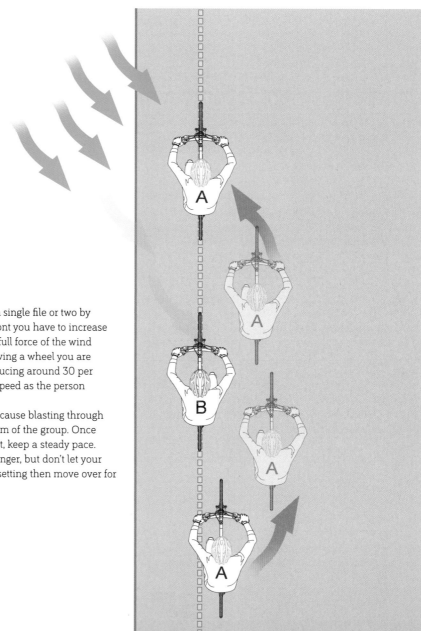

THROUGH & OFF

Whether the group is going along in single file or two by two, when it's your turn to hit the front you have to increase your effort because you will get the full force of the wind and aerodynamic drag. When following a wheel you are sheltered from this and will be producing around 30 per cent less power riding at the same speed as the person leading the group.

Increase your effort smoothly, because blasting through then slowing down upsets the rhythm of the group. Once you've assumed position at the front, keep a steady pace. If you feel strong, stay at the front longer, but don't let your ego take over. Do your turn at pace setting then move over for the next riders to take their turn.

GETTING OUT OF THE SADDLE

An important point to remember when moving from sitting in the saddle to riding out of the saddle is don't stop pedalling between the two. It's surprising how many people do stop. They stop pressing down on the pedals just for a moment as they get out of the saddle. It isn't a problem when riding alone on the flat, but if you are riding in a group your bike will go backward relative to the riders following you. And that can cause crashes. So, whenever you get out of the saddle, push a bit harder with your down leg during the transition.

CLIMBING TECHNIQUE

The best general climbing position is sitting in the saddle, pedalling a gear you can keep on top of, with your upper body raised to help you breathe deeply. Holding the tops of dropped handlebars and sticking your elbows out, nothing too exaggerated, assists deep breathing too.

Switch to holding the brake lever hoods and lower your upper body if you need more power on the pedals, because you can pull with your arms from that position.

Holding the brake lever hoods is the best position for climbing out of the saddle. Pull up with your arms as well as pushing down with your legs, and vary where your upper body is over the bike. If the surface you are riding on is dry and hard, you can get right forward. If it's slippery or loose, keep your upper body further back so its weight loads your rear wheel for better grip.

SHIFTING GEAR

Always keep pedalling when you shift derailleur gears. Stay in the saddle when you shift the chain between chainrings, because if you are making a big effort and the bike is moving from side to side a chainring shift can derail the chain.

On the whole though, modern gear shifters, particularly the electric ones, allow you to make good shifts in all sorts of conditions. Just have a bit of mechanical sympathy with your gear shifts, the same as with braking, and don't try to do the impossible.

It's best to avoid extreme chain positions too, so your large chainring with your largest sprocket, or vice versa, should be avoided. With a double chainring think of your gears as two sets of ratios, and make your big gearing decisions by shifting between chainrings. Then fine tune your selection by shifting between your sprockets. With triple chainrings you have three sets of ratios, and with one life is much simpler, although you may find bigger gaps between ratios. This isn't a problem with off-road bikes, but can be with road bikes.

Use lower gears up the first few hills on very hilly rides to conserve energy. It's a good idea to have one extra low gear ratio for super steep sections of hills, or if you start struggling a bit. It's your "get out of jail" gear.

Whether you're in or out of the saddle, changing gears is an important part of climbing. Through experience you'll learn when and where to shift gears, but try to avoid extreme chain ratios.

1.1 FAST, SAFE DESCENDING

Riding downhill fast is speed for free. It doesn't require fancy equipment or a new bike. It doesn't require any extra effort or an increase in fitness, it just requires a bit of skill and technique. Fast descending is crucial in races, and it improves your performance in cyclosportives. Plus, and this is a bit counter-intuitive, it's safer than going downhill slowly. Your bike is more stable at speed than it is if you go cautiously downhill with your brakes on. And, like many things in cycling, descending fast and doing so safely is all about good technique.

GET LOW

Because drag increases exponentially with speed, to go fast downhill you need to reduce the drag acting on you as much as possible. Hold the bottom of your drop handlebars and bend your elbows to get your upper body as low as possible. Tuck your elbows into your sides and, if you are freewheeling, do the same with your knees, keeping your cranks level and parallel with the floor. If your bike has flat handlebars, miss out the first step.

Lowering your upper body pushes your bottom toward the back of the saddle, which gives good weight distribution, helping to stabilize your bike. This is very helpful with the next thing you have to consider when descending fast – applying your brakes.

Picking your line through corners on a descent is key, but braking techniques are just as important. The overall aim is to descend as quickly and as safely as possible.

BRAKING ZONE

Raise your upper body before you brake, but keep your hands on the bottom of your handlebars as this is the most stable position from which to pull your brake levers. Raising your body also acts as a sort of air brake. Slowly squeeze on your brakes, front first, then rear if you need more braking power.

The steeper the descent, the more you can apply the rear brake, but it should still be front before rear. Never use one brake full on; if you need more braking power divide it between the two brakes, front before rear, but apply more rear the steeper the descent. Always brake in a straight line.

Never descend faster than is safe for the conditions. If the descent is bumpy or wet you should descend slower than if it is smooth and/or dry. You also need to be extra careful and smooth in applying your brakes when it's wet or the road surface is loose, and brake much earlier than you would if it were dry.

Finally, don't overlook pedalling if the descent is not so steep. This works wonders for improving your average speed and costs very little energy. But always stay within your comfort zone and keep within your capabilities while still trying to push the envelope by focusing on good technique.

REMEMBER

- **Use eye protection** – clear lenses in low light and sunglasses when the sun's out. Getting hit in the eye by a fly when you are descending hurts, and it can quickly turn into a drama.

- **Stay loose** – if the descent is very bumpy, reduce your speed and raise your bottom out of the saddle slightly. This lets your legs get involved in absorbing shocks. Keep your weight back over the saddle when you do this, though.

- **Keep tyres and bike in good order** – regularly check that everything on your bike is safe and secure. Pay attention to bottles, as they should fit tight in their cages because they can bounce out on descents. You don't want to be tripped up by your own drinks bottle.

- **No extreme positions** – I know the Tour de France pros do it, but they are racing on closed roads for big stakes. Cycling is their job, bike control is second nature to them, and they still crash and get hurt. They assess the risks against the benefits and make a decision, a decision you don't need to make. On top of that, studies have shown they don't go much faster than they would with a normal low descending position.

Peter Sagan is a master at descending at speed, mixing skill and bravery with plenty of technique. Here he even lowers his body over the top tube, creating even less drag in order to improve his speed. Unless you're a supreme descender or racing on closed roads, that move isn't recommended.

1.1 PERFORMANCE PEDALLING

So, there's a lot more to efficient pedalling than just pushing down with your legs. It's about maximizing the force you can apply and minimizing the resistance through each revolution. This can be achieved simply by spending more time on your bike and by doing the simple drill set out on pages 22–3. At British Cycling we took it even further with special equipment designed to help this process.

THE CLOWN BIKE

This was an ergometer set up in the lab used purely to improve pedalling coordination at extremely high cadences. The "clown bike", as it was affectionately known, had very short cranks (110–30mm/4¼–5¼in), which meant that higher than normal peak cadences could be achieved. We used the clown bike to do unloaded sprints, meaning there was hardly any resistance when pedalling. Each session was short and sweet, typically four to six bursts of maximal cadence pedalling, lasting a mere handful of seconds, with peak cadences reaching 320rpm-plus. These high-cadence efforts were performed simply to improve the efficiency of the contraction/relaxation coordination of the muscles. This drill made pedalling at normal track sprint cadences of around 150rpm seem like slow motion in comparison and really helped to improve our technique and pedal much more smoothly back on the track.

HUMAN FERRARI

Fast pedalling is at one end of the sprinting spectrum, and at the other is how much torque you can apply. A lot of torque (force applied in a rotational direction) is required to get you moving from a standing start in a sprint time trial, but it's also needed to power the initial jump in match sprints, or the various bursts of speed in a keirin. The ability to produce high levels of torque has become even more crucial over the past decade as the gear ratios that sprinters race with have increased dramatically. It's also crucial because of the bigger gears sprinters use now.

It's amazing how much torque a top sprinter produces. Our peak torque at extremely low cadence, from 0–30rpm, was 700Nm-plus, which is more than a Ferrari V8 engine does. And just to underline the fact that the ascending leg plays a vital role in applying torque at slower revs, in tests

we did during the 0–50rpm phase it was found that the ascending leg provides almost 35 per cent of the instantaneous torque of each revolution.

MOBILITY

Good mobility of the hips improves general cycling performance, but it's crucial for sprinters, who must produce power at high cadence in extreme low riding positions. If you are stiff around the hip and lower back then you limit the joints' range of motion, which has an adverse effect when you get low to improve aerodynamics and/or when cadence increases.

What happens in a case of poor mobility is the rider's knees come out laterally, their weight shifts forward on the saddle and their hips and whole upper body start bobbing up and down. Not ideal.

Also, if mobility around the hips is lacking, when you make maximum sprint efforts, either in or out of the saddle, there's a risk of pedalling becoming much less fluid, particularly as fatigue sets in. This is most noticeable in events such as the one-kilometre time trial, when the massive amounts of lactate start a degree of breakdown in muscle function. It's remedied by focussing on pedalling in circles, and maintaining correct form on the bike. This can be seen in many other sports too, such as when the shoulders, neck and arms stiffen up in athletes as they fatigue over the last 20 or so metres of a sprint.

BIOMECHANICS

Minimizing the distance between the pedal axle and the sole of the foot is important from a biomechanics perspective. It's also important in making you feel more closely connected to the bike. The shoes and pedals Team GB used were the nearest to this ideal we could get.

Finally, crank length has an effect on pedalling. Shorter cranks allow increased maximum rpm, while longer cranks increase torque, which helps when using higher ratios (and when accelerating). Sprinting has changed at elite level over the past decades and sprinters are now using much bigger gears and, as a consequence, longer length cranks than they used to.

1.1 **IMPROVING AERODYNAMICS**

More speed for free can be found by improving your aerodynamics.
I've said this before, but it's worth repeating because it's so important in
cycling. The biggest resistive force when cycling on the flat is aero drag.
The relationship between speed and power isn't linear, it's exponential,
which essentially means that the faster you go, the more important your
aerodynamic efficiency will become.

THINK LIKE A FISH

Water is denser than air, so fish have even bigger problems
moving at speed than we do. Their solution was to evolve into
a thin and very smooth shape that slips through the water
with ease. They do this by having a small frontal area, an overall
shape that allows water to flow freely over them as they swim,
and a smooth surface.

So, just like a fish, you should try to reduce your frontal area
and do things that help the air flow smoothly over you. There's
a lot of bike kit that's aerodynamic, but the biggest factor
creating drag in the rider–bike package is you, so although aero

kit helps, it's nowhere near the whole solution. Your frontal area
is the space you take up when viewed from the front, so
lowering your upper body and keeping your elbows in line with
your body, drastically reduces your frontal area.

Adopting that position also helps smooth the air flowing
over you. Lowering your upper body reduces the size of eddy
currents created as you ride along. Eddy currents act as a
dragging force, which effectively try to pull you backward.
If you sit up high, the eddy currents you create are bigger,
and therefore stronger, than if you crouch down low.

Even the smallest changes,
such as lowering your upper
body and tucking in your
elbows, will significantly
reduce drag and make you
ride faster.

FURTHER REFINEMENT

Baggy clothes create drag, which is why cycling jerseys and shorts are made from stretchy materials and are cut to fit close. It's a good idea to pull zips down when you're going uphill to help regulate temperature, but when your speed picks up, such as on the flat and especially when going downhill, doing up open zips stops your jersey acting like a parachute.

Adjust your position according to your speed. The most aerodynamic position on a road bike is where your back is flat and your chest is parallel with the ground. Your hands are on the bottom of your handlebars or the brake hoods, with your elbows bent at 90 degrees, your arms in line with your hands and your forearms parallel with the ground.

However, it's no good riding like that if you are uncomfortable, or if you feel you aren't getting all your power into the pedals. The position I'm recommending is an aerodynamic ideal. If it's comfortable then great, and there are drills (see below right) to help you achieve it. Strive for this position within your limits while working to improve it. A low position takes practice before you are truly comfortable with it.

Finally, never tilt your head down to improve aerodynamics. It's dangerous because it reduces your forward and peripheral vision, plus cycling helmets are designed so they are aerodynamic when your head is up with your eyes looking straight ahead. If you put your head down, your helmet actually creates extra drag.

MARGINAL GAINS

The following are small things you can do, but, like everything with improving aerodynamics, they can have a big cumulative effect. In a wind tunnel test I had once we discovered that if I raised my head by 1cm (less than ½in), my drag increased by 2.5 per cent. Not much you say, but in a 5–6-hour cyclosportive that 2.5 per cent could add more than seven minutes to your finish time. Anyway, these are some things you could do to cut drag without buying new kit.

- **Establish a stretching programme** – focus especially on the muscles of your shoulders, hamstrings, hip flexors and upper and lower back to help you get low.
- **Build core strength** – this is important to increase comfort when you get low.
- **Ensure a good riding position** – get this checked by a specialist.
- **Reduce frontal area** – for example, if you are carrying only one drinks bottle put it in the down tube cage not the seat tube, because then it'll be at an angle which will reduce its frontal area.
- **Reduce clothing drag** – be careful how you pin your number onto your jersey in races. Use extra pins to get it as flat as possible. (We used spray adhesive as well as the mandatory pins.)

Comfort is vital, especially on long rides, but even a small improvement in your riding position will reap huge rewards. Keep your body relatively low, your hands on the drops and your elbows bent.

DRILL

- On a flat straight road, rest your hands on the top of the brake lever hoods
- Bend your elbows to 90 degrees
- Try to bring your elbows in line with your hands
- Keep your forearms parallel to the floor
- Start by riding five minutes in that position
- To progress, do another five minutes later in a ride
- Build up to four stretches of five minutes like this, then increase the duration that you ride in this position until it's your default riding position on flat straight roads

1.1 PERFORMANCE AERODYNAMICS

With all the aerodynamic bike kit available, and all the solid research and design that goes into developing it, it's easy to give too much attention to the bike in the rider–bike package when thinking about performance aerodynamics. However, the bike is only about ten per cent of the whole package, especially with regard to frontal area, a crucial factor in aerodynamics. The rider is where the biggest aerodynamic gains can be made, and it can be done without spending a single penny on fancy carbon fibre bits!

KEEP THEM IN

You've got to be aware of your riding position during high-intensity efforts and do your best to maintain your aerodynamic shape, no matter how hard you are trying. We've all done it. I had a tendency to stick my elbows out when sprinting flat out, but that creates a huge amount of extra drag. I developed this bad habit early in my career and fought against it until the day I retired. Just how much extra drag sticking my elbows out caused was brought home to me one day in a wind tunnel.

We used the wind tunnel for testing specific things, such as a position modification or clothing or equipment update, but we were always given some free time to try things of our own. It's amazing what subtle changes in your position can do to your drag numbers. For example, the difference between having my thumbs up or down on the handlebars made a measurable difference in drag.

The real challenge isn't finding an extremely aero position – anyone can do that – it's finding one that you can still pedal efficiently in. There's a sweet spot where power output and improved aerodynamics meet. Caleb Ewan on the road and Matthew Glaetzer on the track have extremely aerodynamic sprint positions (partly due to their body shapes), but not everyone would be able to emulate them and still get all their potential power down. It's important to be functional.

The current trend in pursuits and time trials is to get your hands as close in front of your face as possible to reduce the air hitting the front of your body, as Charlie Tanfield is doing here. In events where aerobars are used, the riders try to manipulate the position of their hands to break the air.

Getting a professional bike fit can help you get an aerodynamic position on your bike, but if you do it yourself one good place to start is the limit of the Union Cycliste Internationale (UCI) rules. The rules are there to prevent extreme positions, such as the ones Graeme Obree famously created, which threatened to change the way all elite cyclists would ride their bikes in the future. So if you start from the UCI-imposed limits, you are, theoretically, getting all the aerodynamic position advantage allowed. Then work back from the limits to find the bike set up that best suits your body. This is a very good source for interpreting the rules for track cycling: https://www.momnium.com/track-bike-setup-within-uci-rules/

KIT

The best track sprinters can do 76–77km (47–8 miles) per hour in a flat-out sprint, and that means pushing a lot of air out of the way. The riders have to create as little drag as possible, so a lot of thought goes into the design of bikes and clothing.

The leading edges of the rider–bike package (the front wheel and handlebars, the rider's helmet and skinsuit, especially around the shoulders and arms) are crucial as they hit the clean air first and dictate what happens to the air next.

Leading edges need to be as narrow as possible to make the smallest possible hole in the air, and smooth as possible to part the air while disturbing it as little as possible. But once past the leading edges, air is pushed around the sides of the rider–bike package and encounters shape changes.

Shape changes can cause turbulent air, which generally is to be avoided because the detached air travels much slower, producing a pressure difference, which is drag. So the first effort in skinsuit design was to eliminate fabric wrinkles and creases. However, the modern cutting edge skinsuits also have panels, raised stitching or seams, dimples or even different textured fabric to trip up some air and cause controllable turbulence. A lot of effort goes into trying to present air to the rider's legs in a way that means they cause less turbulence than they otherwise would.

A narrow band of turbulence over certain parts of the rider–bike package can cause a greater amount of air around it to keep its streamline flow. This is desirable because it reduces aerodynamic wake. Aerodynamic wake has the effect of trying to pulling the rider back, almost like suction.

All cyclists aim to be as aerodynamic as possible when racing. However, there is a trade-off between aero-efficiency and biomechanic efficacy. In pure sprint events (such as the keirin pictured here) there is a slight compromise in aero position in order to allow the maximum power and torque to be produced.

1.1 WHAT TO WEAR IN SUMMER

I'll avoid being too prescriptive, but you should always wear cycling-specific kit on your training rides. Okay, on short commutes or family rides, everyday clothing is fine, but for longer rides, adventures and training sessions, proper cycling kit works best, and in races it's mandatory. Modern cycling clothing enhances the joy of riding. It keeps you comfortable, improves your performance and helps you stay cool in summer and warm in winter.

HEAD FIRST

Starting from the top, modern cycling helmets are light and well aerated, and some models reduce aerodynamic drag. I would advise wearing a helmet when cycling, but I don't believe it should be compulsory. Based on data from other countries compulsory helmets for cyclists appear to have little effect on our overall safety, whereas improvements in road layout, the provision of more segregated cycle lanes and increased driver awareness statistically make cycling much safer.

Helmets definitely reduce the effects of most head impacts, and they certainly prevent minor bumps being more serious. I've been grateful I was wearing a helmet several times. However, they must fit properly and be worn correctly. Here's how to ensure your helmet does both.

A well-fitted helmet touches all your scalp without squeezing it. When you move the helmet slightly, without securing the straps, your scalp should move with it. Once you've got a helmet that fits, adjust the straps so that when fastened, and you are standing, the bottom of the helmet is parallel with the floor.

Some cyclists choose to wear an old-fashioned cotton cycling cap instead of a helmet to keep the sun off their head. Obviously this doesn't offer protection against knocks though. However, worn under a helmet, it is great for keeping rain and road spray out of your eyes on wet days.

JERSEYS & SHORTS

I'd recommend wearing a light short-sleeved undervest in summer, unless it's very hot, when it's good to undo your jersey zip to prevent your core temperature rising. Cycling undervests are made of material that moves sweat away from your skin, in a process called wicking, to stop a build-up of sweat.

There are cycling jerseys of all sizes, colours and types. They are part of the history of cycling as well as its present. If you race, depending on the rules the race is under, you'll probably have to compete in your club or team jersey, which should be close-fitting to improve aerodynamics. There are loose-fit jerseys and it's up to you what your ride in, but if performance is your goal then close- but well-fitting jerseys are best because they reduce drag.

The same goes for cycling shorts. Most competitive riders go for Lycra because it fits closely and reduces drag, but there are loose-fit shorts made from other materials that are great

to wear. They are cut for cycling and have a cycling-specific liner, just like Lycra shorts do. You can get gender-specific shorts and jerseys too, so women don't have to wear cycling kit designed and cut for men anymore.

SHOES, SOCKS & GLOVES

Competitive cyclists should go for light, supportive shoes with as thin and stiff a sole as you can afford. Thin soles allow your foot to be as close to the pedal surface as possible, which improves biomechanics, but thin-soled cycling shoes are expensive because of the cost of materials needed to make them thin and supportive.

Cycling shoes fasten through many different mechanisms, which all work well. Recently a large number of manufacturers have returned to using simple laces. You can customize and micro-adjust how tight your shoes hold your feet with laces, which is good, but you are stuck with however tight you've done them up throughout your race, whereas you can adjust other fasteners on the fly.

Wear cycling-specific socks because they are made from wicking fabrics and have thin soles to ensure good contact with your shoes. Other sports socks aren't really suitable because they tend to have thick or even cushioned soles.

Cycling-specific gloves called track mitts improve your grip on the handlebars and soak up sweat, so there's no danger of your hand slipping and compromising safety. Their cushioned palms prevent blisters. They don't stop your hands radiating heat, but they can help prevent injury. When you fall, you tend to put your hands out, which then meet the ground palms down. Grazes are inevitable, but track mitts help prevent them.

ADD-ONS

Arm and leg warmers, basically close-fitting sleeves and leggings to fit under cycling jerseys and shorts, are great for spring and autumn rides, and on cooler days in summer. A light rainproof jacket that fits into a jersey pocket is a good idea too. You can get cold very quickly in the rain, but make sure the jacket is made from a breathable material, so you don't accumulate loads of sweat inside when wearing it.

Sunglasses will keep the glare out of your eyes and stop dust or pollen from irritating you in the summer.

An undervest, coupled with a short-sleeved cycling jersey makes for a great combination in summer, spring or autumnal conditions.

The right headgear is vitally important when you're riding on the roads or on the track. Use the adjustable straps to make sure that your helmet is secure but not too tight.

Close-fitting cycling shorts will reduce drag.

It's an advantage to have shoes that allow you to adjust their tightness on the fly in a race.

1.1 WHAT TO WEAR IN WINTER

Winter in the colder zones of our planet can be challenging for cyclists, but advances in cycling clothing mean that riding outdoors is possible and comfortable in all but sub-zero conditions. And I don't recommend riding outdoors on the road when the temperature drops below zero, not because of the cold necessarily, but more because of the danger of skidding on ice.

HEAD START

Ventilation in cycling helmets can be a disadvantage on cold days, but a thin cycling skull cap, or even a cotton cap under your helmet will help insulate your head. Skull caps have the advantage of being made from breathable material, and they often cover your ears too, which is a good idea when it's cold. Buffs are adaptable bits of kit, which can be used as a scarf, a face mask or in place of a skull cap.

Long-sleeved tops are best for winter. They range from thin, simple ones for autumn days to thicker, quite technical tops for really cold weather. A long-sleeved undervest makes a great base layer, then if you have at least one thin and one thick long-sleeved top, you'll learn by trial and error which one to wear over your base layer to match the weather conditions. Sometimes it might even be necessary to wear a thin mid layer, but the thicker tops, often called outer layers, are so good nowadays it doesn't happen very often.

You can dress in layers when it's cold to trap a layer of warm air near the skin. However, modern materials trap warmth within their fabric, which is why we don't need to wear as many layers of clothing as we did.

You can buy rainproof outer layers, but the thin rain and windproof top you have for summer will probably work just as well worn over your winter ensemble if the weather is wet.

Gilets are very useful. They are perfect to wear over thinner long-sleeved tops on days when it's cold but not quite so cold that you need a thick winter top. They also work if you set off riding early in the morning, when it's colder, because you can take the gilet off and carry it in your pocket when the day warms up. Gilets fill in the gaps between your other clothing.

LOOK AFTER YOUR LEGS & FEET

Protect your legs with leg warmers, just like the ones you use on cooler summer days, or bib-tights when it's colder. Bib-tights are like bib-shorts, but have long legs and are usually made from slightly thicker material than leg warmers.

A lot of people are tempted to ride in shorts when it's cold, but it's not a good idea. Your muscles work best when they are warm, and cold muscles are prone to injury. It's the same with ligaments and tendons. Knees are particularly vulnerable in cold weather, as tightness in the muscles around them can alter the way your kneecap tracks within the knee joint, and that can irritate both the kneecap and the tissue around it.

FEET & HANDS

Cold feet are bad news. Start with some cycling-specific winter socks that have thermal characteristics. Normal cycling shoes are okay, although you can buy winter shoes. Most riders use overshoes. They are usually waterproof or water resistant, and they stretch over your cycling shoes. Neoprene overshoes work well, although they wear out quickly if you walk about in them too much.

Neoprene is also a good material for cycling gloves, especially if you are riding in wet conditions. Neoprene traps warmth coming from your hands, and although it lets some water in, that water heats up and forms a protective warm layer. Waterproof gloves are also available, as are thermal ones. Wool gloves are good too. It's a matter of choice, but unless you ride a lot in a very cold climate, avoid bulky gloves because they make braking and shifting gear more difficult.

BE SEEN

In the dark winter days, it's especially important to be visible on your bike. A lot of bike kit comes in black these days, so make sure your clothes have lots of reflective bits on them to alert people to your presence.

---

i

LONGER BIKE RIDES

On longer bike rides you want to strike the right balance between making sure you have the kit to be self-sufficient and not weighing yourself and the bike down. I take all my kit in my back pockets but a saddlebag would be another option. For a long bike ride make sure you have:

- Tyre levers
- Phone
- Multi-tool
- Food/gel

- Pump/CO_2 canister
- Inner tube
- Money

A WORD ON HELMETS

There has been much debate over bike helmets and, at the end of the day, whether you wear one or not is a personal choice. I always wear one, as do my kids, because I like to stack the odds in our favour in case of any sort of fall, but I'm not convinced by the argument for compulsory helmet use. In every place where helmets have been made compulsory, there has not been an increase in overall cycle safety and the effect has often been to reduce cycling numbers dramatically (which, given the health problems caused by sedentary lifestyles and air pollution, is far from ideal). The helmet debate also detracts from the bigger picture, which is that the most significant change we can make to reducing serious cycling injuries and fatalities is to improve road infrastructure, reduce speed limits and invest in cycling awareness education for all road users.

Orange or clear glasses are also a good addition to keep the rain and mud out of your eyes in bad weather.

Multiple layers trap warm air near to the skin.

Neoprene traps warmth but is still breathable.

Overshoes will keep your feet dry.

BIKE CARE

2

1.2 **SAFETY CHECKS**

Bikes are durable but their parts still wear out, which, as well as causing the inconvenience of mechanical breakdown, can compromise safety. Regular safety checks will ensure you replace parts when they are worn and keep your bike running smoothly, avoid equipment failures and keep your training on course. You save money too, because worn parts are not only weak links but they play a significant role in wearing other parts out.

Carry out the following checks at least once a week and replace any worn parts as soon as possible. It's worth buying a spare pair of brake pads, a tyre, inner tubes and brake cables. There are lots of good bike repair books that show you how to fit them.

BRAKES

Check brakes for wear by pulling on the front and rear brakes and pushing your bike forward. If either wheel revolves then its brake pads are worn. There is usually an adjuster on the brake levers or callipers to take up some wear, but when that's no longer effective the brake pads must be replaced.

If your bike has rim brakes you should check the brake pads for uneven wear, which is a sign that the pads are not contacting the braking surface evenly. The effectiveness of your brakes is compromised if that happens, because not all the pad's surface is used. Fit new pads and adjust your brakes correctly.

For bikes with cable brakes, check the cables and cable outers for signs of splitting or fraying. Frayed inner cables can snap, leaving you without brakes. Change the cables before you ride again. Worn or split outers reduce the effectiveness of your brakes by allowing dirt in to wear and potentially clog the cables. Change a split outer as soon as you can.

For bikes with hydraulic brakes, check the exposed length of each brake hose for splits or any sign of leaking brake fluid. The evidence might be as little as a single droplet or a smear of fluid on the hose. Leakages need immediate attention from qualified mechanics, who will replace the brake hose with a new one, unless you are confident you can do it.

TYRES

Check the whole circumference of each tyre for bulges, cuts or splits. Tyres showing any of those symptoms or any form of distortion could blow-out. If you spot any of these failures, replace the tyre immediately.

Look closely at the tread of both tyres for signs of wear. If the tread is worn the tyre has lost structural strength and can break down. A tyre that has been in a skid and developed a flat spot can also be dangerous. Once again, replace the tyre if you see these signs.

WHEEL RIMS

Look for evidence of deep scoring on the rim of your bike's wheels. Rim brakes gradually wear out the rims, especially if you ride off-road or in poor weather conditions. Eventually, the rims will fail and you could crash. Cracks around the nipples of the spokes where they join the rim are a danger sign too. Replace the rim if you see these signs. And always have broken spokes replaced.

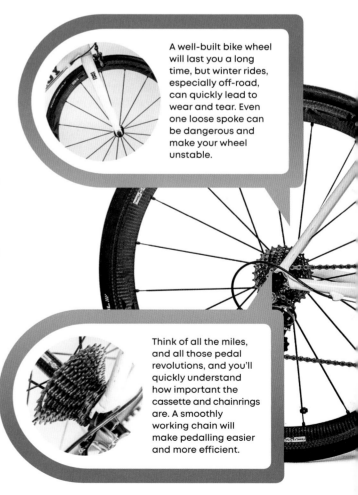

A well-built bike wheel will last you a long time, but winter rides, especially off-road, can quickly lead to wear and tear. Even one loose spoke can be dangerous and make your wheel unstable.

Think of all the miles, and all those pedal revolutions, and you'll quickly understand how important the cassette and chainrings are. A smoothly working chain will make pedalling easier and more efficient.

FRAME & FORKS

Regularly check for cracks and dents, and inspect underneath the frame too. Take the wheels out of the frame regularly to check around the drop-outs, where the wheels are held in the frame and forks. Always touch up scratches or flaked paint on steel frames with enamel paint.

CASSETTES, CHAINS & CHAINSETS

Check for worn or missing teeth on chainrings and cassettes. One sign of cassette wear is the chain jumping when you apply pressure to the pedals, especially if you are out of the saddle. Replace chainrings or sprockets as soon as you see this sign.

Chains wear out, although they wear out less often if you clean and lubricate them regularly. You can buy a gauge that measures chain wear accurately; follow its instructions and replace the chain when recommended.

Modern chains working across 11 sprockets have a lot to do, so they require regular replacement. A top professional road racer might need a new chain every 1,000 miles, and somebody who trains hard and competes should change an 11-speed chain at least every 4,000 miles. Replacing a chain before it gets worn saves wear on sprockets and chainrings.

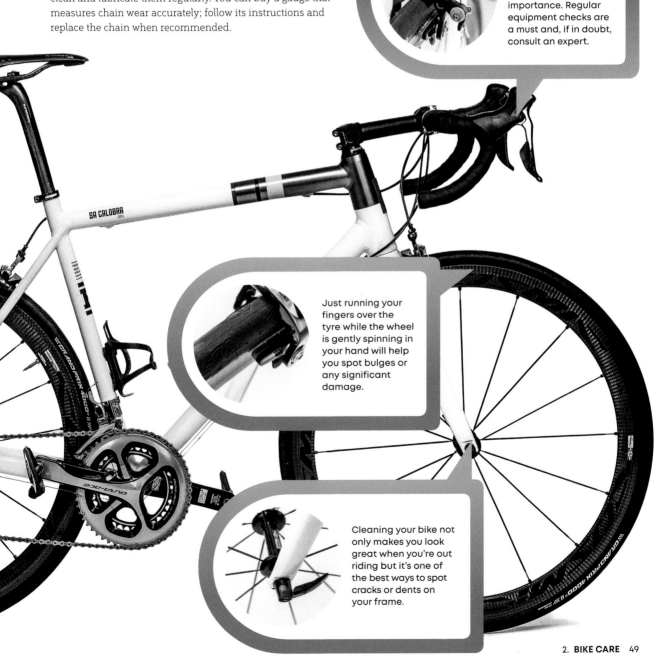

Whether you're competing in a race or just riding to work, brake reliance is of paramount importance. Regular equipment checks are a must and, if in doubt, consult an expert.

Just running your fingers over the tyre while the wheel is gently spinning in your hand will help you spot bulges or any significant damage.

Cleaning your bike not only makes you look great when you're out riding but it's one of the best ways to spot cracks or dents on your frame.

1.2 **CLEANING YOUR BIKE**

Bikes are resilient and dependable provided they are cared for. Although sealed bearings proliferate on bikes today, and they require much less maintenance than they once did, the drive-train – that's the chainset, chain, cassette and gear shifters – is still exposed. Water gets in and can corrode parts, and grit sticks to lubricants forming a grinding paste that can wear out moving parts.

Removing old lubricant and grit from your bike's drive-train is one practical reason for regular bike cleaning. Another is the opportunity that cleaning gives you to check your bike, as detailed on the previous two pages.

Finally, a clean, well-maintained bike is a joy to behold and to ride, and it's dependable. It allows you to get on with your training without interruptions. So follow this step-by-step guide to cleaning your bike, it's quick and easy to do.

YOU WILL NEED

- A hose or a bucket
- Access to hot and cold water
- Some different sized, stiff-bristled brushes
- Degreaser
- Sponges
- Some form of cleaning agent, bike-specific preferably, and lubricant

1
Hang your bike up, if possible, or if you have a work-stand, place it on that. Remove both wheels then wash any excess dirt off the frame and wheels with a hose or warm water.

Top tip
Always try to get someone else to do it!

SHIMANO

2
Spray the chain and cassette with degreaser. Then, with a stiff-bristled brush, work the degreaser into the chain links, applying more degreaser if required. Do the same with the teeth on the chainrings, the front and rear mechs, and the cassette sprockets, using plenty of degreaser and brushing hard.

3

Scrub the chain with hot soapy water. Use a specific chain-cleaning brush to get the best results. The idea is to remove as much old lubricant from the chain's surface as possible. Scrub the front and rear mechs also.

4

Let the chain dry then lubricate it, making sure to get good coverage. Hold a cloth behind the chain to prevent lubricant spraying all over the place. Spray a little lubricant on the rear mech's jockey wheels.

5

Use hot soapy water, or a proprietary frame cleaner, to clean the rest of the bike. Work the cleaner inside the frame angles, and over the handlebars, brakes and brake levers, the pedals and the insides of the brake calipers, underneath the saddle, under the bottom bracket, and around the cable guides. Then scrub the cassette and wheels with hot soapy water as well.

6

Rinse the frame and wheels with water – you can use a hose for this step. Then dry the frame with a soft cloth and check the other components, including tyres, for wear or damage.

7

Polish gives your frame an extra bit of sparkle. Take care not to get polish on the brake pads. Wipe the tyre treads and sidewalls with a dry cloth and put the wheels back in the frame, taking care to secure them well.

1.2 WINTERIZE YOUR BIKE

These steps will help you to prepare your bike for the rigours of winter, for riding in a wet climate and if most of your riding is done off-road. Grit and sand thrown up by the wheels combines with lubricant to form a grinding paste on any moving parts. Water and salt, which is often used to treat roads where ice is likely to occur, will corrode metal parts. Regular cleaning and replacing old lubricant helps prevent damage, but preventing as much grit, sand, salt and water reaching the delicate parts of the bike in the first place helps even more.

SPRAY PROTECTION

Spray-protection devices shield you and your bike in wet weather. When you ride along a wet road your wheels pick up water, the rear wheel sprays it up your back and the front onto your legs. It's even worse in a group if you are following somebody with no mudguards, because their rear wheel sprays water right into your face. This is not too bad in summer, although water coming up off roads can carry germs, which you end up swallowing. Seriously, cyclists have got ill through this.

Spray protection comes in many forms, from simple flaps that clip onto saddles to full mudguards that bolt to the bike's frame. Saddle flaps and short guards that clip onto the bike's seat post will block a lot of spray from the back wheel. There are also guards that clip to the frame and are secured in place with tie-wraps, which catch spray coming off the front wheel.

Clip-on spray catchers are great for summer conditions because you can add and remove them as and when you need to, but full mudguards provide the most protection from spray. There are two types: mudguards that bolt to custom eyes on the bike's forks and rear drop-outs, and temporary mudguards that fasten to the seat stays and fork blades and are thin enough to fit race bikes. Modern race bikes do not usually have mudguard eyes.

WEATHERPROOFING THE DRIVE-TRAIN

Clean your bike's chain in winter as often as you do in summer, plus after every wet ride, which is good practice at any time of year. Apply the same light lubricant that you use in the summer, so it works down into the chain and coats everything, then apply a heavier lubricant over the top to prevent everything washing off quickly.

Dribble oil on the pivots around which the front and rear mechs move. Use a heavier, wet oil instead of the oil you would normally apply during the summer. Every time you dribble oil like this, first flush out the old oil by dribbling some degreaser on the pivots and letting it sink in for a few minutes.

CLEANING & LUBRICATING THE PEDALS

Apply heavier, wet oil to lubricate the retention mechanism of clipless pedals after treating the moving parts with degreaser. The heavier oil will not wash off as easily as dry oil. Regularly clean off old oil with degreaser and apply new oil in order to prevent the accumulation of grit and the consequent increase in pedal wear.

PROTECTING WEAK SPOTS

If you ride a lot in a very wet climate, it might be worth taking some extra steps to prevent water from damaging your bike.

The point where the seat post enters the frame can be a problem, especially on bikes with steel or aluminium frames, because moisture getting in this joint will cause corrosion and can eventually bond the frame and seat post together. To prevent moisture getting in, mark the point on the seat post where it disappears into the frame, then remove the seat post from the frame. Pull a piece of narrow road bike inner-tube over the frame. Insert the pin through the inner-tube to the point where you made a mark, and secure the tube in place with a tie-wrap.

You can also buy waterproof headset covers, which you might consider if you have an older bike from the days before modern A-headsets were fitted, and you ride a lot in the wet. The protectors go over the headset without removing any components and are held in place by Velcro.

In an ideal world you'll have a winter bike with mudguards and a summer bike without. (Although in the UK the weather often takes a turn for the worse, even in the summer.) As you can see, I'm not practising what I preach regarding overshoes and mudguards in bad weather here!

Clipping in and out of your pedals needs to be seamless and without stress, and a build-up of dirt and grit can slow down your pedal action and erode the mechanism.

PHYSICAL

STRENGTH & CONDITIONING FOR CYCLISTS

3

2.3 CORE STRENGTH

You need a strong core otherwise pushing down on the pedals with your legs would lift and twist your body, which wastes energy. To get all your power into the pedals your core must provide a solid platform for your legs to push against. To illustrate this, imagine sitting on the floor and pushing a heavy weight away from you with your legs. Would it be easier with no support behind you or with your back against a solid wall? A strong core is your wall. It ensures that all the push from your legs goes straight down into the pedals, with no lift or side-to-side motion.

WHAT IS YOUR CORE?

Core describes the muscles at the centre of your body. It includes the big one, the notorious six-pack *rectus abdominis* muscles at the front, the erector muscles of your lower back, the sheets of muscle that circle your midriff like a girdle, the much smaller but very important muscles in your spine and the muscles that help to stabilize your hips. They must all be strong for a solid core to perform correctly.

However, injury, strain, sitting at desks and life in general mean that some of the smaller muscles are not used consistently. They lose strength and condition, and larger muscles take over, which causes imbalances that can

manifest in pain. This can lead to a negative effect on your cycling, mobility and health. A strong core doesn't just make you a better cyclist, it gives you a better life.

There are lots of exercises to help strengthen and condition your core. Some use equipment such as a Swiss ball or resistance bands, and they are excellent, but I've chosen five effective exercises that don't require equipment. I've also included an advanced exercise that requires a weighted barbell, to help you get to the next level of core strength.

Remember, core strength must keep pace with your fitness because the fitter and stronger you get, the more power you've got for the pedals.

CORE STRENGTH PREPARATION
ENGAGE YOUR TA

TA stands for *transverse abdominis*, and it's the innermost sheet of muscle in your abdomen. It's crucial to engage this muscle in every core exercise you do in order to get the best effect from it, but engaging your TA is a core exercise in its own right, and one you can do anywhere.

Commit to learning this while standing upright first and then, once you're familiar with the move, you can engage your TA in any position for any exercise. Doing so underpins all other core exercises, as well as lifting weights, yoga, Pilates and stretching. Critically, engaging your TA also improves your cycling. When you get used to engaging your TA during exercises, start doing it when you ride. It will feel odd at first but keep practising. It will soon become second nature, and you will ride faster.

- To engage your TA, pull your navel back toward your spine.
- Keep breathing in and out while pulling your navel back.
- Hold it for 20 to 30 seconds, then repeat three times. You'll quickly get a feel for it.
- Then engage your TA when you do any of the following exercises.

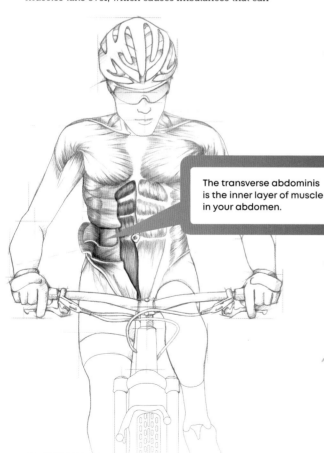

The transverse abdominis is the inner layer of muscle in your abdomen.

CORE STRENGTH 1 FRONT PLANK

Planks engage your core as one.

- For the front plank, lie face down, supported on your toes and elbows. You should have your forearms in front of you, shoulder-width apart.
- Raise your hips off the floor and hold, with your head, hips and feet in one line. Start counting 101, 102, 103...and see how long you can hold this position.
- Let your middle sink slowly when you can't hold it any longer, and record your count. You've got a number to beat next time.

Top tip
If you aren't training with somebody else, use a mirror or video yourself doing the exercises to ensure you are doing them correctly. Most people can't tell that they are doing an exercise correctly while they are doing it. Correct form is key.

1.1

CORE STRENGTH 2 SIDE PLANK

- Lie on your left side, supported on your left elbow and forearm with your forearm in front of you.
- Raise your hips until they are in line with your head and feet. Count 101, 102, 103...and again, see how long you can hold it.
- Lower your hips slowly when they start to dip, and then do the same on your right side. Don't do a longer count on one side than the other, even if you can hold it, as this will create imbalance.

2.1

CORE STRENGTH 3 CRUNCH

- Lie on your back with your knees bent, arms crossed over your chest and hands next to your shoulders.
- Slowly curl your head, then shoulders, then chest, up and forward. Imagine your spine as a string of pearls being raised one vertebra at a time from your head toward your hips.

3.1

Top tip
Do not use your hips or momentum to crunch. This must be a controlled movement using your abdominal muscles.

3.2

- Hold at the top, then return to the lying position one vertebra at a time.
- Try and do ten crunches at first, but always with correct form.
- Never sacrifice form for extra reps on any exercise.

CORE STRENGTH 4 LATERAL SIDE CRUNCH

4.1

- Lie on your back with your knees bent and your arms straight by your sides. Ensure that your feet are far enough away from your body for you to feel the effort.
- Slowly lift your shoulders and mid-back off the ground, vertebra by vertebra, reach your right hand forward toward your right ankle and tap your heel.
- Lower with control.
- Repeat, aiming your left hand toward your left ankle. Try ten crunches on each side for starters.

CORE STRENGTH 5 LEG RAISE

5.1

- Lie on your back with your arms by your sides. Ensure your back is flat to the ground and your legs are straight. Keeping them straight, raise your legs to about 30cm (1ft) off the ground and hold for 10 seconds. Ensure you core is engaged as you lift your legs.
- After 10 seconds slowly lower your legs to the floor. Repeat three times for each set.
- Do four sets with a 10 second rest between each set. Gradually lower the position to which you lift your legs on each set. The closer your legs are to the ground the harder this exercise is.

CORE STRENGTH 6 (ADVANCED) BARBELL ROLL-OUT

- Start on all fours, ideally on a raised surface as shown, with an Olympic barbell (with full-sized plates on either side) in front of you. It doesn't matter how much weight is on it.

6.1

Scan this QR code to see a video showing correct form for the barbell roll-out.

- Grab the barbell with both hands in a wider-than-shoulder-width grip and slowly roll it forward as far as you can.

6.2

- Roll until your hips are fully extended and your body is parallel to the floor. Ensure your movement is slow and controlled through the whole exercise.

- Slowly roll the barbell back toward your knees, initiating the move by contracting your abdominal muscles. Focus on raising and lowering your hips up and down rather than going forward and backward.

- Make sure you hinge from the hip, both on the forward and backward rolls.
- To progress, simply increase reps.

2.3 RESISTANCE TRAINING – WHY YOU SHOULD DO IT

There are only so many hours in a day and you want to ride your bike, so why do resistance training? Well, first there are ways of doing resistance training on your bike (see pages 80–1) but lifting weights is the most effective way to get something every cyclist needs, and that's a bit more torque and power. There are other benefits to be gained from training with weights, such as improved physical balance and, if done sensibly, protection against injury.

WHAT IS TORQUE?

Torque is force applied in a rotational direction. An extra bit of grunt, as it's often called, can really improve overall performance. Having the ability to produce a lot of torque can help you stay seated in the saddle on climbs while others are expending more energy heaving themselves uphill out of the saddle. It helps you accelerate quickly with less effort, it helps you create a gap quickly and saves long, energy-sapping efforts. Grunt also helps you win sprints, and winning sprints helps you win races.

As a track sprinter, I did a lot of weight training as it was central to the performance demands of the events that I rode. For most cyclists, increased torque can be gained by doing a handful of key exercises, using relatively high loads and less than ten repetitions per set (explained below), but always using good lifting form. Never sacrifice form for lifting more weight. If you are unfamiliar with the exercises on pages 82–7, get some coaching before embarking on a weight-training programme.

REPS & SETS

Repetitions (reps) means the number of times you repeat an exercise in one go. Sets is the number of times you do the repeats of that exercise. So three sets of eight repetitions means repeating the exercise eight times for one set, and doing the same number of repeats twice more. There's a specified rest period in between each set, which can be shortened or lengthened to manipulate the training effect.

Some cyclists avoid lifting weights because they think it builds bigger muscles, and bigger muscles means more body weight, which is not what most cyclists want. However, it takes a huge amount of high-resistance training with a high-protein diet to significantly change your body shape. A session or two of moderate load and intensity per week is all the average rider needs to get that extra torque withouth gaining mass. It can also be a welcome break from the bad weather and monotony of dark winter road miles during the off-season in the UK.

OVER 40s

Those over 40 should especially consider incorporating strength training into their programme all year, and consideration becomes need over time for two reasons. The first reason to lift weights in older age is to maintain bone health, and the second is to slow down the drop-off in performance due to decreased production of two key hormones.

Cycling is fantastic exercise for anyone of any age, but one of the things that makes it so good is its biggest drawback too. When you ride, your bike carries your weight, which makes cycling a great choice for anyone with injuries that would be adversely affected by running, or for anyone who is overweight. However, bones are living tissue, their cells are continuously regenerated throughout your life. But cells are replaced in response to load, so if you don't load your bones, your body won't create new live cells at the rate the olds ones die, and you could end up suffering from osteoporosis.

It's something women have a particular tendency to as they age, but studies have found that even some young male professional cyclists have the early signs of osteoporosis. This is because they spend hours on a bike with their weight supported. It can be avoided by regularly putting your bones under load, and weight training does that in spades.

The two key hormones that play a vital role in recovery from training are testosterone and human growth hormone, and production of them both drops at an increasing rate as you age. Luckily, short bursts of hard training, such as heavy lifting or sprint workouts, increase the production of these two vital hormones, even in older people. This is why older cyclists should spend a bigger proportion of their training time doing these kinds of workouts, and cutting back on longer rides.

2.3 **STRETCHING**

A cyclist's body is fairly fixed in position, and there's little to extend your range of motion when cycling. So why stretch? It's because the fixed position of cycling means some muscles aren't used over their full range, so they shorten. Shortened muscles become less effective at applying force, while tension created by shortening inhibits muscles during their relaxation phase.

Scan this QR code to hear about the importance of stretching.

The net effect is a drop in overall efficiency and potential power, as tension causes a reduction in revolutions per minute (rpm). Shortened muscles can also put undue strain on joints, causing pain and further inefficiency.

Stretching also aids recovery by helping to reduce post-exercise soreness, which promotes good sleep, and sleep is when maximum muscle repair takes place. Also, good sleep leaves you fresher and able to take on an increased training load. The feelgood factor after stretching has a positive mental effect too. All these things add up to help you become a better cyclist.

You might be young and gifted with long, supple muscles and perfectly aligned limbs, but don't be misled into thinking you don't need to stretch. Things have a habit of creeping up unnoticed and suddenly there's an issue. Being disciplined about stretching helps you keep on top of things.

The exercises shown here are static stretches, and you'll see where you should feel the stretch in the shaded areas. This is the first level of stretching. However, like almost everything physical, stretching can be advanced, so you eventually become super-flexible, which will help you meet future cycling challenges. More advanced stretching includes dynamic stretches and proprioceptive neuromuscular facilitation (PNF), which requires contraction under tension to elicit the optimal lengthening of the muscles.

Finally, you can do stretches at any time. They are especially good after a ride, or as part of a general mobilization session with core strength, foam roller, and yoga or Pilates.

STRETCH 1 HIP FLEXORS

- Engage you *transverse abdominis* and drop into a lunge position, keeping your upper body upright and your forward knee flexed at 90 degrees.
- To stretch your hip flexor, extend the angle of your forward knee to move your front thigh forward. You should feel the stretch in your back leg at the top of your thigh.
- Hold for a count of 20 then swap to the other leg and repeat.
- Repeat a further one or two times for each leg.

1.1

STRETCH 2 HAMSTRINGS

- Sit on the floor with one leg straight out in front of you, pull your other foot toward your crotch and let the knee on that leg drop to the floor.
- Lean forward on the straight leg side and slowly try to touch your toes with one hand. You probably won't be able to reach your toes at first, but that doesn't matter.
- Keep stretching for a count of 20 and then sit up straight.
- Swap legs and repeat.
- Repeat the stretch at least twice on both sides.

STRETCH 3 QUADRICEPS

- Do this sanding up or lying on your side.
- Bend one knee, bringing your heel as close to your backside as possible, then grab the ankle of your bent leg and gently pull your foot as close to your backside as possible.
- Hold for a count of 20, release and then swap legs.
- Repeat the stretch least twice on each side.

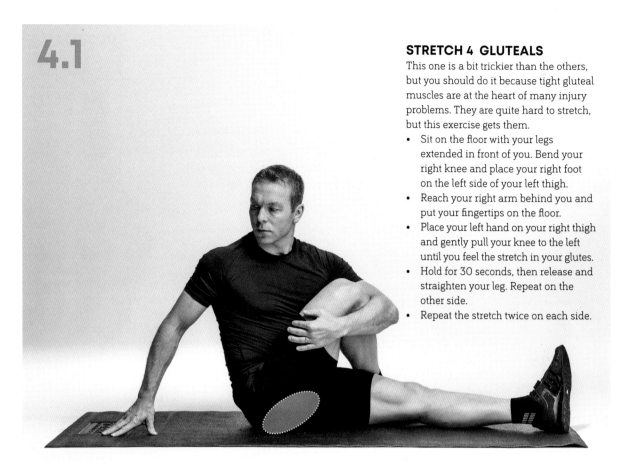

4.1

STRETCH 4 GLUTEALS

This one is a bit trickier than the others, but you should do it because tight gluteal muscles are at the heart of many injury problems. They are quite hard to stretch, but this exercise gets them.

- Sit on the floor with your legs extended in front of you. Bend your right knee and place your right foot on the left side of your left thigh.
- Reach your right arm behind you and put your fingertips on the floor.
- Place your left hand on your right thigh and gently pull your knee to the left until you feel the stretch in your glutes.
- Hold for 30 seconds, then release and straighten your leg. Repeat on the other side.
- Repeat the stretch twice on each side.

STRETCH 5 CALF

- In bare feet, position yourself with your hands flat on the floor and your shoulders over your wrists, with your legs out behind your hips.
- To increase the stretch in your calves, press the heel of one foot down and bend the other leg slightly.
- Hold for a count of 20 in each leg, then come back up.
- Repeat the stretch twice on each side.

5.1

2.3 WORKING WITH FOAM ROLLERS

Working with a foam roller is uncomfortable and can at times border on being painful, but don't let that put you off. So long as the pain isn't too intense, it's actually a good sign. Pain means you are hitting the problem. You can control the pain by supporting your body during each exercise so you control the weight you put down on the roller.

Scan this QR code to see how to use foam rollers for the following muscles.

Muscle fibres work like zips. Under contraction, filaments in the fibres unzip longitudinally, then one side of the zip moves over the other in the direction of the contraction, pulling the muscle fibre with it. The filament then zips together and repeats the process as many times as needed in order to perform the desired contraction. The number of fibres recruited depends on the force of the contraction. The filaments reverse this process as the muscle relaxes. Forceful or repeated contractions create micro tears in muscle fibres, which interfere with the contraction process through the build-up of fluid, and often scar tissue, around the micro tears.

Deep-tissue massage helps squeeze this fluid from the fibres and breaks up scar tissue before it gets the chance to become a problem. However, not everybody has access to or the time for deep-tissue massage by a qualified practitioner, which is where foam rollers come in. Used properly, they do almost the same job, squeezing fluid from muscle fibres and breaking up scar tissue.

They also have an additional benefit. Stretching mostly affects the most supple section of the muscle, but it won't release tension where muscles might be really tight, where there are knots or a build-up of scar tissue. You can target those tight bits with a foam roller and work on the localized tension. They are a fantastic recovery tool.

There are all kinds of foam rollers, and you can do good work with a tennis ball, but I like the cylindrical rollers. They are light, you can take them anywhere, and you can even store clothes inside the hollow ones so they take up little space in a bag.

The feeling you are looking for in your muscles when using a foam roller is best described as a warm release. Keep at it, work thoroughly and regularly, looking for that warm release feeling. The harder you train, the more a foam roller will become your friend.

FOAM ROLLERS 1 BACK ROLL

The back roll doesn't just feel good after you've done it, it feels good *while* you're doing it.

- Lie on your back with the roller under your spine, just below your shoulders.
- Simply roll up the mat until the foam roller is just above your hips.
- Roll back down the mat and repeat until the tension is relieved.

- This relieves tension in the spinal erector muscles, which are worked hard in cycling. If you relax and arch your back over the roller it has a positive effect on mobilizing your lower spine. (You might get a pleasing "pop pop pop" sound while rolling as the vertebrae mobilize. Don't worry, it's normal, particularly if you're old and battered like me!)

FOAM ROLLERS 2 ITB ROLL

ITB stands for iliotibial band. It isn't a muscle but a kind
of connective tissue known as fascia (see page 95),
which is found throughout the body. The ITB extends
down the side of each thigh, lateral to the knee, from the
outside of the pelvis, over the hip and knee, to attach just
below the knee on the tibia bone. In cyclists, the ITB can
become very tight and cause pain, but the problem is
avoided or relieved by regular use of a foam roller.

2.1

- Lie on your side with the roller under your hip, your
  lower leg straight, your upper leg bent behind it and
  your upper body supported on your forearm. Roll your
  body over the roller until it is just above your lower knee.
- Be sure to work right to the ends of the muscle and roll
  up and down a few times on each side. If it hurts – and
  in cases of tightness it will – increase the support from
  your upper body while you roll.

2.2

FOAM ROLLERS 3 BASIC GLUTEAL ROLL

- Sit on the foam roller with your hands behind you for support. Tilt onto one buttock and support your upper body on the corresponding forearm, then just roll that side up and down the roller from the top of your glutes to the top of your thigh.

3.1

- Continue rolling along one side for as long as is comfortable.
- Repeat once on the other side.

3.2

FOAM ROLLERS 4
ADVANCED GLUTEAL ROLL

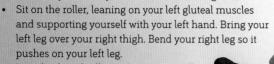

4.1

This really hits all your gluteal muscles, especially the hard-to-reach *piriformis*, which is almost impossible to stretch any other way and is notorious for tightness.

- Sit on the roller, leaning on your left gluteal muscles and supporting yourself with your left hand. Bring your left leg over your right thigh. Bend your right leg so it pushes on your left leg.
- Lean back and roll, trying to present all of your left side gluteals to the roller.
- Repeat once on the other side.

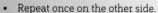

FOAM ROLLERS 5 QUADS

5.1

- Place the roller underneath your quad muscles on the front of your right thigh, supporting your upper body on your forearms.
- Roll up and down on the roller along the whole length of your thigh.

- Work right into the joints to hit the ends of the muscles.
- Repeat once on the other side.

5.2

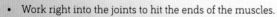

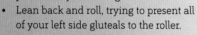
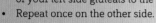

6.1

FOAM ROLLERS 6 HAMSTRINGS

- Place the roller underneath your hamstring on the back of your right leg, with your hands on the floor behind your backside for support.
- Roll up and down on the roller along the whole length of your thigh.

6.2

- Work right into the joints to hit the ends of the muscles.
- Repeat once on the other side.

7.1

FOAM ROLLERS 7 CALF ROLL

- Place the roller underneath your right calf muscle, with your hands flat on the floor behind your backside for support.
- Roll up and down on the roller along the whole length of your calf.

7.2

- Work right into the joints to hit the ends of the muscles.
- Repeat once on the other side.

FOAM ROLLERS 8
UPPER BODY MOBILIZATION ROLL

This roll works on tension in your *latissimus dorsi* muscle, which is worked hard in cyclists.

- Lie on your right side with the foam roller in your armpit and your right arm pointing in front of you. Lower onto the roller and roll between your upper arm to your mid torso and back.

8.1

- Repeat once on the other side.

8.2

2.3 YOGA & PILATES FOR CYCLISTS

The relatively fixed body position a cyclist adopts while riding can cause muscle shortening over time that can reduce joint mobilization in the spine and shoulders. That can create areas of reduced spinal flex, a rounded thoracic spine and round shoulders. Depending on their degree, these might adversely affect cycling performance but, more importantly, they will affect your general mobility, making everyday chores, even things like playing with your kids, more difficult.

We're all susceptible to this and, despite working with some of the best sports experts, I have an area of stiffness in my lower spine that I have to cope with by increased flex further up. It's not ideal. If performance is your aim then good joint mobilization promotes good biomechanics, which means more power to the pedals and less chance of injury. Good mobilization also gives you a better life.

YOGA

Yoga can be excellent for mobilizing your spine and opening up your shoulders. It is also very good for training you to breathe properly because it focuses on deep breathing from your diaphragm.

Accessing your full lung capacity is especially important in sport because there are more alveoli at the bottom of your lungs than at the top. Alveoli are the little sacs where waste carbon dioxide in the blood is exchanged for inhaled oxygen. There is also more blood at the bottom of your lungs, which are a bit like sponges. Imagine a water-filled sponge sitting on a shelf. Gravity will make most of the water drop to the bottom of the sponge, and it's the same with your lungs. Breathing deeply and using the bottom as well as the top of your lungs brings more oxygen into contact with more blood, and that equals more power.

Yoga has to be learned from the basics to be effective, so there's no point in me giving you a couple of exercises to do. It's holistic too, so you will get the benefits I've outlined above by doing a balanced yoga routine. Luckily, there are plenty of yoga books and videos, as well as classes up and down the country. It's well worth giving yoga a try, especially if you have mobilization issues.

PILATES

Pilates has several exercises for small muscles that are crucial for spine function and health. These muscles can waste away when we lead sedentary lives and/or when bigger spinal muscles take over. It happens when the smaller spinal muscles are underused, which they are when you sit with a slumped spine. It can be a particular problem for cyclists because our big spinal muscles are used a lot when riding and can become overdeveloped in comparison to the smaller ones. Cyclists who sit slumped over a computer, or drive a lot, are at particular risk.

The two big spinal erector muscles at the bottom of your back, which are prime movers whenever you stand up, are used a lot when cycling in order to anchor your hips in place, so your legs can push down effectively.

When spinal erector muscles bear heavy loads they develop accordingly. But those big muscles can take over the work of the smaller muscles between each vertebra. Normally the smaller muscles also help flex the spine, but if they aren't being used they shrink and lose their force. They become too weak to resist the big muscles at rest, and the big muscles pull your lumbar spine out of shape, which is a common cause of lower back pain.

Building a stronger core helps share some of the load the spinal erector muscles would otherwise carry, but it won't entirely address the problem of back pain caused by the wasting of the inter-vertebral muscles. Luckily there's a Pilates exercise that addresses the wasting, called the shoulder bridge. >>

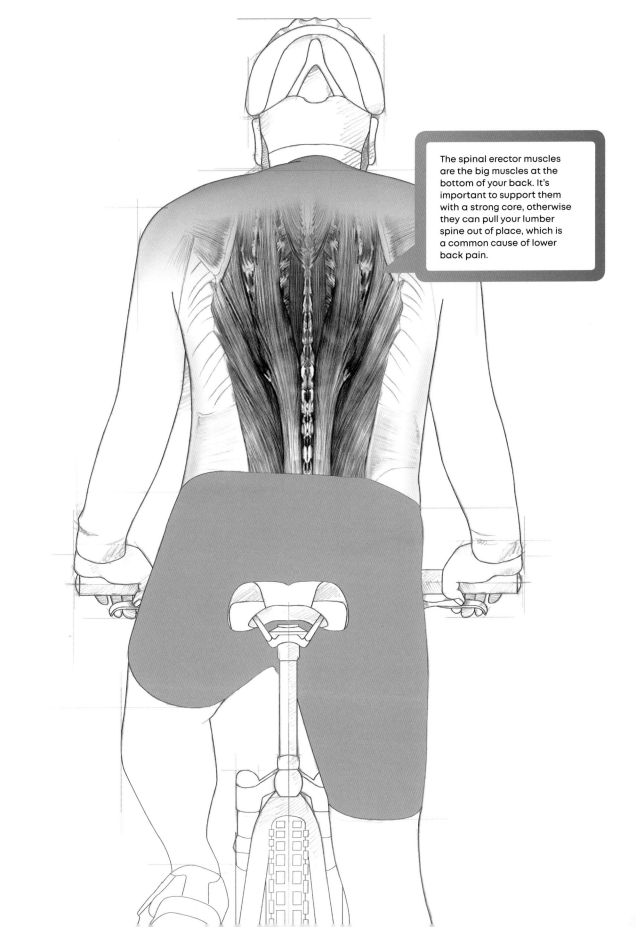

The spinal erector muscles are the big muscles at the bottom of your back. It's important to support them with a strong core, otherwise they can pull your lumber spine out of place, which is a common cause of lower back pain.

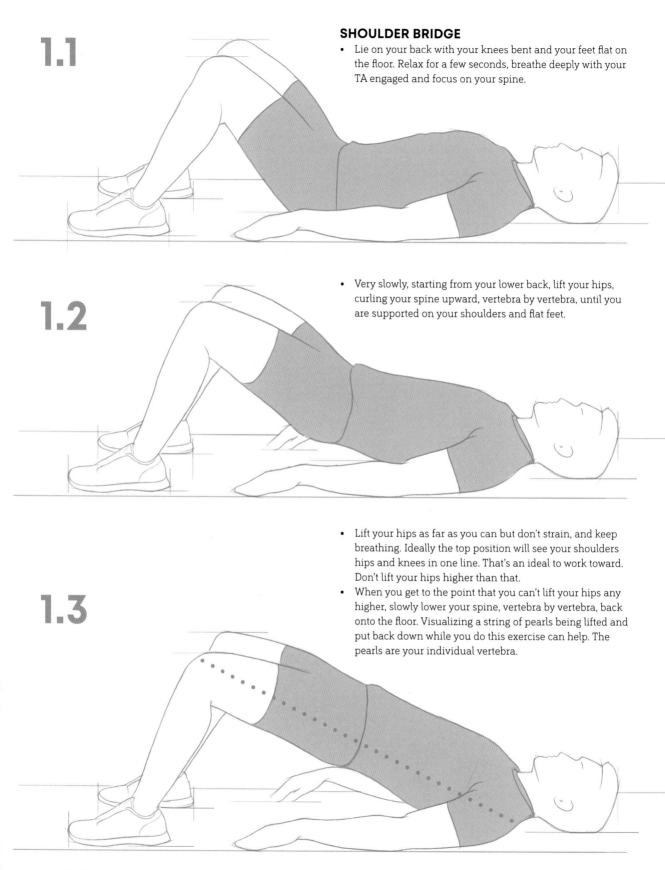

1.1

SHOULDER BRIDGE

- Lie on your back with your knees bent and your feet flat on the floor. Relax for a few seconds, breathe deeply with your TA engaged and focus on your spine.

1.2

- Very slowly, starting from your lower back, lift your hips, curling your spine upward, vertebra by vertebra, until you are supported on your shoulders and flat feet.

1.3

- Lift your hips as far as you can but don't strain, and keep breathing. Ideally the top position will see your shoulders hips and knees in one line. That's an ideal to work toward. Don't lift your hips higher than that.
- When you get to the point that you can't lift your hips any higher, slowly lower your spine, vertebra by vertebra, back onto the floor. Visualizing a string of pearls being lifted and put back down while you do this exercise can help. The pearls are your individual vertebra.

2.3 BUILDING A STRENGTH & CONDITIONING PROGRAMME PART 1

Stretching should become a near daily ritual, ideally performed immediately following training. It's also worth stretching whenever you feel a bit of tightness somewhere, rather than wait until it manifests itself as an injury. Always stretch in a warm place, preferably with your muscles warmed up with some sort of light activity, and work into the stretches slowly. Do a preliminary stretch first, then a full stretch as far as you can. Always stretch slowly and deliberately.

The same goes for hitting pressure points and areas of tightness with your foam roller (see pages 68–75). If you can set aside 10–15 minutes daily for stretching and working with a foam roller, you will reap enormous benefits. Your body will often tell you what needs attention first, but it's good to do all the stretching exercises demonstrated on pages 65–7 because prevention of problems is easier than curing them.

Keeping on top of your physical condition helps you recover quickly from training and avoid injury. This means you can train more often and because of that you will build your fitness to a higher level.

WHEN TO DO YOGA & CORE EXERCISES
A few yoga moves are great for opening up your body before a weight-training session, and you can tag the core exercises onto the end of your weights sessions too. Riders who only follow a strength training programme during their off-season should still do the core routine from pages 58–63 at least once a week.

As I said on page 76, you can learn yoga from books or videos. Try to perfect a couple of moves that help to mobilize your spine and open your shoulders, and do those as part of your warm-up routine before lifting weights, or before your core routine if you've stopped doing weights.

ON-THE-BIKE RESISTANCE TRAINING
Long before we went to our first Olympic Games I used to do a really extreme version of this with my fellow Team GB sprinter Craig MacLean. On-the-bike resistance training can be achieved by increasing gear ratios, riding up steep gradients or adding extra weight to yourself or your bike. Of course, you could do all of these together, which Craig did. At one time his training bike weighed 40 kilograms (88 pounds). He filled the frame tubes with lead shot and put weightlifting plates in the bike's pannier bags.

Craig MacLean (left) was ahead of his time with some of his ideas and concepts for resistance training.

Francesco Moser was a talented rider both on the road and the track. He worked with the late Aldo Sassi and incorporated resistance training into his programme.

Going back a few years most cyclists trained on heavier bikes than they raced on, but it was the Italian road race World Champion and three-time Paris–Roubaix winner, Francesco Moser, who brought high-gear low-rev training to everyone's attention. The idea came from the Italian coach he worked with, Aldo Sassi, when preparing for his successful attempt on the World Hour record in 1984. The session involved repeated rides up the same long climb in a huge gear, which Moser could only pedal at 50 to 60rpm. Craig and I did that too, only with bells on.

We were sprinters, so the hill didn't need to be as long as Moser's, and we only did runs of about ten pedal revolutions to mimic the gym, but in a specific on-bike way. We pulled on our brakes to provide the most resistance possible without actually stopping and falling over (which we still did occasionally!). If the aim is to improve torque production and strength then it has to be a maximal effort lasting only a few seconds, maybe 10–30 seconds at a time, otherwise the output drops down to a level where it's not eliciting maximum fibre recruitment. Short and explosive efforts are key, despite the fact that the resulting speed of crank rotation is very low. It's the same principle as pushing heavy weights as explosively as possible in the gym. The resulting speed may be slow but the intention is always to try to move the bike as quickly as possible.

You can get on-bike resistance training by riding up and down the steepest hill in your area a few times during a ride. You can make the hill even harder, and the training more effective, by going up in a higher gear than you would normally use. Try riding in and out of the saddle.

A word of warning though, make sure you are thoroughly warmed up before you do on-the-bike resistance training, and if you experience any kind of knee pain while you are doing it, stop immediately.

2.3 BUILDING A STRENGTH & CONDITIONING PROGRAMME PART 2

Scan this QR code to see videos showing correct form for all the strength and conditioning exercises.

Bodybuilders look the way they do because the sole aim of their training is to increase muscle fibre cross-sectional area in a process called hypertrophy. Track sprinters have bulkier physiques in comparison to almost all other types of cyclists. However, this is a by-product of their training and diet, they don't aim to get bigger just for the sake of it. Sprinters are the drag racers of cycling. They face special demands requiring rapid accelerations from stationary using very high gears, but even they don't want too much muscle bulk.

STRENGTH & CONDITIONING 1 SQUAT

This is the king of exercises, so if you do one lifting exercise and nothing else, do this one. It builds leg, core and back strength in a very functional way.

- Start with the loaded barbell (we have used an unloaded barbell here to enable a clear view of the positioning) supported on a squat rack or stand, with the bar at collarbone height. Face the bar and step underneath it.
- Hold the bar low down on your shoulders with your hands as close together as your flexibility allows. This bunches up your shoulder muscles so that the bar has a natural shelf of muscle on which to rest (see below).
- Tighten your gluteal muscles together, engage your TA as instructed on page 58, and take the weight of the bar on your shoulders before stepping back. Stand straight with your feet slightly wider than your hips and your toes pointing outward.
- Squat down, lowering the weight slowly, looking ahead and keeping your spine neutral. Don't let your spine go rounded, but don't try to hyperextend it the other way either. Your knees should track your toes.
- Lower until your thighs are parallel to the floor. If you can go lower, all the better. Going lower is something you should work to progress with this exercise.
- Come out of the squat, back to standing, with as much power as you can put into the lift.

A closer grip allows the muscle to bunch, creating a shelf which is both safer and more comfortable.

A wider grip equals a flatter back, meaning the bar grinds against bone and will be uncomfortable.

1.1

FREE WEIGHT EXERCISES

Do three to four sets of each exercise, completing all the sets before doing the next exercise. A good way to ease yourself into free weights is to keep the reps low.

- The first set should be eight reps of a weight you can only just lift ten times.
- Increase the weight on the bar by around five per cent and do a set of six reps of the exercise with that weight.
- Increase the weight by five per cent again, and do a set of four reps of the exercise.

Initially, a good way to ease yourself into a free weights routine is to focus on three main exercises and take time to perfect the techniques before even thinking about loading the bar.

1.2

2.1

STRENGTH & CONDITIONING 2
OVERHEAD SQUAT

This is an advanced exercise, but worth mastering because it's great for hip and shoulder mobility, for improving squat technique and core strength, and for injury prevention. It isn't specifically focussed on strengthening the legs, but physiotherapists often prescribe it for shoulder or thoracic vertebrae problems. It will help strengthen your upper body too.

- Approach the bar in the rack, lift it onto your shoulders with a wide grip, and then press the bar into an overhead wide-grip stand for the start position. (In contrast to the squat, a wide grip is important here for better balance.)
- Keep the bar directly above your head, lower down into the squat and then push back up. The bar should track straight up and down, never moving from the centre point.
- Come out of the squat, back to standing, with as much power as you can put into the lift.

2.2

STRENGTH & CONDITIONING 3 DEADLIFT

This is a functional movement that strengthens the kinetic chain used in cycling, as well as other sports. If performed correctly it also provides greater resilience to injury. It's important to use an Olympic barbell loaded with one large plate, rather than lots of smaller-weight plates. Large plates raise the bar to the correct height off the floor to start the exercise.

- Start with the barbell on the floor. Stand facing it with your feet hip-width apart and your toes pointing slightly outward. With your legs straight, bend over and grip the bar with your thumbs behind it. Lower your hips, keeping your arms straight and your spine neutral, until your shoulders are in front of the bar.
- Engage all your posterior chain muscles and your core, and drive upward through your heels.
- You should be able to wriggle your toes all through the lift, until the barbell is at hip height. Keep your arms straight and don't arch your back.
- Return the barbell to the floor in a smooth and controlled manner.

3.1

3.2

3.3

STRENGTH & CONDITIONING 4
ROMANIAN DEADLIFT

This is a posterior chain exercise that targets the lower back, gluteal and hamstring muscles. Large plates aren't as important for this one because you're starting from a standing position. You don't lower the weight as far as in a regular deadlift (see page 85), but it's a much safer exercise in respect of risk of injury to the lower back. It really helps develop hip extensor strength, which is very important in cycling.

- The barbell should be on a rack at hip height. Lift it off the rack with a double-overhand grip. Stand upright with your feet hip-width apart and your toes straight (they can be slightly pointed outward but by no more than 15 degrees).
- Keeping your arms straight, lower your torso until the barbell is just below your knees. Move your hips back slightly and bend your legs slightly as you do this. Keep your chest and shoulders back.
- Once the bar is at knee level, activate your gluteal muscles by clenching your buttocks together and return to standing upright. You should be using your hips to lift and activating your glutes and hamstrings. You shouldn't be feeling this exercise in your arms, which should be straight.

4.1

4.2

5.1

STRENGTH & CONDITIONING 5
DUMBBELL LUNGE

This is a unilateral exercise, which makes it more specific to cycling. It's important to perform it in an explosive manner, pushing off the ground dynamically to get the most from it.

- Start by standing upright with a dumbbell in each hand, looking straight ahead.
- Step forward with either leg, leaving the other foot stationary behind you. The step should be far enough forward so that when you lower your body, keeping your torso as upright as possible, your lead shin is at 90 degrees to the floor. Breathe in as you go down.
- Stand up by pushing through your lead heel and bring your rear foot forward to the start position.
- Repeat the move with your other leg for one whole repetition.
- Be as explosive as you can when you stand. Try to keep your balance so you don't wobble at all because that helps strengthen your core. If you find you can't keep your torso upright during this lift, that could indicate tight hip flexors or a weak lower back. More stretching and foam roller work (see pages 65–75) will help improve the former, and the Romanian deadlift (see opposite) will help strengthen your lower back.

5.2

6.1

6.2

STRENGTH & CONDITIONING 6 CALF RAISE

This exercise improves ankle strength, which is especially important during accelerations or low-cadence/high-torque pedalling, such as when climbing steep hills. You can use both legs, or alternate between legs to create a greater load. Don't expect to notice a drastic change in muscle size, regardless of how many of these you do. It is notoriously difficult to gain muscle mass in the calf area.

- Stand on the edge of a step or low aerobics platform. Pull in your abdominal muscles and shift backward until you are standing with the ball of your foot on the step.
- Lower your heel over the edge, then raise your heel a few inches above the step.
- Continue until you feel a pull in your calf muscles.
- Repeat on the other side.

CORRECT FORM

I cannot stress enough that it is crucial to do all exercises with correct form. This is true not only for safety reasons, but also because they are most effective when done correctly. Never sacrifice correct form for more weight, because doing so won't make you stronger but drastically increases your risk of injury. I recommend you get qualified one-to-one instruction on how to do each of the strength and conditioning exercises. Finally, always wear the flattest shoes you can when weight training.

RESULTS

It might not feel like it when you're putting your all into a climb, but you will really notice the benefit of all these strength and conditioning exercises on your performance, especially in challenging ascents.

TRAINING THEORY

4

2.4 THE CIRCULATORY SYSTEM

The circulatory system, also known as the cardiovascular system, is your body's multitasking organ. It delivers fuel, the metabolites from food and oxygen to burn it. This provides energy for muscles and organs to work. The circulatory system also carries waste products from muscles and organs, and it helps maintain your body temperature within its narrow optimal band. On top of that, it transports the materials and chemicals required for repairing and rebuilding your body.

THE MECHANICS

The circulatory system comprises the lungs, heart and blood. It's actually two systems working together: pulmonary circulation and systemic circulation. Pulmonary circulation takes place between the heart, which is a double pump, and the lungs.

Blood is pumped around your body, delivering oxygen to muscles and organs. Once oxygen is delivered, blood becomes deoxygenated. The deoxygenated blood carries carbon dioxide waste back to your heart. To continue the cycle, deoxygenated blood must be pumped from your heart to your lungs, where a gas exchange takes place. Carbon dioxide is transferred to lung tissue, removed by exhalation and replaced by inhaled oxygen. Newly oxygenated blood returns to your heart and systemic circulation takes over. Oxygenated blood enters your heart and is pumped around your body, giving up oxygen in response to the body's demands and picking up waste carbon dioxide.

ELEMENTS OF THE CIRCULATORY SYSTEM

• Blood is made up of red and white cells and it carries nutrients, electrolytes, hormones and oxygen around your body. Oxygen binds to a metalloprotein, iron being the metallo part, called haemoglobin, which is responsible for the red colour of red blood cells.
• Arteries and arterioles are the blood vessels that carry oxygenated blood around your body in a continuous branching network. The arteries are surrounded by smooth muscle and supplied with nerves, these expand and contract the arteries to regulate blood flow according to the body's energy and oxygen demands. Arterioles branch off from the artery system. They are narrower than arteries with no nerves or surrounding muscle. The arterioles feed blood to a network of capillaries that surrounds all muscle fibres.
• Capillaries are tiny, with walls just one cell thick. They are where oxygen leaves the blood and enters muscle tissue, with the blood collecting carbon dioxide from the muscles at the same time. Blood changes from oxygenated to deoxygenated in the capillaries.
• Veins take deoxygenated blood from the capillaries. Veins are closer to the skin than arteries and you can see them just beneath the skin. Their blue colour is due to the deoxygenated blood. Veins have tiny valves in them that open and close between heart beats to stop gravity from causing blood to pool in lower limbs. Venal blood plays a part in your body's temperature regulation system.

WHAT HAPPENS WHEN YOU TRAIN?

Training improves your circulation by increasing the efficiency with which gases are exchanged in the lungs, which means more oxygen is picked up and more carbon dioxide is taken out. Endurance training, in particular, increases the size of the heart's chambers, so it pumps a large volume of blood around your body per beat. More intense training increases the strength of the cardiac muscles, so the heart is more powerful and has a bigger stroke volume (SV).

Both adaptations mean a trained heart pumps more blood further around the body per beat than an untrained one. Training can also improve the quality of blood. Responding in particular to endurance training, your blood volume increases, and so does the amount of haemoglobin in it.

Endurance training stimulates capillary growth in muscles and organs, including your heart and lungs. This increases the amount of oxygen that can be absorbed during inhalation, and it increases the amount of oxygenated blood and nutrients that can be delivered to muscle tissue, allowing muscles to work harder and repair quicker.

Artery walls become more flexible after each bout of exercise, which lowers blood pressure. If exercise is done regularly then relaxation of the artery walls becomes permanent, and so does lowered blood pressure.

The net result of all these adaptations is more oxygen and fuel for working muscles, which culminates in more power on the pedals, as well as improved general health.

HOW TO STIMULATE CHANGE

Any endurance exercise programme stimulates capillary growth, increases haemoglobin and improves the efficiency of your blood. However, it's thought that riding long distances stimulates capillary growth the most, while training at your maximum oxygen consumption point, or VO_2 max, optimizes the amount of oxygen it can carry. I'll show you how to do these with great accuracy, and in ways that help you achieve your personal cycling goals, as well as making you fitter and healthier for life, in chapters 5 and 6.

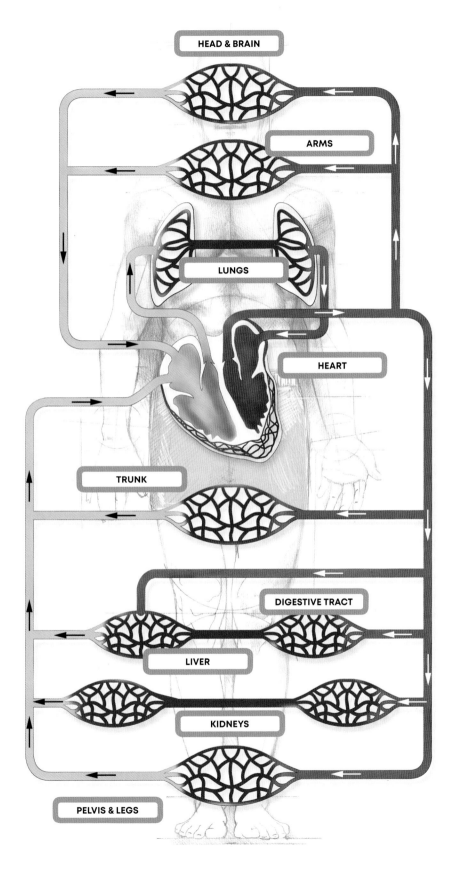

HEAD & BRAIN

ARMS

LUNGS

HEART

TRUNK

DIGESTIVE TRACT

LIVER

KIDNEYS

PELVIS & LEGS

2.4 **MUSCLES**

Muscles move our bodies and help some of our internal organs do their work by contracting and relaxing. Muscles are powered by energy from chemical reactions inside them.

There are three types of muscle:

1. CARDIAC
2. SMOOTH
3. SKELETAL

Cardiac and smooth muscles move through involuntary mechanisms. Cardiac muscles keep the heart beating, while smooth muscles do lots of things, including pushing food through the gut. Skeletal muscles move by voluntary mechanisms, even if we might not be aware of them, such as blinking. They are also used to maintain posture, walk, run, lift, swim and pedal.

MUSCLE NUMBERS

There are approximately 693 skeletal muscles in the whole human body.

On average, individual skeletal muscle fibres can exert a force of 25 Newtons per square metre (per 11 square feet).

The power output of the human heart per beat is between one and five watts, which, because it beats continuously throughout life, makes the cardiac muscle the hardest-working muscle in the body.

Skeletal muscles are 20–25 per cent efficient, meaning that only a quarter (max) of the energy going into them comes out as work. Most of the rest is lost as heat.

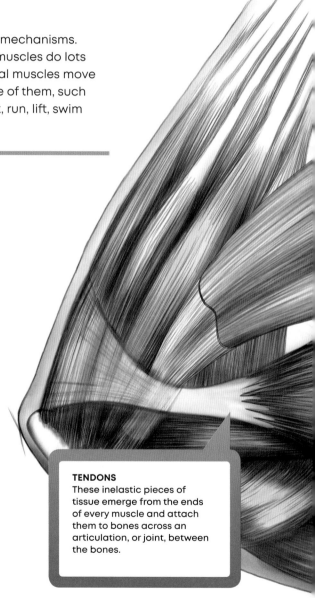

TENDONS
These inelastic pieces of tissue emerge from the ends of every muscle and attach them to bones across an articulation, or joint, between the bones.

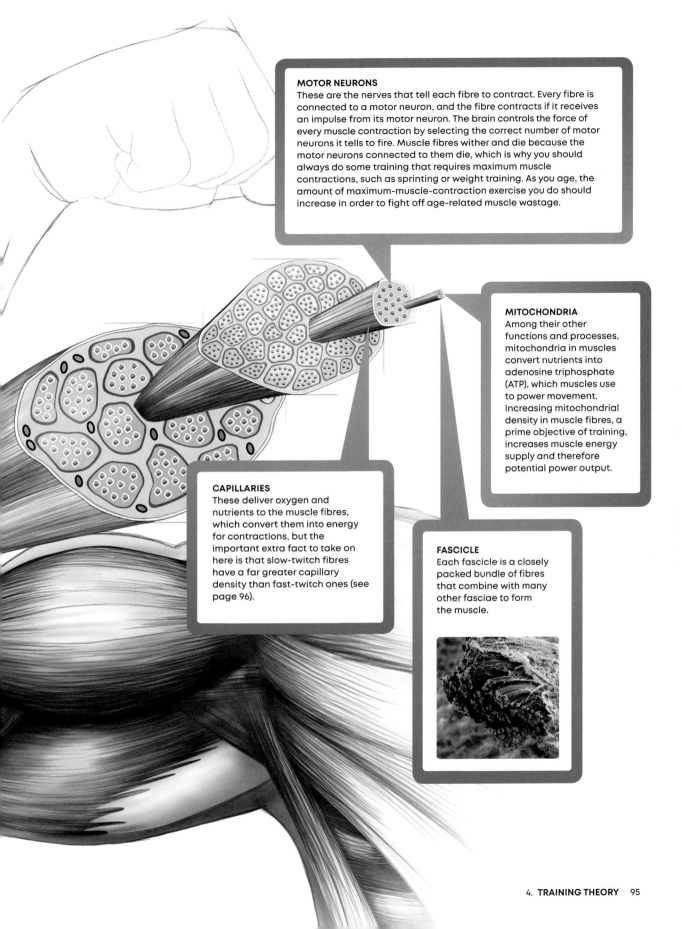

MOTOR NEURONS
These are the nerves that tell each fibre to contract. Every fibre is connected to a motor neuron, and the fibre contracts if it receives an impulse from its motor neuron. The brain controls the force of every muscle contraction by selecting the correct number of motor neurons it tells to fire. Muscle fibres wither and die because the motor neurons connected to them die, which is why you should always do some training that requires maximum muscle contractions, such as sprinting or weight training. As you age, the amount of maximum-muscle-contraction exercise you do should increase in order to fight off age-related muscle wastage.

MITOCHONDRIA
Among their other functions and processes, mitochondria in muscles convert nutrients into adenosine triphosphate (ATP), which muscles use to power movement. Increasing mitochondrial density in muscle fibres, a prime objective of training, increases muscle energy supply and therefore potential power output.

CAPILLARIES
These deliver oxygen and nutrients to the muscle fibres, which convert them into energy for contractions, but the important extra fact to take on here is that slow-twitch fibres have a far greater capillary density than fast-twitch ones (see page 96).

FASCICLE
Each fascicle is a closely packed bundle of fibres that combine with many other fasciae to form the muscle.

2.4 **MUSCLES IN TRAINING**

This section focuses on how muscles respond to training, and how the nature of their contractions can be changed through action. However, the number of muscle fibres a person has, and the composition of types – slow twitch, fast or intermediate – cannot be changed by training. It is determined by genetics. Certain specialized training will increase fibre diameter, but nothing increases the total number of fibres. On the other hand, muscle fibres can be lost if their motor neurons die, which happens through age or if they are underused. Fibres can also be lost during illness.

WHAT HAPPENS WHEN YOU START TRAINING?

Taking part in any aerobic exercise increases the number of capillaries that supply your muscles. It also increases the number of mitochondria within them. This means that the muscles are getting more fuel and have increased capacity to burn it, so you get fitter. If you do any kind of aerobic training, you will soon be able to ride longer and harder on a bike.

The force a muscle can apply is determined by its cross-sectional area and the amount of energy available in its fibres. The cells within muscle fibres are constantly being replaced, and certain types of training stimulate a response that creates an increase in muscle-fibre diameter. Other forms of training increase mitochondrial density.

The proportion of slow- and fast-twitch muscles we are born with broadly governs the sort of cyclist we can become. People with a large proportion of fast-twitch fibres will be better sprinters, whereas those with a high percentage of slow-twitch fibres will be better at longer distances. However, intermediate fibres can be trained to act like fast- or slow-twitch fibres, so everybody can improve their endurance and/or the sprint side of cycling by doing training that targets the specific need.

The two muscles used most in cycling, the *quadriceps femoris* and *gluteus maximus*, are the two strongest muscles in the human body in the total force that they can apply.

WHICH TRAINING DOES WHAT?

Long-distance riding stimulates a disproportionate increase in capillary growth, whereas riding hard for 3 minutes increases the number of mitochondria in a muscle cell. Riding close to the pace you can maintain for one hour also stimulates these, but its main purpose is to improve efficiency of muscle-fibre chemistry. The net result is that your steady one-hour pace gets faster.

Fast-twitch muscle fibres are generally only fired into action by the brain when we make fast or forceful movements, so riding at a comfortable pace means fast-twitch fibres won't be trained. But even long-distance cyclists need to develop their fast-twitch fibres to help them climb very steep hills.

There is a natural trend of under-used muscle fibres to wither and even die with age. That process can be slowed dramatically by doing some training that fires fast-twitch fibres. Some sort of sprint, weight or hard hill training is important for all cyclists, but especially those over 40. It's also thought that stimulating fast-twitch fibres increases the efficiency with which all muscle fibres convert energy into work. Finally, muscle fibres need protein to grow stronger. If you are training hard, you need to increase the amount of protein you eat, but more of that in chapter 8.

i

MUSCLES AT WORK

Muscles contract and relax through the behaviour of actin and myosin within the cells of muscle fibres. Myosin is a molecular motor that acts like an active ratchet. Chains of actin proteins form high-tensile passive, thin filaments that transmit the force generated by myosin to the ends of the muscle. Each myosin paddles along an actin filament by repeatedly binding with it, pulling and letting it go, thereby sliding the thick filament over the thin filament. This repeated ratcheting or pulling of the actin filaments causes a muscle to contract.

The energy for contractions comes from ATP. This is created by a number of complicated processes, either in the presence of oxygen (aerobic) or without oxygen (anaerobic). Muscles store nutrients to make ATP in the form of fat globules (glycogen), which can be rapidly converted to glucose, and creatine phosphate.

The nutrient that is used when a muscle contracts depends on the speed and force the brain requires from the contraction. Creatine phosphate converting to ATP powers immediate, fast or very forceful contractions. Fat converting to ATP powers the least forceful contractions, while glucose converting to ATP powers all those in between. There isn't a given point where one system stops and another starts, it's more of a continuing gradient of reliance from one system to another as contractions intensify. As you will see later in the book, the proportion of different fuel types a skeletal muscle uses for any given force of contraction can be influenced by training and/or dietary manipulation.

2.4 **BONES**

Bones are the body's levers and chassis. They protect vital organs, determine basic body proportions and allow movement around joints, which are amazing pieces of delicate yet hard-wearing engineering. Bones also play a role in the production of blood cells, the storage of minerals and a number of other metabolic processes. Bones are an overlooked factor in the fitness equation. We imagine the skeleton being pretty inert, but bones are very much alive and play a significant role in our health, fitness and wellbeing. They must be looked after, and because a cyclist's bones are under particular threat they must be given an extra dose of exercise to help them maintain their structure and function.

BONE NUMBERS

There are about 206 separate bones in the human skeleton, although it depends how you count them, as authorities differ on how many bones form the pelvis, for example. Bones mature to full strength at around 20 years of age, so younger riders especially should seek out good coaching advice.

When they are mature, bones are extremely tough with an average compressive strength of 170 megapascals. Their average tensile strength is 104–21 megapascals and they have a sheer stress strength of 56 megapascals, and that's strong.

A CYCLIST'S BONES

One of the many metabolic processes bone tissue is involved with is the storage of growth factors, such as insulin-like growth factor. These hormones are very important in recovering from and adapting to exercise. Bone tissue also stores alkaline minerals used to restore the body's chemical balance when its acidity rises, as it can during exercise.

Bone tissue dies, and while new tissue is born, the rate and quality of new bone depends on two things. One is eating an adequate supply of bone-forming minerals, particularly calcium, and the other is doing load-bearing exercise.

A well-balanced diet and staying fit helps satisfy the nutrient demands of bone tissue, but cycling might not satisfy the load demand required to build healthy tissue. Cycling isn't load-bearing because the bike supports your body weight. Studies have shown that some professional racers competing at a Tour de France level have a bone mineral density well below average for their age. To counter this, cyclists should do load-bearing exercises once or twice a week, involving either impact (jogging) or constant loads (lifting weights). There is some evidence that off-road cycling over rough terrain can stimulate good bone growth through impact loading, particularly if you raise your body out of the saddle and support it with your arms and legs in order to absorb impacts.

One further factor with bones is that the best endurance athletes tend to have slim bones, whereas the best sprinters have thicker ones. Bone thickness more than length determines skeleton weight, which is significant for endurance athletes. Also, heavy-boned people have larger areas for the sheet-like muscles of the body to attach to, so they potentially have bigger muscles. Consequently, heavy-boned cyclists are more likely to be successful at the sprint end of the sport's spectrum. There isn't anything anyone can do about this because bone thickness, as opposed to the quality of bone tissue, is an entirely genetic trait.

TUNING UP

Apart from doing load-bearing exercises, eating a balanced diet and getting your bone density checked if you are in a group prone to osteoporosis, you need to look after your joints.

Muscle tightness is a major cause of joint pain because tight muscles can pull joints out of line. A thorough and regular programme of stretching, foam roller work and Pilates will help prevent muscle tightness and balance your body.

I've already covered what happens when your large spinal erector muscles take over from smaller muscles in flexing the spine, and how to prevent them causing back pain (see pages 58–63). This can also happen around your knee joint, when muscles on the outside front of your knee develop more than those on the inside front. If that happens the outside muscles might pull the kneecap out of line, or out of track as it's called. Lifting weights regularly with good technique helps balance leg muscle development, but if you start suffering from kneecap pain then you may need treatment and special exercises from a qualified practitioner, once a correct diagnosis is obtained.

Finally, joints don't like being cold. They are filled with a fluid that gets thicker in cooler temperatures, and that can cause pain. Muscles can tighten in response to the cold as well, and tight muscles can affect joint alignment. The lower back and knees are particularly vulnerable to the cold. Always keep your lower back covered when you ride. Keep in mind the great Irish racer, Sean Kelly, who used to wear shorts only when the temperature was above 15°C. Okay, he was a top pro with really low body fat, which makes muscles even more susceptible to the cold, but it's worth thinking about.

Bones have an outer layer composed of compact bone with minimal spaces inside their structure. Within this hard, white outer layer is a cover of trabecular bone, which is spongy and has spaces in it for blood vessels and bone marrow.

Red bone marrow is found within some bones, notably the femur, and it's where red and white blood cells are made. Yellow marrow stores fatty acids.

Cartilage is a white, smooth and shiny material that coats the ends of many bones and facilitates the smooth movement of joints.

The plate-like bones that form the skull are fused at their joints. Their job is to protect the brain, eyes and tiny bones inside the middle ear, of which the stapes, also known as the stirrup, is the smallest bone in the human body.

Ribs, along with the sternum or breast bone, protect the heart, lungs, liver and other organs. The ribcage moves upward during inhalation to allow lung expansion. Humans have 24 ribs arranged in 12 pairs. The first seven pairs are called true ribs and are attached to vertebrae at the back, and to the sternum through the costal cartilage. Of the next five, three pairs are attached to the sternum through a common cartilage, and the last two are attached to vertebrae only.

The femur, or thigh bone, is the largest bone in the human skeleton. An adult male's femur is on average 48cm (19in) long and 2.8cm (1⅛in) in diameter. Long bones such as the femur act as levers, either increasing the speed at which a limb moves or the force each muscular contraction applies.

Research carried out in the 1980s suggested that it is beneficial for cyclists to have a high femur-to-tibia-length ratio, and a survey of pro racers at that time showed a significant number of top racers had those characteristics. However, people with shorter femurs can compensate by using shorter cranks and increasing their pedal cadence.

Sesamoid bones, of which there are several sets withiin your skeleton, are embedded in tendons. They act to hold the tendon further away from the joint, so the angle of the tendon is increased and because of that the leverage of the muscle's contraction is increased.

The patella, or the kneecap, is a good example of a sesamoid bone, and is susceptible to injury for cyclists.

2.4 HORMONES

Hormones are chemicals that control cellular functions. They are particularly important to athletes because they control a number of physiological reactions, including energy metabolism, tissue growth, hydration levels and the synthesis and degradation of muscle protein.

Hormones can be anabolic, meaning they help build new tissue, or catabolic, meaning they play a part in breaking down tissue. The important thing for people in training to know is that certain training and/or dietary protocols can boost anabolic hormone production, while you can organize your training in a way that avoids boosting catabolic hormones.

Here are some of the most important hormones that play a part in exercise. These are the ones where production can be manipulated through training and/or dietary protocol.

GLUCAGON

This is another pancreatic hormone, but one that is released in response to low levels of sugar in the blood. It stimulates the release of free fatty acids from fat tissue, and the conversion of glycogen stored in the liver to glucose. Both are then used as fuel.

This is also a good hormonal response to know if you are trying to lose weight. It's one reason why fasted rides (on an empty stomach), if used sparingly, hold value in a fat-loss programme. Glucagon response can also be stimulated by long rides, and when food is taken sparingly, but always adequately.

INSULIN

Insulin is secreted by the pancreas in response to excess glucose in the blood, converting that glucose into glycogen, which is then absorbed into muscles or stored as fat tissue. The glycogen and fat are then available as an energy reserve.

This is important to know if you are trying to lose weight. Spikes of sugar created by ingesting simple carbohydrates above immediate needs cause spikes in insulin production and the possible conversion of glucose to body fat. During exercise insulin production falls, allowing energy stores to be converted to glucose and used in working muscles.

So it's important not to consume too many simple carbohydrates in one go because anything in excess of immediate requirements could be stored as fat. It's also important not to consume simple carbohydrates immediately before exercise, because that will cause an insulin spike that robs your body of energy. Balancing carbohydrate consumption with exercise is something I'll go into further in chapter 8.

TESTOSTERONE

Produced by the testes in men and the ovaries in women, testosterone plays a part in muscle protein resynthesis and repair. Testosterone helps build stronger muscles. Its production is increased by bouts of very intense training, such as sprinting, short hard intervals or lifting heavy weights. It's a good idea to include all three in your training, especially after the age of 40 when testosterone production tails off unless it's specifically stimulated.

HUMAN GROWTH HORMONE (HGH)

This is another potentially muscle-building and muscle-repairing hormone. It's secreted by the pituitary gland. HGH also increases bone mineralization, supports the immune system and fires up the fat metabolism. Like testosterone, its production is increased by bouts of intense exercise, although it's actually secreted during the rapid eye movement (REM) cycle of sleep. That's one of the reasons why many full-time athletes take an afternoon nap, to get an extra dose of HGH.

INSULIN-LIKE GROWTH FACTOR

This has a similar structure to insulin, is produced by the liver and works with HGH to repair protein damaged during exercise. It's an important hormone in promoting muscle-fibre growth.

CORTISOL

This is a tricky hormone for athletes. During long bouts of exercise, cortisol aids the breakdown of triglycerides, which are the main constituents of body fat in humans. This breakdown is a good thing because triglycerides are derived from the body's fat stores to form glucose, which is burned in the muscles. However, if you exercise for too long, especially without adequate food intake, cortisol can start breaking down protein, which can lead to muscle wasting.

That's not all. Chronic stress without the release of physical activity causes a sharp rise in cortisol levels. In this situation cortisol increases hunger and promotes the desire for high-calorie foods. It can also cause muscle tissue to be lost from arms and legs, and fat to be stored in the abdomen, which is a major health concern. This is because high levels of cortisol cause blood glucose to rise, so insulin is produced to control this by turning the glucose to fat.

However, when we talk about high levels of cortisol what we mean is high levels relative to testosterone and HGH production. So, if you boost the testosterone and HGH side of the relationship, by doing intense efforts such as sprinting and weights, while controlling the causes of high cortisol production, such as stress, you get fitter, stronger and leaner all in one go.

2.4 IL-6 FITNESS SWITCHES

Muscles burn glucose and fat to fuel their activity, however, as you exercise harder the ratio of glucose to fat used increases. That means when you ride really hard your muscles are almost totally fuelled by glucose. This is a potential problem for anyone who wants to perform well over longer distances because our bodies can only store enough glucose to fuel two hours of hard effort. However, even the skinniest person has enough fat reserves to keep going all day. If only there was a way of changing the way the body works so muscles would use fat for fuel at higher power outputs. Well, there is, and it involves an immune system compound called interleukin-6 (IL-6), which was previously thought to just play a part in the body's inflammatory response to infection and injury.

HOLY GRAIL

When it is produced by your muscles during exercise, IL-6 works like a hormone, promoting a number of chemical reactions, the most important of which in exercise terms is the burning of fats as fuel. Even more amazingly, this not only happens while IL-6 is being produced, but it continues to trigger adaptations that increase an individual's fat-burning capacity for quite a long period of time after exercise.

Overall it means that an athlete can exercise at a higher intensity using fats as fuel, which is a bit of a Holy Grail as far as endurance exercise and performance is concerned. Normally the body uses fat as fuel only when exercising lightly, but if this fat/glucose see-saw can be tilted in favour of fat being used at higher exercise intensities it would provide an immediate boost to endurance performance.

As well as being in finite supply, glucose cannot be replaced at the rate it's normally used when exercising hard, even using the latest sports nutrition products. The human body can't process ingested carbohydrate quickly enough to fuel working muscles with glucose once the body's stores are exhausted.

Ingested carbohydrates can delay the glucose exhaustion point, and push it back significantly. Using fat for fuel at higher outputs is the only thing that can spare glucose stores for when they would best be used, such as during really intense bits of races or on hill climbs. You can do that if you can flick the IL-6 switch.

THERE'S MORE

As well as tipping the fuel supply see-saw in favour of fats, IL-6 is thought to speed up glucose output from your liver and inhibits insulin resistance. So, as well as raising the intensity threshold at which you burn carbohydrates, it improves the top end of your body's fuel delivery system. It's a bit like a physiological turbo charger.

IL-6 also exhibits leptin-like effects on the body, leptin being the hormone that controls appetite. So, increasing the amount of IL-6 your muscles produce could help to control weight, which is always useful.

There is something important to stress about IL-6, and that's to define the difference between muscular production of IL-6, which is a good thing, and IL-6 produced by T-cells (a type of white blood cell) and macrophages. This is because high levels of IL-6 are found among cancer sufferers and people with other illnesses and major injuries. It has also been found in athletes who are showing over-training symptoms. However, in those situations the IL-6 is not secreted by muscles, and it works in a completely different way, doing a completely different job.

HOW TO FLICK THE SWITCH

Although the positive effects of IL-6 sound good, getting your muscles to produce it is a fine art, and it's very easy to get it wrong and do more harm than good.

In tests on fit athletes IL-6 release was maximized when very little glycogen was available. It was also found that IL-6 production was suppressed when carbohydrates were consumed during exercise.

One surefire way of doing that is a long ride in which you include several bouts of hard riding. Eat a small meal beforehand, and although you should drink plenty during the ride, try not to eat until you really feel you have to. The aim of this ride is to really deplete your glycogen stores, so you feel you can no longer maintain the hard level of effort you are making. At this point you will have gained the IL-6 effect from the ride.

You will feel shattered afterward, but the good news is there is evidence to suggest that its effects last, so you won't have to do it again soon. In fact, it's unwise to do it often. Consider it a flavouring, something worth adding but not a big ingredient of training.

2.4 OTHER FITNESS SWITCHES

A lot of cutting-edge training focuses on gene activation. Adaptations that improve your fitness are controlled by genes, and these adaptations are signalled by gene activators. Many advanced training sessions are designed to stimulate production of enzymes and other chemicals that signal specific gene activators, but done with such precision they provoke a specific response and don't stimulate reactions that might work against their objective.

Training, even at the top, used to be fairly hit and miss. Athletes relied on hard work to throw all their physiological plates in the air with the hope of catching as many as possible. They probably did some sessions that compromised the steps forward in fitness they were aiming for. Even what they ate and when they ate it occasionally worked against them. Things have changed dramatically since then.

TRAINING TO INCREASE MITOCHONDRIA

PGC-1a is a gene activator. The more PGC-1a there is in a muscle fibre the more mitochondria there are. PGC-1a production is controlled by an enzyme called AMPK, and AMPK is produced when our muscles work very hard. Therefore, AMPK production increases during high-intensity training. However, consuming carbohydrates during such exercise works against AMPK production.

High-intensity intervals, such as six by 1-minute sprints with 2 minutes of easy pedalling between each one, done in a short bout of cycling, say 1 hour on a turbo trainer, is a very effective way of increasing AMPK production and, therefore, mitochondrial density. Just make sure that you warm up and cool down, and that you don't take on any carbohydrates during the effort.

TRAINING TO INCREASE FAT ENZYMES

PPAR alpha is one of a number of chemicals called transcription factors, but what PPAR alpha controls is the amounts of enzymes that break down fat into a useable energy form. PPAR alpha production is stimulated by forcing your body to burn fat instead of carbohydrates, which could be done by hours of easy riding. However, a quicker way is to do some training in a fasted state.

Training for an hour at a fairly steady pace first thing in a morning without eating breakfast is a good way to do that. And you only need to do two or three of these rides in a 10–14-day period to get a large and reasonably long-lasting increase in PPAR alpha production.

STRENGTH TRAINING

It's been known for some time that human growth hormone and testosterone play a role in muscle repair and in achieving a muscle's potential. However, it's now understood that although those hormones play a part in it, they don't control protein synthesis, which is a crucial aspect of building muscle strength. A protein called mTORC1 does that.

Its production is stimulated by loading muscles, which means lifting heavy weights, and by the presence of amino acids. However, AMPK blocks its activation, and AMPK is produced in endurance training sessions. That's why it's hard to train for strength and endurance at the same time, but developing both is very important to a cyclist. Understanding the interaction of mTORC1 and AMPK enables coaches to plan more effective training sessions by timing them better, and by understanding the nutrition requirements of different training modes.

KEY POINTS TO TAKE AWAY

Don't do endurance and resistance training on the same day. If you do, however, do the endurance training before the resistance training.

High-intensity intervals of 3–5 minutes riding flat out and at a constant pace for the duration of each set dramatically increases the number of mitochondria in your muscle cells. Increased mitochondria density allows you to ride harder for longer. It's like the Holy Grail of fitness.

Boost your endurance with 1 hour of steady riding before your first meal of the day. Two or three of these sessions spread over ten days will enable you to ride harder while burning fat for fuel instead of carbohydrates. This spares your carbohydrate stores, reserving them for the harder parts of a ride, such as the hills. Occasional carbohydrate-depleted rides are enough to preserve this adaptation.

Eat a complete protein source or take an amino acid supplement before and after any resistance-training session.

PERFORMANCE CYCLING DEMANDS

5

2.5 CYCLING FITNESS

To simplify matters, in this section we are going to break down cycling fitness into five key facets, or abilities. They can be defined by the maximum effort you can maintain for the following periods of time:

6 SECONDS
30–60 SECONDS
3–5 MINUTES
1 HOUR
2+ HOURS

The importance of each ability depends on what kind of cycling challenge you take on. As a sprinter, most of my training was focused on improving the effort I could maintain for just a few seconds.

The sprint events require training predominantly in the maximal effort end of the spectrum, while most other cycling disciplines focus on sub-maximal efficiency over varying durations. A track pursuit rider focuses on the 3–5-minute range, but still works on 1-hour effort and endurance, while road racers should hone all five areas due to the variety of situations they face in their event.

Different cycling abilities are enabled by different physiological systems, and these systems require training because they are what makes you a better cyclist. Let's look at how they fit together.

6 SECONDS

This represents the maximum power you can perform on the bike. Even the best sprinters in the world can only hold a true peak power for 2 or 3 seconds.

This is a purely anaerobic effort requiring the conversion of creatine phosphate to ATP without using oxygen. This process fuels the most powerful muscle contractions, but even in a top sprinter, in top condition, the ATP is completely depleted after 6 seconds, and will require a relatively long time to replenish and recover.

Although all this sounds like the realm of sprinters, training to improve peak power is useful for a whole range of cyclists. Improving maximum power means you can kick out a few pedal revs and quickly close gaps in bunch races. It also helps you launch attacks and sprint faster at the end.

Upping peak power output also increases pedalling efficiency. This is because no matter the intensity, you put down more power for less fuel cost per pedal revolution than somebody with lower peak power. That can give you a significant energy saving over a long distance.

30–60 SECONDS

This is sub-maximal sprinting. The one-kilometre time trial on the track and keirin events demand training to improve this ability, but all cyclists benefit from training in this area. Training designed to improve your 30–60-seconds ability increases your body's lactate tolerance, which is its ability to process high levels of lactate and continue working in a high lactate state. Do that and you can deal with what cyclists refer to as "going into the red", which is something you have to do sometimes to make and withstand attacks in races. An effort of this duration can look harmless on paper but in reality causes the biggest pain to the legs if performed properly. Kilo riders can hit levels of 22 millimoles per litre of lactate in the blood after 60-second efforts. Not a pleasant sensation!

3–5 MINUTES

Riding as hard as you can at a constant pace for 3–5 minutes, where at the end of that period you can hardly ride any further, is a measure of something called your VO_2 max. It's the maximum amount of oxygen your body can process while exercising, and is a big performance limiter in endurance sports. Every individual has a predetermined genetic VO_2 max limit, but VO_2 max is very trainable up until that limit.

Endurance track riders train quite a lot at this level, but a little bit goes a long way, and even endurance track riders do blocks of VO_2 max work. For everyone else, used sparingly, training that pushes your VO_2 max toward its potential helps road racers make and withstand attacks, it improves time trial performance and it helps increase endurance and pedalling efficiency.

1 HOUR

Years ago, exercise scientists discovered that there is an optimal pace that cyclists can ride at which their bodies just about keep up with processing the fuel they need and removing the by-products of exercise. The pace can be maintained for roughly 1 hour before other factors come into play that tend to slow you down. Go any harder within that hour and you have to slow down to recover.

This pace has been referred to in various different ways, the most common being anaerobic threshold, although as I said, it's more a zone of transition. All cyclists dip in and out of this zone of transition, so improving the effort that you can maintain for 1 hour is important. It's very trainable too, and training it will also help increase your VO_2 max and efficiency.

2+ HOURS

This covers your ability to keep riding at a steady pace for a long time and marks the point at which your energy stores would become empty unless you start taking on fuel during the ride. It's a crucial capacity to train if you fancy doing a long-distance cycling challenge, but even ultra-endurance cyclists shouldn't spend all their time working on this. They need to work on the other abilities too.

2.5 SPECIFICITY & PROGRESSION

Specificity is one of the most important things to keep in mind when designing your training programme. That doesn't just mean riding your bike a lot, it means riding in a way that targets the specific abilities outlined on the previous two pages. Consider the duration, intensity, terrain, riding position and cadence of your target event and tailor your training accordingly.

If you are aiming for a particular objective, such as one of the challenges discussed later in the book, you should build toward it progressively and in a manner that targets the specific requirements of that challenge. Physiological adaptations occur in response to the body being pushed out of its comfort zone. Simply doing the same thing over and over, at the same intensity, will eventually result in minimal physiological adaption, as the body becomes accustomed to the training stress. Over time, in order to see progression, the training volume, intensity and frequency must continually change.

You should also think of your training as a pyramid, where each of the physiological capacities on pages 108–9 supports the next. You can achieve this through a process called periodization, where you spend separate periods of time focusing on training a particular physiological process to make significant gains, while still doing some training of the other processes to maintain any advances made there.

CLASSIC PERIODIZATION

For many years classic periodization was the way to train. You picked an objective, say a target race, and looked at how far ahead your target was. Then you divided the time you had to prepare for it into separate periods. The structure followed the simple guidelines of high volume/low intensity at the start of the season, progressing through to much higher intensity but lower volume of work as the big day approached. This formed your "pyramid" of training.

The biggest block was the base of the pyramid, and it was dedicated to endurance training, the ability to ride steadily for hours, also known as long steady distance training. This first period formed the foundation of the pyramid because it underpinned everything else. Apart from the shortest sprints, everything else in cycling has an element of endurance.

It's important to understand that periodization isn't linear. It's a tricky challenge for athletes and coaches to get the right balance, and ensure the overall progression is happening to achieve peak performance on the day that counts. So it's often something of a "plate spinning" exercise trying to ensure that you don't neglect one component of fitness for too long while focussing on another.

i

TRACK SPRINTERS & POWER ATHLETES

For track sprinters and any power athletes, their base is strength. It is the foundation of their performance from which power and speed can be developed. Typically, they would do large volumes of strength-based work in the early phases of their season. The exercises themselves would begin with high-resistance basic gross motor skills, which would become more cycling specific over time, to help convert this basic strength into on-bike power. The ability of the muscles to apply power in as explosive and efficient a manner as possible is the challenge, and this development of speed comes in the final stages of the periodized cycle.

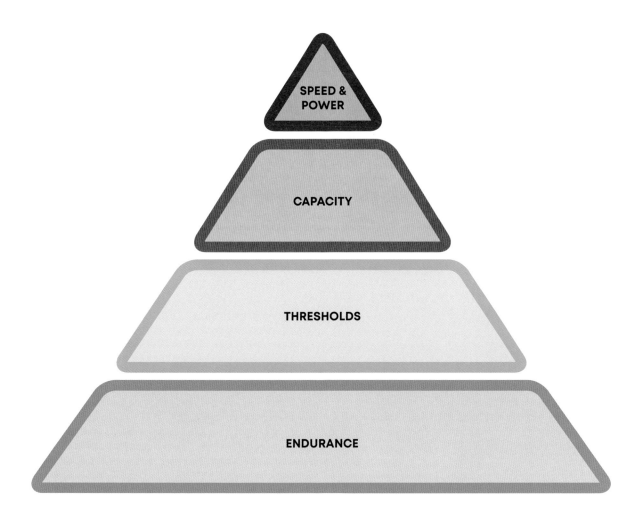

With all other disciplines, after a base period of long steady distance rides, training turned to improving the rider's one-hour pace. Then, while still while maintaining some training and one-hour pace, and doing longer rides, riders started training at VO$_2$ max pace to improve that ability. Then, after a period of focus on VO$_2$ max, riders would do some speed training, usually quite close to their target race pace. During all of this the riders would include some long rides and the other types of training they'd already practised.

MODERN THINKING

Classic periodization worked, but nowadays riders are more likely to include all the different types of training in each period, while focusing on one. That means they might do a base period of endurance training, but still be working on VO$_2$ max and pure speed to maintain previously made gains.

A reverse pyramid can also be effective for people living in parts of the world where their off-season is cold, and where short-distance, hard-effort training to improve VO$_2$ max, power and speed can be done indoors. Once the power and speed is put in place over the colder months, longer rides can be done when the weather improves to increase endurance.

PROGRESSION

Adjust periodization to suit your circumstances, but focus on really improving one ability during each phase while doing some work to maintain gains made in others. The key, though, is to keep progressing in each period, and you need to do that by making the individual training sessions you do harder each time, a process known as overload.

This is where a training diary comes in. By recording all your training sessions, including how you performed and felt in them, you have information that can help you to ensure the following sessions can be made more challenging. Then by factoring in adequate rest and good nutrition, you will improve the specific abilities you need. Next, I'll go deeper into each ability, how important they are for specific objectives, and how you know you are making the right efforts to target them.

2.5 ENDURANCE

Endurance underscores much of cycling performance. Most cyclists need endurance training to reach their potential, the exception being sprinters, for whom strength underpins their performance.

However, for some, endurance is an end, not just a means to better performance. Ultra-endurance challenges explore a world beyond what most enthusiasts would call "normal" cycling. It's a fascinating world too, where mental as much as physical strength plays a big role in the outcome.

WHAT'S OUT THERE?

Ultra-endurance events fall into two categories. There are those determined by distance and those determined by time. So, challenges such as 400 or more kilometres (250 or more miles), or 12- or 24-hour events. There are also records to go for, so distances including 500 and 1,000 miles, or time records, such as how far can be ridden in 12, 24 and 48 hours. Then there are races that go even further, like the Race Across America (RAAM), or the "most miles cycled in a year" record, something that has gained in popularity since the advent of GPS tracking apps such as Strava.

The numbers involved in ultra-endurance cycling are staggering, and it's a side of cycling that's growing. There have always been cyclists who ride long distances; after all, it's where the roots of the sport lie. The first races were designed to test the durability of a new invention, the safety bicycle, and those riding them were portrayed as superheroes battling terrible roads and awful conditions for hours on end.

Some ultra-endurance events are held on the same routes as the first races, such as Paris–Brest–Paris. There are also lots of new events that fall under this banner, and it's become a global phenomena. Increasing numbers are getting into ultra-endurance cycling, but what's the attraction and what sort of people do it?

THE OLDER THE BETTER

Ultra-endurance events tend to suit older cyclists. Mike Secrest is a doyen of the ultra-endurance world. He's in his 60s now and is the winner of the 1987 RAAM. He's held some amazing World records, the last of which he set when he was 54. "People who love cycling do ultra-endurance, and in particular it appeals to older riders because the major factor in success is in the mind, and long distances suit older riders physically as well," he says.

The mind is incredibly important in ultra-endurance, and more experienced riders tend to have a better sense of pace, while older people are often better at breaking a challenge down into manageable sections. Experience is essential, but long distances may suit older cyclists physically too.

With respect to shorter disciplines, there's generally a lot of bad news for cyclists as age increases: VO_2 max declines, muscle mass declines, fat deposits increase and power drops off. However, there is one physical capacity that can improve with age, and that's efficiency. This is the physical key to unlocking success in ultra-endurance challenges.

Efficiency is the metabolic cost of each pedal revolution. You apply power to the pedals, but a given amount of power doesn't exact the same physiological cost from every cyclist. More efficient cyclists can provide the same power to the pedals by using less fuel, and producing less waste. They are lean burn engines, they spare their energy supply and, even more importantly, they use a greater proportion of fat than glucose as fuel than less efficient riders. Provided they have a good nutrition strategy, efficient cyclists won't run out of fuel during a challenge.

Professional road racers with a good few Grand Tours in their legs are usually very efficient, but so are most cyclists who've done regular long rides for a number of years. Having said that, ultra-distance doesn't just belong to older riders. Young ones who have the right muscle-fibre composition (lots of slow-twitch fibres) are born for ultra-distance cycling. If you can keep going all day, going until your ride partners beg for mercy, but you are always last in the sprint for the café, then ultra-distance is waiting for you.

And there's more. Woman appear particularly suited to ultra-distance events in a number of sports. If you look at cycling and running World records, and express the men's time/distance as a percentage of the women's, the male and female percentage difference gets closer as distance increases. A great example of how the playing field can level with distance was seen in Britain during the late 1960s, when Beryl Burton set a new British record for a 12-hour time trial. However, not imagining that a women would ever ride that far in 12 hours the rules stated that the record was specifically a men's record, so the man she beat, who also rode further than the old record, was officially accorded the new one.

2.5 **THRESHOLDS**

Athletes have known for years that there is a limit to their fast cruising speed, and although they could exceed that limit for short stretches of time, it would eventually lead to a slow-down and recovery period. To find out why this happened sports scientists put athletes on treadmills cyclists on stationary bikes, and asked them to run or ride at a progressively faster pace. They recorded body temperature, blood chemistry, respiration, power output and heart rate. The answer to their question came from the athletes' blood chemistry, and a chemical by-product called lactate was thought to be the culprit.

THE SCIENCE

Scientists concluded that athletes could continue increasing their power output as long as they used oxygen to burn the fuel needed for their muscles. However, once they had maximized that system they started producing energy without using oxygen, and it caused a sudden and huge increase in lactate production, which they thought caused the slow-down.

Scientists called exercise powered by oxygen aerobic, and exercise without using oxygen anaerobic. The crossing point from one to the other was called the anaerobic threshold. However, it was still a tricky thing to quantify because it involved taking blood samples during tests in which subjects exercised at increasing intensities. The tests showed that blood lactate increased at a constant rate with increasing exercise intensity, but as the intensity continued to rack up, there came a point when blood lactate concentration rate increased suddenly. This was called the deflection point.

Then an Italian exercise physiologist, Professor Francesco Conconi, discovered that heart rate also deflected at the lactate deflection point. This therefore meant that the lactate deflection point could now be determined by heart rate. While Conconi was doing this work, portable heart rate monitors were being developed, which was timely.

Conconi also discovered (and to be fair, other people knew this intuitively too) that training at or fractionally under each athlete's individual anaerobic threshold (deflection point) pushed the threshold upward. So, by undertaking fairly precise training sessions using information displayed on a heart rate monitor, cyclists were able to increase the pace at which their physiology applied the brakes.

LACTATE THRESHOLD TRAINING TODAY

These days, scientists and coaches know a lot more about anaerobic threshold. For a start, it isn't lactate that puts the brakes on, it's hydrogen ions. This is because as you exceed your anaerobic threshold, lactate does build up, but it's broken down and used to produce more energy. Lactate isn't a limiter, but at the point where lactate suddenly builds, so do hydrogen ions, and they limit how hard you can ride because they increase the acidity of your muscles. Increased acidity interferes with the way muscle fibres work, and with energy turnover.

It's also accepted that heart rate is so variable from day to day that it's not the best indicator of where an individual's threshold lies. Some cyclists use power meters and power output tests to determine where their anaerobic threshold lies. They then use that data to improve their threshold power by training with a power meter.

Training with power is more accurate than heart rate, but even power output has variables, and the tests to determine it have to be exact. Most power meters also require regular calibration. That all adds extra cost and effort, so I think that despite all the breakthroughs in ways to monitor your training, training by feel still has a place.

Once you've learned what particular training intensities feel like, then how you're feeling becomes a sound reflection of what's going on inside your body. I'll talk more about using "feel" to monitor your training in the next two chapters, but one thing I think is very important to point out now is that training by feel helps you focus and keep in the moment of any effort you are making. It puts you in touch with what is going on inside your body.

---

i

THE OTHER THRESHOLD

There is another exercise threshold, or to give it its proper name, a zone of transition, and it also needs working on. It's the point where the body moves from relying on fats for fuel to using a mix of fats and glucose. After the fats-to-glucose switch is thrown, as exercise intensity increases, so does the percentage of glucose used to power your muscles.

This threshold is important because if you can raise it – and there are ways of doing that – then you can ride harder for longer because you will use a bigger proportion of fats for fuel, which are plentiful even in the skinniest person, and you save your limited glucose stores for harder efforts.

2.5 **CAPACITY**

Capacity describes the size of your engine, and training at capacity improves your performance potential. Training at this level is really hard, and you must be really committed, even though the sessions are short. Most cyclists, no matter what they are training for, will benefit from doing some capacity work, and in some disciplines capacity is a massive performance limiter.

WHAT IS IT?

Roughly speaking, capacity describes a maximal effort over a 5-minute duration. A capacity effort is close to a person's VO_2 max. It's a measure of the maximum amount of oxygen an individual can process during intense exercise.

An athlete's VO_2 max is measured during a controlled ramp test. During these forms of efforts athletes ride against increasing resistance. They use the same gear ratio, and are asked to keep up the same pedal revs throughout the test. As you can imagine, it becomes harder and harder as the resistance increases. The athletes carry on, pushing as hard as they can until they can no longer maintain the required pace. At that point, the test is over.

The ramp test measures where the athlete's thresholds are, then close to the end of the test, close to where the athlete can't continue, the testers are able to determine the VO_2 max. This is measured in millilitres per kilogram, per minute, which is expressed as ml/min. The VO_2 max is a very good predictor of an athlete's potential in endurance sports, but it's not the only predictor.

For example, VO_2 max is the potential size of an individual's engine, but it doesn't measure how efficient that engine is. A cyclist with a massive VO_2 max will always be good, but not as good as they could be if their efficiency is poor. That means that efficient cyclists often beat competitors capable of producing much higher VO_2 max numbers.

Potential VO_2 max is genetic, but it is also much higher than untrained VO_2 max, so training in a methodical, disciplined manner allows you to access a greater percentage of your potential. Someone with less genetic potential can beat someone with more, just because they train more effectively.

CLOSING ON POTENTIAL

The most powerful way to nudge your current VO_2 max toward its potential is by doing capacity training sessions. They help increase your sustained maximum power, which you use when making or withstanding attacks in races. But capacity sessions also drag up your thresholds, which means you will be able to cruise at a higher percentage of your VO_2 max. Basically, you'll be able to ride harder for longer.

This is because capacity sessions done at above anaerobic threshold improve your body's ability to mop up excess hydrogen ions. However, the training required to elicit this

is tough, and should be used sparingly because too much causes a phenomenon called over-training. This is a place you don't want to go, and it's more than just being tired.

Being tired after a training session is good, it's what sends messages to your body to adapt during periods of recovery, but over-training means experiencing fatigue long after a period of recovery. There's a massive difference. A lot of cyclists mistake over-training for a lack of fitness, so they train harder. That can lead to chronic fatigue, a medical condition that can take a long time to overcome.

So, capacity is a crucial area for most competitive cyclists to work on. It's a massive performance limiter in single-day road races, in which even sprinters have to survive attacks by going very hard and processing a lot of oxygen before they get to the end to unleash their finish. Capacity efforts split up races; they get breakaways established, both uphill and on the flat, and they are key to performance in cyclo-cross and cross-country mountain biking.

All those types of cyclists must include capacity sessions in their training, but it is strong stuff and must be used sparingly. Capacity efforts also improve time trial and long-distance performance, although if that's the only competitive cycling those riders do they need less capacity work. Finally, capacity is the chief performance limiter in endurance track cycling.

2.5 SPEED & POWER

Scan this QR code to see a video of me riding at my maximum sprint effort.

No cyclist can be too fast. Clearly, it is the be-all and end-all for track sprinters, but having the ability to make short, sharp bursts of speed can help anyone. Bridging gaps, attacking and going for stage wins in road racing all require speed and power.

It's the same in other disciplines. Cyclo-cross riders and cross-country mountain bikers must be fast to get off the grid quickly. Throw in downhill mountain bike racing, and all off-road cycling disciplines require repeating sprint-type efforts. While BMX is pure speed.

Improving basic speed and power even helps cyclists stay safe in traffic. Acceleration is vital in getting away smoothly from traffic lights, and it helps decisive moves in traffic.

SPIN TO WIN

Even riders who specialize in the smoother efforts involved in a time trial, or those who take part in ultra-distance challenges will benefit from doing speed training. The reason is that riding fast for a very short time means you have to focus on perfect pedalling technique. That's because a perfect pedalling technique is the only way to get maximum power into the pedals.

It's also worth including some really fast pedalling bursts in your training, using a lower gear than you are comfortable in but spinning it really quickly. Track sprinters do this a lot and it means that they get comfortable with the cadence they ride at in competitions.

Fast pedalling and sprint intervals promote and reinforce the correct neuromuscular pathways for pedalling, which in turn improves cycling efficiency, which is a crucial for all cyclists including time trialists and ultra-distance riders.

POWER

I included power in the heading for this section, first because it has a bearing on sprint speed, but also because it covers efforts lasting a bit longer than a pure sprint, so from 30 seconds to 1 minute. These prolonged bursts of speed are also efficiency improvers, and they are a crucial skill to have in many cycling disciplines.

By increasing the absolute power that you transmit to the pedals, you increase the efficiency of your cycling. In short, this means you can put in more power for less fuel, which is a significant factor in long-distance riding. Plus, done in a certain way, very short intervals are good for building core strength. You don't need much training at this intensity, but it is very important.

Being able to make and sustain short bursts of power is crucial in a variety of race situations. It's much easier to sprint across any gaps in the peloton if you are fast, rather than make a sustained effort to cross them. No matter how strong you are, if you take too long to close gaps it will cost you.

Every road and track racer needs a snap speed. It will get you out of trouble, help you move up quickly in the bunch and get back up to speed after corners. It's a crucial ability in all sorts of situations. When I started my cycling career and was competing in a much wider range of events, the coach at my local cycling club always said that it didn't matter whether you were racing mountain bikes, on the road or on the velodrome, never neglect your speed training.

FULL ON

To get the most from speed and power training you should be fresh for each session you do, so do them after an easy day, but the sessions must be full on. You must start each effort without thinking of the rest of the session. Just focus on doing one effort at a time and getting as much speed and power into it as possible. As far as building pure speed and getting the efficiency benefits from speed training, it's better to do three at one hundred per cent than do six or more at only ninety-five per cent. Commit fully, as though each effort is your last.

HORMONAL EFFECT

There is a lot to be gained from sprint and power training. It increases efficiency for long-distance riders, improves off-road performance and even accelerates recovery and fat loss.

This is because it stimulates testosterone production immediately afterward and stimulates later growth hormone production. These are two things that greatly aid recovery and promote fitness boosts. Although sprint training is fuelled by glucose, it increases resting metabolic rate for up to 24 hours afterward, which has the net effect of not only burning more calories than a steadier session would, but also of taking a large proportion of those calories from fat reserves.

TRAINING TOOLBOX

6

2.6 ENDURANCE TRAINING SESSIONS

The best way, the inescapable way, to increase endurance is by doing some long steady distance training. It's not the only way – endurance can be improved in shorter sessions and with the help of dietary manipulation. However, if you ride long races or do other types of endurance challenges, you need regular long steady rides in your training, and there is an important secret to getting the most out of them.

LONG STEADY DISTANCE SESSIONS

This is a long ride, although how long depends on your previous cycling experience and current fitness. It can be anything from 1–6 hours, and more for anyone preparing for an ultra-distance challenge. The distance is less important than the intensity of this session. It must be below the point where the body switches from using mostly fats for fuel in the fats/glucose mix, so that in these sessions fats are dominant in the fuel mix. Drift above this intensity and the benefit of the session is lost.

Luckily, it's quite easy to feel when you're riding at the correct long steady distance intensity. It should feel easy, so a pace where you could hold a conversation without taking big gulps of air. If you are riding alone, try reciting the words of your favourite song under your breath. If you start gasping between the words, slow down until you can say them easily.

This is an easy session, but easy to get wrong, and a lot of cyclists go too hard on long steady distance rides. They end up training in a grey area that's too hard to improve their fat metabolism, and not hard enough to improve anything else.

All endurance training, including long steady distance, increases mitochondrial density in muscle fibres, which provides muscles with access to more energy.

GO FAST TO GO LONG

There are many studies on the effects of interval training. In 2008 Burgomaster and Howarth et al studied the effects of micro-interval training, and found that as well as causing anaerobic adaptations and increased muscle mass, which is what you would expect, after performing high-intensity intervals skeletal muscles expressed large amounts of a protein known to induce mitochondrial genesis. Mitochondria are the cells where energy is produced to keep muscles working.

When he was one of British Cycling's coaches, Dan Hunt suggested that one major reason for the success of so many riders trained in the British Cycling system could be: "The way we can train speed and endurance at the same time without ever focusing on either of the two."

Furthermore, experiments with micro-intervals have shown that they increase the levels of proteins associated with the oxidation and transport of glucose and fatty acids. The net result is that fat is burned as an energy source at higher exercise intensities and for longer periods of time. These are all endurance, not speed adaptations. Therefore, short intervals (see pages 130–1) do more than their main purpose of boosting top-end performance.

A COMPRESSED LONG STEADY DISTANCE SESSION

The physiological effects of a 6-hour ride can be evoked in a much shorter session by creating glycogen depletion, but still doing most of the ride at fat-burning intensity. The body stores glucose as glycogen, converting it to glucose when the body demands. Depleting the body's glycogen stores reduces the amount of glucose available for fuel, and so forces it to work by using fats as fuel. Doing that increases the intensity at which glucose is the body's predominant fuel choice, so sparing glycogen stores for really intense efforts.

Reducing the duration of a long steady distance ride cuts over-use injuries, reduces exposure to bad weather and prevents the immune system becoming depressed, which happens after long rides. You can repeat a compressed long steady distance session more often, and therefore stimulate a greater response and adaptation to it. It's advanced training, though. Most riders improve endurance just by eating fewer carbohydrates and doing occasional long steady distance rides. Compressed long steady distance is for keen competitive racers wanting a bit more.

You start by eating very little carbohydrate at breakfast. Then, after warming up by slowly increasing your effort, ride hard for 10 minutes to reduce some of your glycogen stores.

Then drop down to your normal long steady distance intensity for the long middle part of the ride. The final trick is to do the last 10 minutes at high intensity, but pedalling very quickly – 100 to 110 rpm, or more if you can. Fast pedalling creates a high oxygen demand without loading your muscles. It tricks the body into thinking it's working hard, because by this stage of the training session there is very little glucose left to fuel this sudden elevated oxygen demand.

If you get this training session right you can boost the body's ability to use fats as fuel at higher intensities, the major adaptation brought about by riding long distances.

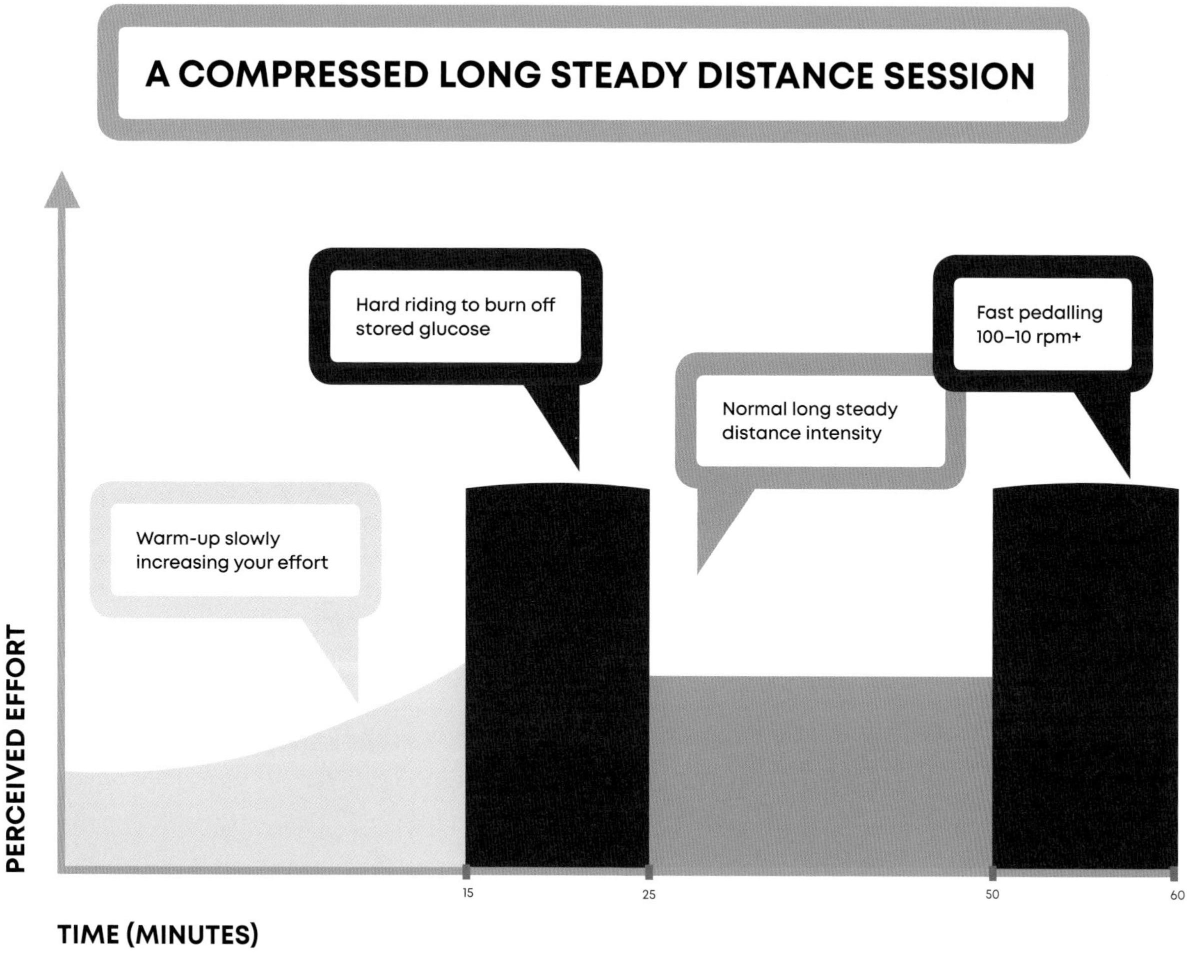

A COMPRESSED LONG STEADY DISTANCE SESSION

Hard riding to burn off stored glucose

Fast pedalling 100–10 rpm+

Normal long steady distance intensity

Warm-up slowly increasing your effort

PERCEIVED EFFORT

15   25   50   60

TIME (MINUTES)

2.6 **THRESHOLD SESSIONS**

Endurance training sessions, such as the ones described on pages 120–1, will increase the intensity of effort you can make before you cross your first threshold, in which you predominantly burn fats for fuel. The following session addresses the second threshold, the one that was called the anaerobic threshold. This is where a sudden increase in blood lactate concentration occurs. The training session described below, or variations of it, help you increase the intensity you can ride at before the sudden increase of blood lactate concentration occurs. You'll be able to ride faster and push harder before your physiological brakes slow you down.

FEELING THE BURN

"Feel the burn" was a phrase used in aerobics, a form of exercise that was once very popular. It encouraged participants to push hard until they could feel a pleasant warming sensation in their muscles, which, it was believed, was when it was doing them the most good. It helped people focus when they were exercising, and learning to feel where your upper threshold intensity is helps you improve your threshold.

The riding intensity at which blood lactate levels start rising rapidly feels like a very hard but manageable effort. You will breathe deeply and quickly and your legs will feel like they are pushing hard, but it's workable hard. Threshold intensity should feel hard, but you should feel on top of it. When fully fit, rested and really committed, you could probably ride like that for 1 hour. That's the pace you are looking for.

However, you don't have to train at your threshold intensity to increase it. You can push the threshold up by riding at an intensity that many coaches call the sweet spot. The threshold can also be pulled upward by riding at intensities above it, as will be explained on pages 125–6, but that form of training is very hard.

You get much more fitness return from riding at sweet-spot intensity. Sweet-spot training isn't as fatiguing as threshold or above-threshold training, so you can do more. Finally, most coaches agree that it is training volume that has the biggest effect on improving fitness, so long as it doesn't exceed the total amount of work your body can handle.

THE TEST

Before you start sweet-spot training you need to establish a benchmark effort, so you can become familiar with what it feels like. The test establishes your lactate threshold riding intensity. Repeat it three times, equally spaced, in a period of seven to ten days so you become familiar with it. It's a good training session in its own right, so it won't harm your fitness by doing these three tests.

Do the test on a circuit of flat to undulating roads. A long hill is even better, but it must be long enough to take 20 minutes to ride. If you can't find a stretch of road like that then try a flat to undulating off-road circuit, or use a turbo trainer. The latter has the advantage of providing precision and a controlled environment, plus a threshold test on a turbo trainer is easily repeated.

Warm-up for the test by riding progressively harder for 20 minutes. Then ride very hard for 20 seconds, then easy for 40 seconds, and repeat that 20 seconds hard/40 seconds easy five times. Ride easy for 5 minutes, then start the test.

You have got to ride as hard as you can at a constant pace for 20 minutes, so don't start too fast. The pace you are after is what you could manage, at a push, for 1 hour. Holding it for 20 minutes is long enough for you to get a feel for it, but not so long that it becomes a real suffer-fest. Finish by riding progressively more easily for the last 5 minutes.

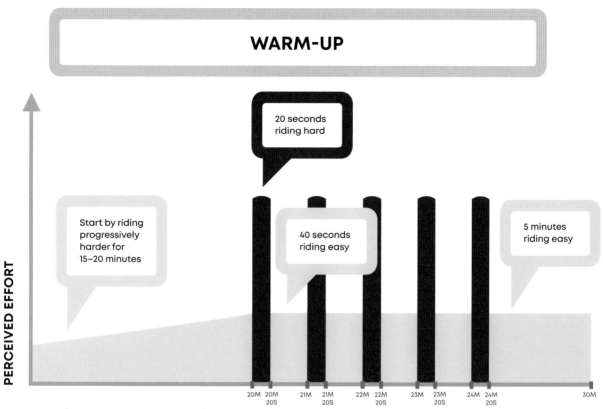

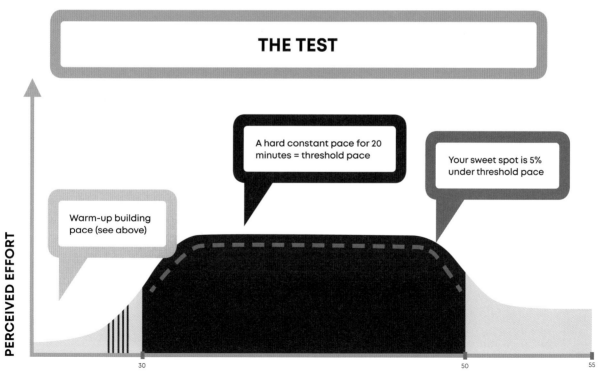

THE SESSION

You need some self-knowledge for this, which is why
I recommend repeating the test three times. Once you have
the feel for it, your sweet spot is just under (about five per cent
under) the test pace, so when you do sweet-spot repeats, start
each one at threshold pace, and then quickly back off to just
under it.

The session itself is simple. You warm-up for 10–15
minutes by riding progressively harder. Then do two
10-minute repeats at sweet-spot intensity, with 5 minutes
easy pedalling between each one. Stay in the zone and
concentrate during the repeats. Build up the length of time you
ride at sweet-spot pace to 20 minutes, repeated twice, giving
you 40 minutes at near-threshold pace. That will start pushing
your threshold upward.

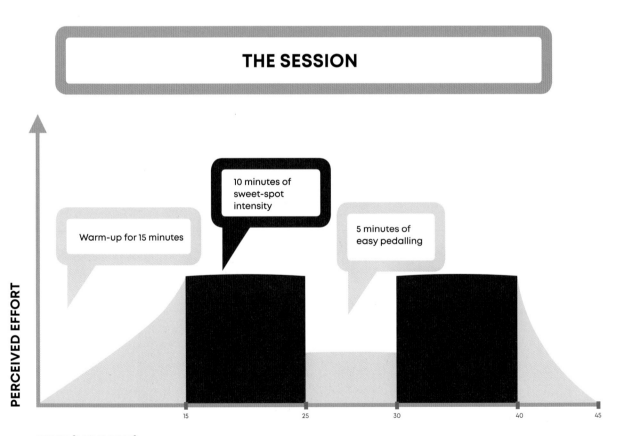

THE SESSION

Warm-up for 15 minutes

10 minutes of sweet-spot intensity

5 minutes of easy pedalling

PERCEIVED EFFORT

15   25   30   40   45

TIME (MINUTES)

2.6 CAPACITY SESSIONS

These are training efforts designed to move performance closer to genetic VO_2 max potential and are particularly popular with Great Britain endurance coaches. Performance at close to VO_2 max, and the ability to recover quickly from doing so, is the lynchpin of road-racing success, especially in single-day road races. It is also crucial in circuit races, shorter time trials, cyclo-cross, cross-country mountain biking and endurance track racing. Working at close to VO_2 max also improves your overall efficiency and endurance, and it drags up your thresholds.

Capacity sessions demand a lot from your body, which responds during recovery by increasing the efficiency of mitochondria in muscle fibres, as well as their number. These sessions also improve lung and heart function, have a positive effect on muscle fibres, and help increase the efficiency with which oxygen and fuels are delivered to and taken up by working muscles. This kind of work is a very powerful tool, but it should be used sparingly. Do too much training at capacity and you risk chronic fatigue.

CLASSIC VO₂ MAX INTERVALS

As I said, you are trying to push your capacity toward your genetic VO₂ max limit. Each interval lasts 3 minutes, and its intensity should be as hard as you can maintain at a constant effort for those 3 minutes.

A good way to dose your effort, and get the most effect from this training, is to do the first minute of the three at an intensity you could keep up for 5 minutes. It should feel harder than a threshold effort, but manageable. In the second minute, try to lift your pace and push a little bit harder on the pedals. For the final minute, try to maintain the intensity of the second minute. You should feel like you are hanging on for the final 30 seconds of the 3 minutes, desperately watching each second tick by until the 3 minutes are up.

Aim to do three 3-minute classic capacity intervals, working up to five, with 3 minutes of easy riding recovery between each one. There's no need to do more than five, because progression comes by always riding as hard as you can for 3 minutes. So, you are always pushing toward your limit.

There are several ways of doing these intervals. Some riders do them on the flat, others on a climb or even off-road, but whatever terrain you choose, you must allow each 3-minute effort to be constant. That's why doing them on a turbo trainer is a good idea, because you can focus totally on pacing the effort.

VARIATIONS

British Cycling endurance riders do capacity intervals, such as the 3-minute ones, but sometimes extend them to 5 minutes. They are full-time bike riders, so they can factor in sufficient recovery from these longer efforts.

For variation, you can shorten your capacity efforts and do more of them. For example, six to eight 2-minute intervals, done on a turbo trainer, with 3 minutes of easy pedalling between each. Control the first 30 seconds of each effort, then give it everything for the rest of the interval. You should be going as hard as you can by 1 minute, then hanging on through the next.

Whatever type of capacity intervals you do, make sure you are fresh when you do them, and that you recover fully afterward. Do them after an easy day and follow them with another easy day. Don't do capacity efforts more than once a week and refuel straight afterward. I'll go into training frequency and nutrition later in the book.

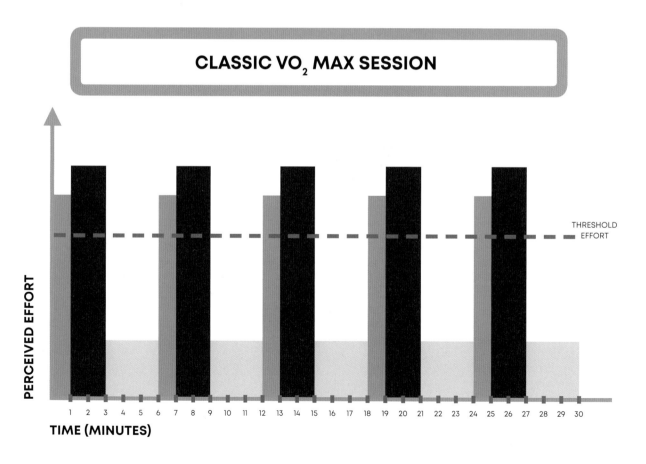

CLASSIC VO₂ MAX SESSION

THRESHOLD EFFORT

PERCEIVED EFFORT

TIME (MINUTES)

1 2 3 4 5 6 7 8 9 10 11 12 13 14 15 16 17 18 19 20 21 22 23 24 25 26 27 28 29 30

SPIKE EFFORTS

Team Sky riders use spiked efforts, a name coined by their coach Tim Kerrison, when preparing for big road races such as the Tour de France. They do them to simulate some of the efforts they will have to make during a race, but they also have a profound effect on improving capacity performance.

The Tour de France guys do them on long climbs, but they can be done on various terrains or on a turbo trainer. The idea is to ride at threshold, then jump up to a much higher pace, as if they were making or answering an attack in a race, for 30 seconds to a minute, then drop back to threshold for a while, then do another spike effort, and so on. This is hard training and should not be attempted until you are very fit. Use it to find a bit extra in the weeks before you taper your training for a big race.

2.6 SPEED & POWER SESSIONS

At the risk of repeating myself, no cyclist can be too fast or too powerful. Speed and power are essential in race situations, but training the physical systems that improve both have lasting effects on other areas in the body. It will help you became stronger and boost your ability to deal with and process lactate.

10 seconds flat-out

MICRO-INTERVALS

Professional cyclists have been doing micro-intervals for years, and they are increasingly used by fitness coaches and personal trainers when working with busy clients. Micro-intervals are short but intense efforts of 60 seconds or less, repeated several times with varying lengths of active recovery between them. They have a wide range of very potent training effects, but some of the reasons behind those effects are only just being discovered.

It's fairly obvious from their short but full-on nature that micro-intervals will have a positive effect on the basic power a cyclist transmits to the pedals. And if the recovery intervals between them are kept short, micro-intervals are really potent at training the sort of "attack, recover and attack again" ability required for many forms of bike racing.

However, it's recently been discovered that micro-intervals also train the physiological processes that support much longer efforts. They boost the level of VO_2 max potential an individual can access with a positive effect on absolute fitness. They can be a great core training method and significantly increase cycling efficiency by strengthening

core muscles and perfecting the neurological links that fire the muscles we use when pedalling.

An interval training session like this, with full-on efforts sprinting out of the saddle, then reducing the power and keeping recovery short, is road-race specific. Many circuit-race specialists do a version of this on a short circuit by sprinting out of corners, sitting and keeping the power on, then slowing for the next corner, and sprinting out of it.

PRO-POWER SESSIONS

This is a standard pro road-racer session. After a good warm-up, do a set of ten times 40 seconds hard and 20 seconds easy (see opposite below).

Experienced pros will repeat the set of ten reps four times, with 5–10 minutes easy pedalling in between each set (see below). You can do them during a longer ride, or you can do them on a turbo trainer. Some riders vary this session by doing 20 seconds flat-out with 40 seconds easy, which changes the session's emphasis toward increasing your raw power output. One set of ten of either of these is enough to get a solid response from your body.

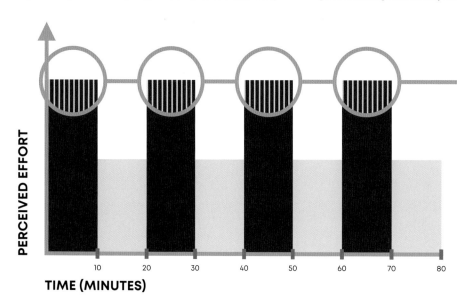

PERCEIVED EFFORT

TIME (MINUTES)

TRACK SPRINTER TURBO SESSION

There are hundreds of different ways to approach training for track sprinting, but a good starting point for beginners is to repeat the following four times: 10 seconds flat-out, then 1 minute and 50 seconds recovery. Your flat-out sprint needs to be done at 100 per cent. Repeat the set three times, with 5–10 minutes recovery between sets.

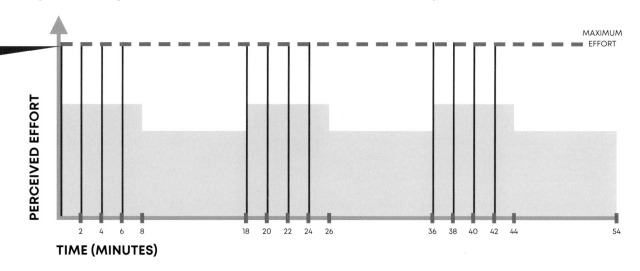

PURE SPRINTS

Improving raw top-end speed is what my racing world, track sprinting, is all about, but occasional training sessions based on the principles track sprinters use are worthwhile for any cyclist who wants a bit of extra zip in his or her legs. Remember, even the toughest road races are often decided by a final sprint for the line.

Pure sprint training is simple. You sprint flat-out, then take a long recovery – at least 5 minutes – then do it again. An easy ride with friends to a café and back, with a few sprints for village signs or other predetermined points, is an excellent sprint session for a road racer.

For something more structured, after a solid warm-up, do five 30-second all-out sprints with 5 minutes of easy pedalling between each one. You must really go for it in the sprints, which is why a bit of competition from a riding friend or friends often helps with this session.

The day before a race is a good time to do this, so long as you don't do too many. You won't ruin your chances in the race – only track sprinters can go hard enough to do damage that would need longer recovery in a sprint. For all other competitive riders, a few sprints the day before a race can sharpen up their legs and help them prepare mentally for the upcoming race.

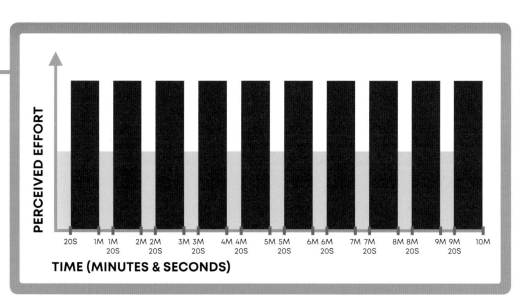

2.6 **TIME-SAVING SESSIONS**

Magazines and books are always coming out with headlines, such as "you can get fit in 20 minutes a week". My favourite was the Seven-Minute Abs workout that promised a six-pack by doing 7-minute training sessions!

Of course, it's easy to get elitist about these things, and anything that gets people exercising is great. Any amount is better than nothing, but anyone taking on any sort of cycling challenge needs more time than 20 minutes a week.

However, there is a very effective training method that gives you a good workout in less time. It's called high intensity interval training (HIIT), and it involves doing repeated short sprints, separated by short intervals of rest. It's perfect for a day when you haven't much time for training.

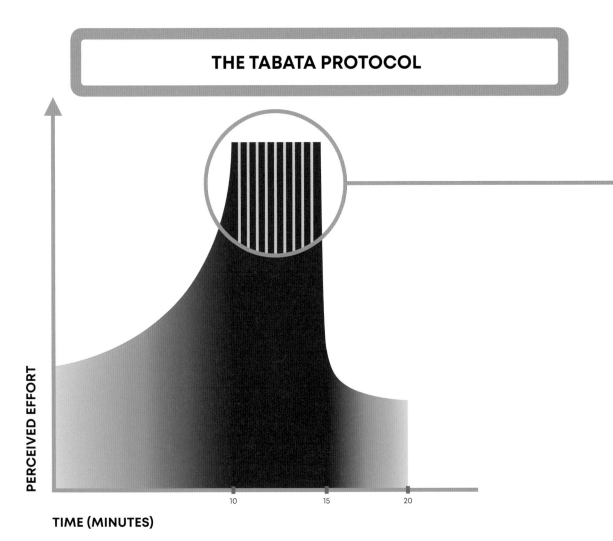

THE TABATA PROTOCOL

PERCEIVED EFFORT

10   15   20

TIME (MINUTES)

THE TABATA PROTOCOL

This is perhaps the most famous study done on micro-interval training. In 1996 an exercise scientist, Izumi Tabata, found that bouts of 20 seconds of flat-out exercise followed by 10 seconds easy, repeated continuously for 4 minutes, increased the VO_2 max of a group of subjects. These bouts of exercise were repeated four times a week, while the group did one steady-state ride on another day. At the same time a similar group did steady-state rides only and showed no improvement in VO_2 max.

This method of training has been seized on by the gym community and is used as a way of training with almost any exercise you can think of. For cyclists though, it's heartening to know that if you can get on an exercise bike, say in a hotel gym, you can do an effective training session in 12 minutes.

- Do 5 minutes riding progressively harder to warm up, 10 if you have time.
- Then do eight 20-second maximum efforts, riding as hard as you can, with 10 seconds easy between each one. That takes 5 minutes, but it's a painful 5 minutes.
- Finally, cool down with 5 minutes of easy pedalling.

I used to do Tabata when I was training for the one-kilometre time trial. I would do two sets with half an hour of rest in between them. I did them on a turbo trainer with low inertia, so I went straight into flat-out sprinting for 20 seconds. Then I stopped pedalling for 10 seconds, then went straight into the next 20-second sprint, and so on.

For me, this was a real lactate tolerance session. Because I'm a sprinter I went deep in each 20-second sprint, producing a lot of lactate. Stopping pedalling between each sprint helped it build up in my legs so the levels rose during the 4 minutes, nearly getting to where they are at the end of a one-kilometre time trial.

I kept my average for each 20-second sprint at above 600 watts, giving me 2 minutes and 40 seconds above 600 watts. I dreaded this session. Each 20-second sprint felt harder than the last, until the last one, which was terrible. I'd end up with huge levels of lactate in my legs, which really hurt. It was like having barbed wire pulled through my veins.

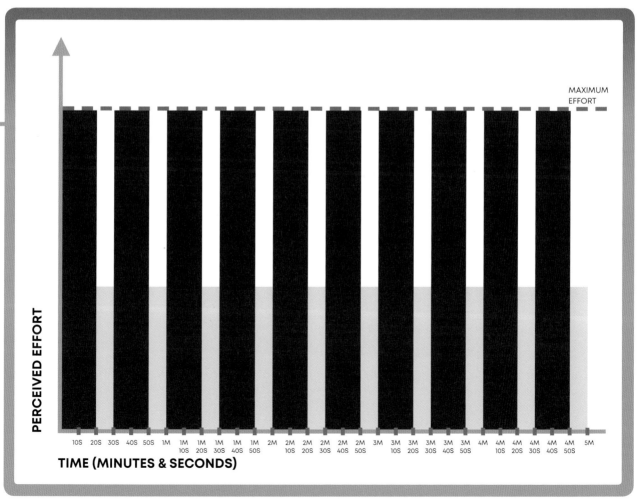

MAXIMUM EFFORT

PERCEIVED EFFORT

10S 20S 30S 40S 50S 1M 1M10S 1M20S 1M30S 1M40S 1M50S 2M 2M10S 2M20S 2M30S 2M40S 2M50S 3M 3M10S 3M20S 3M30S 3M40S 3M50S 4M 4M10S 4M20S 4M30S 4M40S 4M50S 5M

TIME (MINUTES & SECONDS)

THE QUICK POWER BLAST

This is a really effective short training session that can only be done on a turbo trainer. It's very effective at improving your power output, efficiency and core strength.

- Warm-up for 10 minutes.
- Stay firmly seated in the saddle, don't move your upper body, and pedal hard for 10 seconds.
- Pedal easy for 20 seconds.
- Repeat the 10 seconds hard, then 20 seconds easy for 15 minutes.
- Pedal easy for 5 minutes.
- Do another 15 minutes alternating 10 seconds hard and 20 seconds easy.
- Finally, pedal easy to cool down.

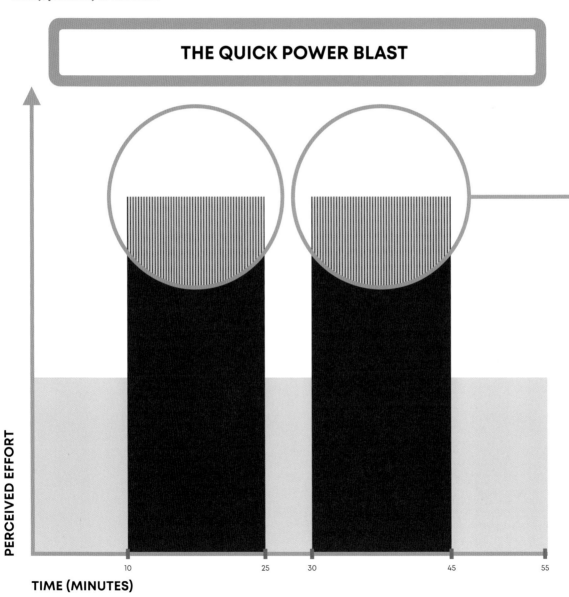

THE QUICK POWER BLAST

PERCEIVED EFFORT

TIME (MINUTES)

10   25   30   45   55

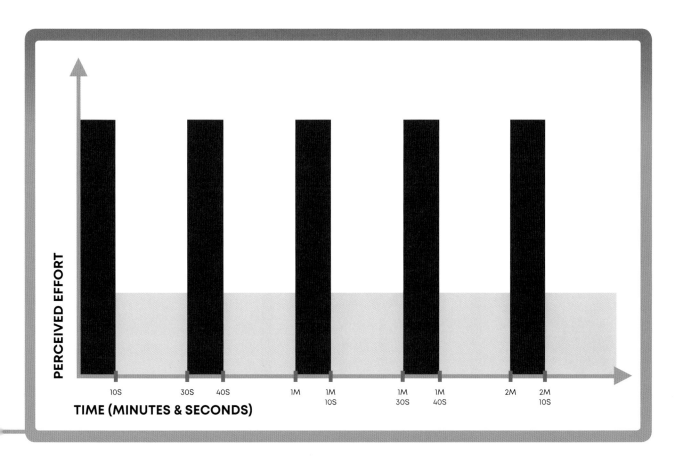

PERCEIVED EFFORT

TIME (MINUTES & SECONDS)

10S 30S 40S 1M 1M 10S 1M 30S 1M 40S 2M 2M 10S

THE SCIENCE

A number of scientists have compared the effectiveness of micro-intervals to more traditional forms of interval training. For example, in 2006 Gibala et al demonstrated that 2.5 hours of sprint interval training over the space of one week produced similar biochemical muscle changes to 10.5 hours of endurance training, and it produced similar endurance performance effects. So, micro-intervals are a great time-saver.

Micro-intervals may also help with losing weight, since they raise post-exercise resting metabolic rate for up to 24 hours. This is as well as the benefit already mentioned about boosting the production of testosterone and human growth hormone (see page 101). Micro-intervals were also found to train muscles to oxidize fats at higher intensities of effort, which in turn means more body fat can be used as fuel.

It's useful to know that a session as short as the Tabata Protocol (see pages 130–1) which can take 12 minutes to perform, will have a positive effect on your fitness. But saving time isn't the be-all and end-all of micro-intervals. They are worth including in your training for their own sake, because as well as giving a lot of training for your time, they produce well-documented training effects of their own.

Finally though, perhaps the biggest benefit of micro-intervals is their reduced cost in terms of wear and tear on your body. Longer intervals still have their place and they are very effective at raising your threshold pace and helping you to access a greater percentage of your genetic VO$_2$ max. However, longer intervals are very costly in terms of the physiological damage they cause, which requires long periods of recovery to compensate and allow fitness benefits to take hold. Micro-intervals do many of the same things, but without the high physical cost, which is why there should be a place for them in everyone's training toolbox.

2.6 **RECOVERY**

It's important to recognize that you don't go through physiological adaptations during a training session. The act of exercise sends messages, but you get fitter during your phases of rest. The fundamental training equation is as follows:

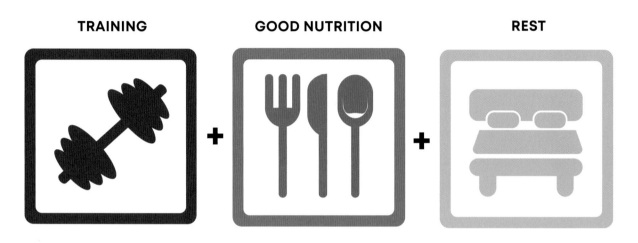

TRAINING + GOOD NUTRITION + REST

INCREASED FITNESS

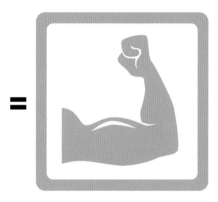

All of the elements above need equal attention, and while it's easy to overlook, quality rest is important. It's also crucial to remember that rest must be proportionate to the arduousness of each training session.

While training in the right manner is key, taking in some easy rides and enjoying your rest days will help your mind recover too. You will want to ensure that the bike doesn't just become associated with effort and pain. An easy ride to a café with friends preserves the association between cycling and fun.

Recovery can be divided into three parts:

- Recovery after each training session
- Recovery after each target race or challenge
- A longer recovery period as part of your yearly training cycle

POST-SESSION RECOVERY

After hard training the speed with which you replenish nutrients will dictate how quickly you recover. Your body is particularly receptive to absorbing these nutrients in the 30-minute window following exercise and therefore it's crucial to start this process as soon as possible. This is when shakes and gels are particularly useful – not only are they convenient but also the body can assimilate the nutrients from them faster than from solid food. In practice, this usually means having a recovery shake immediately after getting off your bike, then having a proper meal within 90 minutes.

POST-RACE RECOVERY

After a race you'll probably have pushed yourself that little bit harder than in normal training and you have to tackle your post-race recovery according to what you have coming up; it might be a single race or you might have just completed a stage of a race with more sections to come. Either way, make sure you rehydrate and replenish your nutrients as soon as you finish the race or section. Planning and preparation before a race is key to ensure that you have the appropriate nutrition ready to consume as soon as you can. Make sure you have a high-quality source of protein to aid repair and regeneration, carbs to refuel and fluid to rehydrate.

THE OFF-SEASON

If you have trained hard all year, then a complete rest after your last challenge is a good idea. However, don't stop training all at once. Instead, cut back for a couple of weeks, only riding your bike when you really want to. It's a good idea to start alternative forms of exercise as well.

Road race and time trial competitors traditionally compete through the spring, summer and autumn, which is when most cyclosportive events take place. That means late autumn or the start of the winter is the best time to take a complete rest. Ten to fourteen days should recharge your batteries, although ultra-distance riders need longer and more regular time off after really long challenges. In fact, after any big target races or challenges, an easy week or two, with maybe some extra days off, is a good idea. Winter is also a good time to get a bike fit and evaluate your kit for the season ahead.

Once you start training again, focus on a 12-week strength and conditioning programme. After that, try to fit in one session a week at the gym, even during summer. Older riders should do one strength and conditioning session religiously throughout their competition season, only missing the session during the week of a target race.

To kick off your bike training during the winter, start riding outside only when the weather is good and you feel like it. Make the rides enjoyable and relaxed, and don't be caught up with distance or effort. The off-season is also a good time to start running, if you enjoy running that is. It's a great cardiovascular exercise that's convenient to do anywhere, and it has some direct crossover benefits for cyclists. Running up hills is particularly good. However, in order to help prevent injuries, make sure that you invest in proper running shoes from a specialist shop.

After your initial 12-week plan it's time to start a more formal, bike-specific training programme, 12 weeks before your first race or challenge. One or two months is enough time to fit in off-season recovery, non-specific fitness work and at least begin your strength and conditioning programme. It doesn't matter if the latter overlaps with the start of on-the-bike training.

DAY TO DAY

The first step in recovery is nutrition. There's a full discussion on the role of nutrition later in the book, but the golden rule, unless you are trying to improve fat metabolism, is fuel your rides and watch what you eat post-exercise.

Training correctly doesn't work unless you provide your body with the building blocks it needs to get fitter and stronger. So, a post-ride snack comprising proteins and carbohydrates is the first block to put in place. After that you should eat commensurate with the size and type of effort you made in training. Eat enough carbohydrates to replenish energy stores, which isn't all that much by the way, and some good-quality proteins and other micro-nutrients that play a part in recovery. I'll go into much more detail in chapter eight.

You must also factor in enough rest to allow the recovery process to occur. The harder you train, the more quality nutrition and quality rest you need. Pro cyclists are legendary at resting.

Try to get 8 hours sleep at night because when you sleep your body produces human growth hormone, which helps your muscles build and recover. It's also been discovered that most growth hormone is secreted just after you fall asleep, so a daytime nap can provide an additional burst of the hormone, bringing about speedier recovery.

Sleep quality is important. Reading in bed is fine but looking at screens isn't conducive to quality sleep. Don't rush about before bedtime and avoid exercise. It might be better to miss a session if you are so pressed for time that you have to train just before going to bed. Breathe deeply when you want to go to sleep – in on a count of four, and out on a count of four. Bedrooms should be cool and as dark as possible. Top-quality mattresses and bed linen help too.

2.6 ADVANCED TRAINING

If you want to take your performance to the next level then the advanced training methods below are for you. They are more in line with what professional cyclists do when they are trying to find that bit extra for a target race, but I've included them as a primer for those wanting to go that little bit further.

ALTITUDE TRAINING

This can be done by living high up for a while, or by training in a hypoxic chamber, but there's a lot of debate about training at altitude, and the plusses and minuses associated with its use.

The positive effects include a temporary increase in red blood cells, and a more lasting increase in the number of blood capillaries, both in the lungs and muscles. More capillaries mean more oxygen can be taken in by the lungs, and more oxygen can be delivered to the muscle fibres, which results in a performance boost.

Some cyclists use hypoxic training in a chamber or by wearing a mask to challenge the cardiovascular system and create the response they would get at altitude. It's also claimed that hypoxic training improves the testosterone-to-cortisol ratio compared to doing the same session in normal air, although when riders go to altitude there is a drop-off in testosterone production at first, with levels returning once they acclimatize.

There's also evidence that altitude, or hypoxia, can help with weight loss. Everything in your body works harder at altitude, or simulated altitude, which burns calories and increases metabolic rate. Some studies show that leptin, a hormone that inhibits appetite, is increased by altitude too.

The current thinking with altitude training is it's best to live high and train low, so riders eat, sleep and recover at high altitude, but do most of their training low down in the valleys. They then end each session with a climb back up to altitude to acclimatize to the effects. That's a very important consideration when training for races with mountain climbs in them. Some riders take longer to acclimatize than others too.

MOTOR PACING

While European riders can do it with appropriate insurance, in the UK motor-paced cycling is only allowed on the track. Mark Cavendish is a great believer in motor-paced training and has even done 6-hour sessions behind his coach Rod Ellingworth's scooter (see opposite).

This is what Ellingworth told the journalist Chris Sidwells about their training in 2011: "Most of my work with Cav has not been on his sprint, but on the rest of the race. He has to be there at the end to win, so we sit down and look at what might prevent him getting there and work on it. To help him cope with hills, for example, we'll use the scooter to replicate everything that might happen on them. We'll hit a hill hard, or start steady and accelerate at the top, or I'll simulate attacks. That way Mark is used to every situation that could happen in a race.

"Another thing we do is sessions on the track of an hour or maybe a bit more, at 55kmph. That way when a race is fast, like Milan–San Remo was when Cav won it in 2009 and riders are thinking 'this is fast' and they feel uncomfortable, Cav isn't uncomfortable at all. He can tap away all day inside a bunch going 52kmph because he's used to a much higher speed. He doesn't waste nervous energy when a race is fast like some do."

TRAINING THE CENTRAL NERVOUS SYSTEM WITH BREATHING TECHNIQUE

The role the central nervous system plays in fatigue is interesting. The German sports scientist, Sebastian Weber, who has worked with some of the world's best professional road racers, thinks central nervous fatigue is often the reason why a rider cannot answer a series of attacks. Have you noticed that the third attack in a short space of time is often successful? Some riders can't survive three or more attacks, and Weber thinks that the central nervous system plays a part in that.

Hormones interact with the central nervous system during fatigue, and Weber believes it's possible to use breathing techniques in training to saturate the body with oxygen and stimulate the hormonal system into what it detects as a stressful situation. That might train the central nervous system into dealing with stress better.

Up to a certain level your breathing muscles get stronger as you get fitter, but when you are fit enough to push really hard and your breathing becomes laboured, the act of doing so has the potential to limit your progress due to something called the metaboreflex.

This is when your brain registers that you are struggling to breathe and it diverts oxygen from your peripheral muscles, your legs for example, to your breathing muscles. If this happens when you are cycling it means that you might be sucking in all the oxygen you need to keep riding hard, but your brain won't send it to your legs, where it's needed most.

To push up the intensity of effort where metaboreflex kicks in, you can do specific strength and conditioning for your breathing muscles, by using a breathing resistance device. There are a few on the market.

TRAINING PROGRAMMES

7

2.7 CHOOSING WHAT TO TRAIN FOR

Scan this QR code for tips and advice on preparing for a big cycling event.

There are many goals you could set in cycling, and there are thousands of races lasting anything from a few seconds to several days. There are also wonderful places to ride, and there's the simple joy of pushing yourself that bit further, or exploring new places, both geographically and spiritually. Above all, when you pick a goal, make it a big one.

Okay, it has to be realistic. Anyone starting cycling at 40 probably isn't going to win the Tour de France, but you will be surprised by what you can do, and what you can achieve if you really try and go about it in a methodical way.

Later in the book I'll be talking about how to be rational in training and in competition, how to control certain aspects around you and ignore the rest. If you are not rational then your emotional side takes over, and that's got to be avoided, except when setting your ultimate goal. Then you are allowed to dream a bit. Go for something big – achievable, but big.

To ensure that you have set yourself the right goal, ask yourself the following questions:

- Does the goal scare you?
- At the same time, does it make you smile, and feel good when you visualize achieving it?

Goals like that get you up in the morning, get you out of the door and get you training. They also help you train and prepare diligently.

WHAT SORT OF CYCLING

Some people take up cycling because they've seen or read about something they want to do. For others, cycling itself is enough. For them, the feeling of freedom and the joy of improved fitness are what they crave. You might want to try many different disciplines, you might want to race, you might even want to win Olympic gold medals or the Tour de France.

If you want to simply enjoy cycling, or take on a challenge, follow the area of the sport you enjoy best, the area that enthuses you. Do you get a kick out of speed? Then track and road racing are for you. If you think cycling off-road is great fun, something you probably did as a kid, then the competitive world of mountain biking and cyclo-cross is perfect for you. Or do you enjoy covering long distances? If so, cyclosportives or even ultra-distance challenges should suit.

You enjoy what you are good at, which is a good guide to what discipline of cycling you are best suited to. Conversely, you avoid what you are not so good at. So, if the thought of doing a series of sprints on a turbo trainer makes you shudder, then ultra-distance might be your cycling métier.

GETTING SERIOUS

There's nothing wrong with success, and if you want to win medals and titles, that's a good thing. Society has become a bit averse to saying so, but there is a joy in winning, and if winning motivates you then go for it. However, winning is demanding. To come out on top, you need to show precision in training and total commitment, both in terms of training and in life around it. To give yourself the best chance of winning, you need to pick the cycling discipline that suits you best. Lightly built riders are genetically suited to going uphill. Heavy muscled riders are more likely to be sprinters.

What sport were you good at in school? If you won sprints in athletics then sprint cycling will suit you, while middle-distance runners often make good endurance track and road racers. The best at cross-country running find they can become good time triallists.

However, other sports are not always a guide. Cycling has special demands, and this is where working with a coach comes in. If you want to progress then invest in some quality coaching, whether on a talent identification programme, where it is provided for you, or by paying for it yourself. Good coaching is crucial if you have big ambitions.

A good coach is your superego. He or she should be invested but detached, loyal but also fair. A good coach is a third eye, standing back and observing you and your performance as a third party. Finding a coach with that sense of idealism is crucial if you want to aim high.

THIS IS JUST THE START

The following training cycles should act as guides to show you examples of how you can work toward your goals and improve your fitness, but I don't want to be too prescriptive and they shouldn't be taken as hard-and-fast rules if that doesn't fit in with your lifestyle. While a pro-athlete's training is only limited by their body's recovery, 99 per cent of people's training frequency and volume is dictated by their work, family and social commitments, and general lifestyle. Creating your own training programme will involve a bit of trail and error, but the following plans provide great starting points to give you an idea.

2.7 TRAINING FOR CYCLOSPORTIVES

Cyclosportives are great challenges to take on. They are a modern phenomenon that has brought many people into cycling. Often run on demanding courses, the biggest cyclosportives trace the routes of great professional road races. They are also mass-participation events, so they attract a wide cross-section of riders, and many are well organized with a unique and exciting atmosphere.

LONG RIDES

These are the lynchpin of cyclosportive success. You don't have to do all that many, but they must be done, and there is an art to doing them. First though, how far and how many? For a 100-mile sportive your longest rides need to be around 4 hours. You will be able to complete a 100-mile sportive without doing them, so long as you have done some structured and progressive training, but long rides bring another dimension to your performance and experience on the day.

Taking in two or three rides like the long steady distance session on pages 120–1 in a 12-week build-up to a 100-mile event is ideal. You could also fit in one or two compressed long steady distance sessions too. Or simulate the effects of long rides by doing two shorter steady-state rides in the same day. That fits well with people who commute to and from work by bike.

OTHER TRAINING

A 12-week strength and conditioning programme forms the base of off-season training, with maintenance sessions done through the period when you take part in events. Ride whenever you can during this 12-week strength and conditioning phase, then 12 weeks away from your first event, start a more formal on-the-bike training programme. Fit in a once-a-week strength and conditioning session whenever possible (and ensure that you have at least three strength and conditioning sessions over each four-week period, taking a complete break for the easy week five). Plan your training backward from the target event. Fit in as many cycles as possible (including your easy weeks), trying to do more or go faster in each session as the cycle of training progresses.

As well as a weekly long steady distance ride, which doesn't have to be 4 hours every week, include the threshold session from pages 122–4 twice one week, and once the following week, and continue doing that until you start tapering for your first event (see page 153 for tapering).

In the weeks when you do only one threshold session, do a capacity session (see pages 125–6) to replace the missing threshold session, then a micro-interval session (see page 128) on the next single-threshold-session week. See opposite for your training plan.

Repeat the above cycle until you taper for the first event. After the event do another easy week, only riding when you feel like it, and then resume the above cycle of training until your next event taper.

EVENT SIMULATION

It's a good idea to turn at least one of the classic steady-state sessions you do in a 12-week training build-up into an event simulation. Don't do it on one of the 4-hour long steady distance rides, as they are just about getting miles in your legs and building your confidence about handling the distance of a big cyclosportive. And don't do it too close to the event – about four weeks before is perfect.

Begin the ride with 15 minutes at a standard steady-state pace, but after that start pushing a bit harder on any hills. Drop back to a steady-state pace for 5–10 minutes every half hour. This simulates what happens when you ride in a group in the actual event. A good duration for this ride is 3 hours.

PROGRESSION

Cyclosportives are not competitive events, but you are timed, and if you want to be competitive and do a fast time, or beat your time from the previous year, that's entirely up to you. Some cyclosportives award medals according to which time band you complete the distance in, but adjusted to take account of your age. A gold medal in an event such as l'Étape du Tour, which traces the route of a stage of the Tour de France each year, is a prize worth having.

It's good, healthy competition, and one thing you can do to improve your all-round cyclosportive performance is to get involved in group rides with a local cycling club. Or go one step further and take part in competitive road races. Both will hone your group riding skills and sense of pace and effort, things that can slice minutes off your ride time in a cylcosportive. You can learn how to train for road races overleaf. They open up another world of racing and challenges.

CYCLE OF TRAINING

WEEK OF TRAINING CYCLE	STRENGTH & CONDITIONING SESSION	MICRO-INTERVAL SESSION	CAPACITY SESSION	THRESHOLD SESSION	LONG STEADY DISTANCE SESSION
1	1	0	0	2	1
2	1	0	1	1	1
3	1	0	0	2	1
4	1	1	0	1	1
5	easy week (just take gentle rides when you feel like it)				
6	1	0	0	2	1
7	1	0	1	1	1
8	1	0	0	2	1
91	1	1	0	1	1
10	easy week				
11	0	0	1 (at least a day apart from the threshold session, with half your usual work periods)*	1 (at least a day apart from the capacity session, with half your usual work periods)*	1
12	0	1 (mid-week, with half the number of intervals)**	0	0	1

*e.g. a 3-minute capacity interval would be 90 seconds
**e.g. 10 × 15 seconds becomes 5 × 15 seconds

2.7 TRAINING FOR ROAD RACES

Road racing extends from short circuit races to the single-day cycling classics and Grand Tour stage races such as the Tour de France. Tactics, physics and skills of racing in a bunch are basically the same in all formats. The difference is that the world's top professionals have it down to a fine art.

In road racing you're basically trying to beat riders who are together in one bunch, but cyclists drafting in a group or even behind one other rider save a huge amount of energy. To win you have to leave the rest, even if it's just for a few seconds at the end, and take on the wind and air resistance yourself. To do that you use a combination of tactics, speed, terrain and pure strength.

PREPARE FOR A SHOCK

With so much coverage of cycling on TV today a lot of people's introduction to road racing is seeing the world's best professionals in action. They roll out of town in a controlled and orderly manner and then the racing starts. They make it look smooth but in reality it's brutal, and it gets faster and faster all the way to the end. They make it look easier than it is because they are conditioned to it, and because they try to maintain their composure, so no one knows if they are struggling.

That's not how most races go. If you are new to cycling your first road races will probably be on a short, closed circuit, and the riders will start like greyhounds out of the trap. The first 10–15 minutes will probably be the hardest and fastest of the race. You must be ready for that. It's no good being strong and lasting the distance if you get dropped soon after the start, and believe me it happens to a lot of newbies and experienced riders. The following training will help you to prepare and is based on a commitment of three sessions a week. This is what you will need to see a real difference.

BASIC ROAD TRAINING

As with all aspects of cycling, basic strength and condition is where you need to start for road races. A 12-week strength and conditioning programme during the off-season (see pages 80–9) will build all-body strength. Then one session every week or so during the competitive season will maintain it. You need the extra torque and grunt that weight training gives you in road races. It helps you cope with fast starts, close any gaps in the bunch quickly and make decisive moves later in the race.

Some long steady distance rides are essential, but the key to road racing is making and surviving attacks. So, on top of the threshold session on pages 122–4, try to do one of the capacity sessions on pages 125–6 each week too. Do the capacity session before the threshold one, with at least one easy day between them.

Every three weeks replace the threshold session with one of the speed and power sessions on pages 128–9. I'd also advise doing some speed and power sessions throughout the year. Do the speed and power session before the capacity session, again with at least one easy day between them.

GROUP TRAINING

You've got to get comfortable riding in a group with all the etiquette and skills involved. As you progress in cycling you'll hear about chain-gang training sessions, and there is a lot to be said for them. Many have been established for years and they simulate race conditions by riding in a pace line. This is where one rider sets the pace at the front and then drops to the back of the line while another rider sets the pace.

Chain-gangs are like interval training with skills thrown in. You are riding at threshold, then capacity, then back to threshold or a bit less. There's even a speed and power effect when you have to give an extra kick to catch on at the back after you've done your pace-setting turn.

A great in-season weekly training plan would be a weekday chain-gang and a threshold session, separated by a day of easy riding. Then a race at the weekend, or a club ride. Joining a good cycling club is important if you want to succeed in road races. Most established clubs are a mine of knowledge, so you can learn about road-race skills while practising them on organized rides.

TRACK FOR ROAD

The final element of road-race training is to take part in some track races. Although they're not essential, they help improve your speed, power, capacity and bike handling. Racing on indoor velodromes continues through the winter, and that's the best time for a road racer to fit in some track.

I could go on about what track racing can do for a road-race performance, but instead I'll leave you with this.

CYCLE OF TRAINING

WEEK OF TRAINING CYCLE	STRENGTH & CONDITIONING SESSION	MICRO-INTERVAL SESSION	SPEED & POWER SESSION	CAPACITY SESSION	THRESHOLD SESSION*	LONG STEADY DISTANCE SESSION
1	1	0	0	1 (at least a day apart from the threshold session)	1	1
2	1	0	0	1 (at least a day apart from the threshold session)	1	1
3	1	0	1 (at least a day apart from the capacity session)	1	0	1
4	0	1 (mid-week)	0	0	0	1
5	1	0	0	1 (at least a day apart from the threshold session)	1	1
6	1	0	0	1 (at least a day apart from the threshold session)	1	1
7	1	0	1 (at least a day apart from the capacity session)	1	0	1
8	0	1 (mid-week, with half the number of intervals)**	0	0	0	1

*you can substitute a chain-gang session for a threshold session
**e.g. 10 × 15 seconds becomes 5 × 15 seconds

Britain's first Tour de France winner, Sir Bradley Wiggins, was one of the best track racers ever before he focused on the road. Britain's first elite World Road Race Champion, Tom Simpson, was an Olympic track medallist at 19 years old. Finally, the only other British rider to win the elite World Road Race title, Mark Cavendish, has a terrific track pedigree.

2.7 TRAINING FOR TIME TRIALS

Time trials have been called the Race of Truth, and it's easy to see why. In a time trial it's just you, the road and your energy. The keys to success are through boosting your steady-state power, reducing the drag you create, skilful bike handling and spreading your effort efficiently.

REDUCING DRAG

Having a strong core is important for every cyclist. It's the platform that carries power down into the pedals, and the platform must be solid in order to maximize that power. But a time triallist's core muscles have other forces to contend with. Their muscles must hold an aerodynamic position while their upper body remains as still as possible. So, time triallists should train specifically to condition their core muscles to those forces.

Be really diligent in doing all-year-round core strength training, as outlined on pages 58–63. Leg strength is crucial too because it's aerodynamically efficient to pedal higher gears in a time trial. A 12-week off-season strength and conditioning programme, with regular in-season maintenance sessions is crucial for time triallists. Then the more flexible you are, the lower and more aerodynamic you can get when you ride, so year-round stretching (see pages 65–7) must be part of your training.

CRUISE CONTROL

Long steady distance rides should be year-round, but the key to success in most time trials is through training sessions that increase the intensity that you can maintain for the duration of the race. As a guide, this can be anywhere from 20–60 minutes.

Time trial training should be aimed at increasing the speed you can ride at threshold. You do this by pushing the threshold up from below with the sessions on pages 122–4, and by pulling it up from above by doing capacity sessions on pages 125–6.

CYCLE OF TRAINING

WEEK OF TRAINING CYCLE	STRENGTH & CONDITIONING SESSION	MICRO-INTERVAL SESSION	CAPACITY SESSION	THRESHOLD SESSION	LONG STEADY DISTANCE SESSION
1	1 (as early in the week as possible)	0	0	2	as many as possible
2	1 (as early in the week as possible)	0	1	1	as many as possible
3	1 (as early in the week as possible)	1	1	1	1 (short version at low intensity if time allows, or none at all)
4	easy week (just take gentle rides when you feel like it)				

One to two threshold sessions a week, depending on your level of fitness and experience, along with one capacity session to replace a threshold session every two weeks, is a good basic training programme. Do long steady distance rides on your other training days, plus one day of strength and conditioning every week if possible, but at least every two weeks.

Every third week, on a week when you haven't got a race, do the micro-interval or pro-power session on pages 128–9. Then have an easy day, then do a capacity session, then an easy day and finally the threshold session.

Again, I'm using the week as a measure for writing convenience and you can spread these sessions out to suit your circumstances, but it's the order in which you do them that's important. Generally, you should go from short to long sessions through the week (or whatever your training period breaks down into). See opposite below for how your training should look:

SKILLS & HABITUATION

Many time trial specialists train on a turbo trainer because it gives them the control they need in order to get the best from their sessions. That's good, but specific sessions, like the ones listed above, even if they are carried out on a turbo trainer, should be done on the bike you race on. If you do them on another sort of training device, such as a Wattbike, it must be set up as close to the position you use in time trials.

You also need to get used to riding whatever bike you use for time trials, so if it's a specialist time trial bike with an aerodynamic set up and riding position, then the key training sessions should be done on that bike. You not only need to train your body to perform optimally when riding in your aerodynamic time trial race position, but you also need to become familiar with how your time trial bike handles uphill, downhill and around corners.

Former Olympic and time trial World Champion, Fabian Cancellara, used to regularly ride his time trial bike for 140 kilometres, nearly 90 miles, in one go. He said it was the only way to "reach the support muscles that work hard when you ride a time trial. Long rides overload the muscles, and they super-compensate by getting really strong, strong in a way you couldn't do in a gym."

Fabian Cancellara (seen here in the stage nine individual time trial in the 2012 Tour de France) regularly practises long distances on his time trial bike, enabling him to adapt his support muscles to be really efficient.

2.7 TRAINING FOR TRACK RACING (ENDURANCE)

I spent 20 years of my life racing on the track and it's where I won my World and Olympic titles. Flying around a velodrome as fast as you can go, with the noise of the crowd, and under the glare of the lights, is an amazing, visceral feeling. Although it's also a very painful one in the case of the kilometre time trial!

The track is a great place for kids to start racing and training. Being away from traffic is one thing, but skills learned on the track, as well as the fitness, confidence and sheer speed gained, carry over into all disciplines of cycling. As I've already pointed out, many of the world's top road racers have had a solid track background.

WHAT YOU CAN DO

You can adapt the Wiggins track training (see opposite) by doing the following sessions, in order, during a week to ten-day period

This is the sort of weekly training an endurance track rider can do between races. Gradually increase the intensity of your sessions each week until the week before a race, when you should take it easy to enable recovery. On the week of a race, leave out the resistance day and just try to fit in a short speed and power session and a threshold session between any races.

Road racing should be part of an endurance track rider's regime. In fact, most endurance track riders flip between the two with ease. The occasional time trial helps with pace judgment too. Race often, especially on the track, because that's how you build experience. You can also use cyclosportives and group rides as some of your training sessions, but you need to have the discipline to stick with the type of ride that you have on your programme. Don't get swept up in competition and start sprinting when you should be practising a long steady distance session. Endurance track riders in British Cycling's performance programme race a lot, and even in training they simulate races.

CYCLE OF TRAINING

MON	TUE	WED	THUR	FRI	SAT	SUN
Rest	Track league (weekly local track racing series)	Strength & conditioning session	Threshold session	Rest	Speed & power session	Local road race or hard group ride

ENDURANCE TRACK TRAINING

A programme used regularly by Sir Bradley Wiggins when he was an Olympic and World Champion pursuiter was a two-day cycle, repeated three times, followed by a rest day, and so on. The two days went like this.

Day 1

Morning session: Two hours on the track, often behind a Derny, at a bit below the sweet-spot intensity of the threshold session on pages 122–4. British Cycling called this intensity tempo training.

Afternoon session: After a long warm-up, he did a series of five standing starts. This was to practise a core skill of pursuit racing, and the best way to improve starts is to practise them. It also served as an informal resistance training session. After that, either alone for the individual pursuit, or with others for team pursuit practice, there would be four flying-start time trials of 1–2 kilometres (½–1¼ miles) The full distance being trained for was 4 kilometres (2½ miles). Each time trial was done at race pace, over race pace, or in a higher-than-race gear ratio in order to build strength.

Day 2

A three-hour long steady distance ride.

2.7 TRAINING FOR TRACK RACING (SPRINTS)

SPRINT TRAINING

I'd like to think that sprinters are special, but different will do. If you think of the energy in your body as water in a bath, endurance cyclists pull out the plug and the water drains out over the distance of the race. When a sprinter sprints they rip out the bottom of the bath and the water goes out all in one go.

Track sprinters train differently from most other cyclists. The emphasis is always on quality over quantity and much of the time is spent in the gym and in the lab, as well as on the track.

In addition to lifting weights and using machines to increase their torque and power production, track sprinters do a lot of work on leg speed by doing under-geared sprints, or rev-outs, to improve coordination and pedalling efficiency.

On top of that, there's a lot of sprinting practice on the track – sprints from slow speed or medium speed, high on the track to low on the track, from behind a Derny bike or against other sprinters – and every sprint is always performed flat out at 100 per cent, as though it's for Olympic gold.

A basic weekly mid-season programme, for a rider looking to improve their performances in the track sprint disciplines, could look something like this:

CYCLE OF TRAINING

DAY OF TRAINING CYCLE	GYM WORK	TRACK WORK	ROAD
Mon am	• Foam rollers on areas of stiffness. • Stretches on areas of stiffness. • Dynamic warm-up, leading into lower body exercises (e.g. squats, deadlifts, lunges etc). Do 4–8 reps of each with high loads. • Core work and assistance exercises to address niggles or identified weaknesses. • Cool-down, foam roller exercises and stretches, targeting areas of stiffness.		
Mon pm	• 15-minute cool-down from track work on foam rollers, targeting areas that have been identified as stiff or sore during the training session.	**WORK ON STARTS** • Warm-up of 20 minutes cycling, starting slowly then gradually working up to fast riding to warm the body's systems up progressively. • Flying-start* 50m then flying-start 100m, done on small-to-medium gear ratio. • Standing-start** or slowly rolling start*** 50m. • 3 × 4 sets of standing-start efforts, the first 3 sets over 65m, the final set over 125m, with roughly 5 minutes between each start for full recovery, and 30 minutes recovery between sets. Use a race gear on the first set, a bigger gear on the second set, and an even bigger gear on the final set. • Gym cool-down of general exercises.	

Tues am			1-hour recovery ride on the flat using easy gears.
Tues pm	• 15-minute cool-down from track work on foam rollers, targeting areas that have been identified as stiff or sore during the training session.	**SPEED SESSION** • Warm-up of 20 minutes (see Mon pm). • 2 × 100m then 2 × 200m flying-start efforts. Use a slightly lower-than-race gear for the first flying 100m, then progress up the gears through the session, so the final effort is using an above-race gear. Rest for 30 minutes between efforts for full recovery. • Gym cool-down of general exercises.	
Wed am			1-hour recovery ride on the flat using easy gears.
Wed pm	• Foam roller work on any areas that feel stiff. • Stretches on any areas that feel stiff.		
Thurs am	Repeat Mon am session.		
Thurs pm		• Warm-up of 20 minutes (see Mon pm). • 5 × rolling-start three-quarter lap efforts. Use your race-gear ratio for the first, progressing to higher gears throughout the session. Make minimal effort until starting to sprint at the 200m line, then full-on out-of-the-saddle acceleration. Rest for 25 minutes between efforts. • Standard cool-down procedure, riding slowly until breathing normally and hardly pushing on the pedals.	
Fri am			1-hour recovery ride on the flat using easy gears.
Fri pm		• Warm-up of 20 minutes (see Mon pm). • 4 × 500m rolling-start efforts at roughly 30kmph. Use race and higher gears, increasing through the session. Stay seated throughout each effort, maintaining posture. Allow full recovery (30 minutes) between each effort.	
Sat			2 hours at a steady pace.
Sun			Rest.

*starting a timed or distance effort from a sprint speed
**starting a timed or distance effort from a standstill
***starting from a slow speed (16–24kmph/10–15mph)

2.7 TRAINING FOR AN ULTRA-DISTANCE CHALLENGE

Ultra-distance is where the body meets the mind, and the mind has to win. You have to have the strength, the miles in your legs, and the all-round conditioning, but the mind is as important as all those things.

MENTAL STRENGTH

One of Michael Secrest's most amazing performances was a World record in 1996 of 534.75 miles (860.6km) in 24 hours set on a 250-metre (275-yard) indoor track. Not only did he have the distance to contend with, but he also had the mind-numbing boredom of circling a sterile track 3,422.5 times, while shifting as little as possible from his aero position. That requires huge mental strength as well as physical strength.

John Marino, another American ultra-endurance legend, who was an official at Secrest's 24-hour record, said: "Mike is tough, so tough that early in his RAAM career he got called the Bull Dog, but even he began to come apart after 18 hours. He slowed, I could see he was uncomfortable, but then something kicked in. He got it back together, increased his pace, and he just toughed it out for the rest of the ride."

Ultra-endurance cyclists use a number of mental skills, although most challenges end in simply toughing it out. Two key skills are being in the moment, and visualization. Everybody who does endurance events breaks them down into sections. So, imagine riding for 1,000 miles in the RAAM and thinking that you still have over 2,000 miles to go. You can't let that thought creep into your head because you will already be experiencing extreme fatigue after 1,000 miles. Thinking about 2,000 more could stop you dead. Your mind and body have to be totally focused on the section of road you're riding. You need to concentrate on eating and hydrating, on your riding position and monitoring how you feel. Those thought processes will keep you occupied and in control. Thinking about how much is left to ride is too scary.

Visualization techniques divide into what you can do before, and things you do during the event. The ultra-running legend Ann Trason says; "Visualize how you will feel at halfway and three-quarters, imagining the discomfort, heat, cold or whatever and then change how you feel about those things. Thinking about them and then making yourself confident about how you feel is one way of beating them, so you have pre-planned a strategy for dealing with them."

Visualization during a challenge depends on calling up mental cue cards. Say you admire a particular climbing specialist in the Tour de France. When you come to a hill, call up the mental image of them riding, and use it to make your pedalling quick and purposeful. It's the same on the flat. Think of a powerful rouleur-type rider, and keep their style in mind. It will transfer to the way you are riding.

PHYSICAL

Long rides are the core of preparing for an ultra-endurance challenge. It's very hard to replicate the duration of the longest challenges, but a good way to approach that is back-to-back long rides over two days. Otherwise, sprinkle one threshold session a week into your training, and alternate between one capacity and one speed session on alternate weeks.

You're only as strong as your weakest link, so do a 12-week strength and conditioning programme, including as many full-body exercises as you can. The around-the-world record holder Mark Beaumont once said: "I do at least a third of my training in the gym, and by doing hill running. I ran a lot because I wanted to train the support muscles in my legs. If they are weak then the main muscles pull on your joints, causing pain over the sort of distances I was doing and potentially stopping the record."

NUTRITION & MATERIAL

I'll go into nutrition in more depth later in the book, but ultra-distance nutrition is special. There are lots of resources from which you can get information on the internet, but one thing that's common in ultra-distance is the use of real food rather than sports products. Stomach problems need to be prevented, and eating things you are used to will help prevent them, but eating food you enjoy is good for morale too. For an example of what can go seriously wrong, just type "The Crawl" into YouTube!

The things that could stop you in an event are difficult to replicate in training. Strained neck muscles are one, saddle sores are another. There are things you can do to prevent them. Find a saddle that suits you and use the same model on all your bikes. Thicker tape and changing hand position often reduces numb fingers. Good shorts and using chamois cream are best for preventing saddle sores.

TAPERING

Tapering is the last tier of training to get right before you can give an optimal athletic performance. Nutrition provides the building blocks, training creates the stimulus to improve, rest and recovery provide the time and conditions for improvement to take hold, but a good taper helps you find that extra one per cent. Tapering helps your body compensate for all the training you have done, but you have to get it right. It's not just a matter of stopping training for a few days, and then racing flat out, because getting the taper wrong can make you worse.

GENERAL PRACTICE

The length of taper before your race or challenge depends on how long and hard the race is, as well as how important it is to you. For example, somebody who races regularly will have target races, which require a full taper. They may also have races that they are using as interim goals or tests before their main objective.

For an interim race, the taper should start four days before. So, if the race is on a Sunday then the taper would start on the Thursday. The golden rule of tapering is to maintain some intensity in training but cut the duration. So, if you would normally do four capacity intervals in 1¾ hours on a given day, you do two intervals in a 1-hour ride.

Take the next day off with complete rest from the bike or any form of exercise other than walking. Then the day before the race, ride at a long steady distance pace for an hour or so, doing no more than five flat-out sprints to rev your engine. Do at least 5 minutes easy pedalling between the sprints. As well as preparing your body for the race, you are improving your fitness with these sprints. Remember, flat-out sprints are a good speed training session.

Above all, though, tapering is personal and something you develop with experience. It's where the art and science of training meet. Don't be afraid to try different things. Also, bear in mind that if you race often you should use some races as training sessions, and train right through them. If you compete a lot and taper for every race you won't build up the volume of training you need to improve.

More important objectives, such as target races or challenges, require a longer taper. For an ultra-distance challenge, the two weeks leading up to the race should see a big drop in training duration. Keep some of the intensity and adjust your diet to your training. If you eat the amounts you need to support full training you'll put on weight. Periods of complete rest are fine in your taper but don't rest all of the time, and you should always ride, making a few short efforts the day before a race.

Target road races require a taper of about one week, maybe less. Again, cut the duration of training sessions but keep some of the intensity. Maybe have one complete day off from training six days before the race, and another four days before. Don't forget to ride and do a few sprints the day before the race.

PERFORMANCE EATING

2.8 **FOOD GROUPS**

We eat a mix of the big three food groups: carbohydrates, proteins and fats. They form the bulk of our diet, along with micro-nutrients, which are consumed in tiny amounts but are necessary for optimum health. We'll start off by looking at macro-nutrients, then cover micro-nutrients on the following pages.

CARBOHYDRATES

Also known as starches and sugars, and sometimes referred to as carbs, carbohydrates are found in grains, root vegetables, fruit, milk sugars and other sugars. Fibre is a carbohydrate, but an indigestible one. During digestion, carbohydrates are broken down into glycogen, which breaks down further into glucose when your body needs it for fuel, such as when you exercise. Glycogen is stored in your muscles and liver. Your body's glycogen stores are quite limited, so any carbohydrates you consume above what's needed for immediate action, and to replenish glycogen stores, is stored as body fat.

Some carbohydrates are processed quickly, so potentially their energy is available faster. Other carbohydrates are absorbed more slowly. Those that are processed quickly will be stored as fat if there isn't an energy demand equivalent to their calories and glycogen stores are full. But because slowly absorbed carbohydrates release their energy slowly, there's more chance of your body needing that energy and not converting it to stored fat.

There is a measure called the glycemic index (GI) which assigns a number for how quickly foods are digested and available for energy. Carbohydrates can be classed as low, medium or high by their GI value, with a high GI associated with the carbohydrates that provide energy quickest (so those more likely to be stored as fat if consumed in amounts greater than your body's immediate need).

EXAMPLES OF LOW, MODERATE AND HIGH GLYCEMIC INDEX FOODS

RATING	GI RANGE	EXAMPLES
Low GI	55 or less	Most fruits and veg, legumes/pulses, whole grains, oats, nuts and fructose.
Medium GI	56–69	Whole wheat, basmati rice and sweet potatoes.
High GI	70+	Baked potato, white bread, white rice, added-sugar or refined breakfast cereals and refined pasta.

PROTEINS

Proteins are broken down by digestion into amino acids, which your body uses to build new proteins in the form of body tissue, including muscle fibres. The muscle fibres are damaged during hard training sessions and competition, and the damage is detected by your body, which uses amino acids to repair it. However, full repair cannot take place unless you eat adequate amounts of protein.

Typical protein recommendations for sedentary populations would be 0.8 grams per kilogram of body mass per day, and those undertaking exercise should have 1.4-1.8 grams per kilogram per day. Then more than 2-2.5 grams per kilogram per day for anyone in very heavy training, looking to promote lean muscle gain or maintain muscle mass during targeted times of weight loss.

Don't think eating lots of protein in one go works as a safety net because excess amino acids can either be broken down into compounds that can be used in energy production or, if not a requirement for energy, stored as fat. So spread your protein intake throughout the day. You need to drip-feed protein to promote the synthesis of muscle protein and avoid fat gain, which is useful because protein has a satiating effect. Proteins, particularly those found in eggs and dairy products, make you feel full and can help stave off hunger pangs, which is helpful if you are trying to lose weight.

Good protein sources for athletes are lean meat, dairy produce, fish, eggs, pulses, beans and nuts. Animal protein contains all eight essential amino acids, but no plant protein sources contain all eight. There are 20 different amino acids, but all except the eight essential ones can be synthesized by your body. Vegans must try to address the question of getting all eight essentials by combining plant protein sources. There are useful books and online guides on how to do that.

FATS

Don't be afraid of fats. Your body uses fat for fuel, and it needs certain fats to function. The thing to be aware of is the distinction between good and bad fats. There are three groups of fats: unsaturated, saturated and trans fats.

Saturated fats are usually solid at room temperature, so there is saturated fat in meat and cheese. It was thought that eating too much saturated fat caused a build-up of plaque on the inner walls of arteries, but after extensive studies, no real link has been found. However, saturated fats are high in calories, which is worth keeping in mind when you are planning your meals. As with carbohydrates and protein, adjust your fat intake to the amount and intensity of training you do.

Unsaturated fats are liquid at room temperature, so they are generally oils. Unsaturated fats have long been associated with health benefits, such as cardiac health and reducing inflammation. There's even evidence that some fats, those in fish oils, for example, help preserve muscle mass. Oils with poor heat tolerance can be rendered harmful by heating them, but olive oil resists heat degradation, as does safflower oil and semi-refined sesame and sunflower oil.

Trans fats are bad fats and they aren't good for you in any quantity. They are also called hydrogenated fats and oils, and hydrogenation is a food production process that extends the life of fats and oils. You won't find hydrogenated substances in fresh food, but having said that not all processed food contains hydrogenated fats, so read the labels. Avoid hydrogenated fats as much as possible

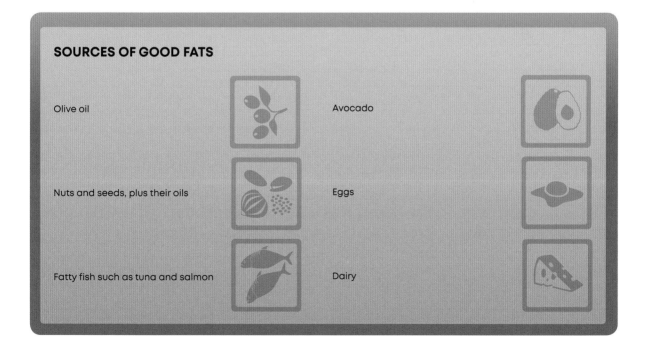

SOURCES OF GOOD FATS

Olive oil

Nuts and seeds, plus their oils

Fatty fish such as tuna and salmon

Avocado

Eggs

Dairy

2.8 VITAMINS, MINERALS & MICRO-NUTRIENTS

A lot has been written on this subject, but suffice to say that vitamins, minerals, micro-nutrients and antioxidants play many vital roles in your physiology. They keep your body functioning optimally, which for athletes, all things being equal, helps them get the maximum benefit from their training. However, vitamin, mineral or micro-nutrient supplements, apart from some exceptions, should only be taken after medical guidance where a deficiency has been diagnosed.

The best way to ensure you get adequate amounts of these essential nutrients is to eat a wide variety of fresh food. All the nutrients you need are found in the main food groups, everything from meat to vegetables and fruit, but some foods contain more than others. A varied diet is best, but processed food is best avoided. Processing, and to a certain extent cooking, can destroy some vitamins, minerals and micro-nutrients.

THE BASICS
You hear the phrase "five a day" a lot in nutritional advice. It refers to eating five portions of fruit and vegetables every day for optimal health. But if you are training hard then consider five a day as a minimum. Eat at least five portions of different fruit and veg a day, and aim for more.

If possible make each plate of food you eat as varied, colourful and bright as possible. Bright and strongly coloured fruit, berries and vegetables are the best sources of vitamins, minerals and antioxidants. Without going into which food contains which micro-nutrient, simply including the widest variety of these, plus a wide range of foods from the three macro-nutrient groups, puts you on the way to maintaining optimum health. It will also boost your immune system and help you recover from and adapt to your training.

GUT HEALTH
Gut health is crucial because eating quality fresh food won't give you the benefits it could if your gut isn't healthy. The best nutrition strategy in the world won't work if your gut is in poor condition. It just won't absorb the micro- and macro-nutrients needed in order to benefit from the training you do.

Staying hydrated helps the gut do its work, and it's important to maintain the gut in a narrow pH band where it works best. The pH is a measure of acidity, with pH 7 being neutral, while below 7 is acidic and above 7 is alkaline.

Ideally the pH of the small intestine, which is where most nutrients are absorbed, should be slightly alkaline. The problem with achieving that is that the stomach, where food is mashed up and broken down before it passes into the small intestine, is highly acidic. Its contents are still acidic when they enter the small intestine. In a healthy gut, the pH changes from acidic to alkaline through the length of the small intestine.

To support gut health you should cut down on the consumption of foods that increase gut acidity. They are alcohol, soft drinks, caffeine, vinegar, ascorbic acid, cheese, white sugar and medical drugs. You also need to eat more foods that counter gut acidity conditions. They are raw vegetables, ripe fruits, bean sprouts, water, milk (goats' is best), onions, figs, carrots, beetroot and miso.

GOING FURTHER
If you're really ambitious and looking for further, albeit smaller improvements, you might find them by having a blood test. However, you need to work with a qualified nutritionist or similar practitioner to make gains from information supplied by it. Blood tests can reveal deficiencies that affect performance, although excesses of some micro-nutrients in the blood can cause problems too.

Excess iron in men is more common than you might think. It can have a genetic basis (for example, when somebody's ancestors lived in an area where there wasn't much iron in their diet, causing the signalling mechanism that reduces iron absorption when iron stores are high to be defective). Even a normal diet can result in excess iron storage by people with that genetic trait, and excess iron can be toxic. Meanwhile, women of childbearing age often have iron deficiencies, but iron should only be supplemented when a deficiency has been diagnosed by a doctor. It is also wise for women to eat iron-rich foods (red meats, leafy greens, raisins, lentils and spirulina).

A blood test might also show a deficiency in selenium for both men and women, but rectifying it isn't as simple as taking a selenium supplement. Selenium has a very narrow toxicological range, so it's easy to take too much. There are gains to be made by fine-tuning nutrition, but it's expensive and you've got to work with a qualified third party to get it right or you can do more harm than good. You also need to have everything else in your training and preparation sorted out first.

2.8 **WEIGHT LOSS**

Many people take up cycling to help them lose weight or, more precisely, lose body fat. That's good because there's plenty of evidence that excess body fat is linked to a number of diseases, some life-threatening and most life-impairing. There are healthy ways to lose body fat, but it's quite a long process so be patient. Firstly, I want to outline why you shouldn't become too obsessed with losing weight to improve cycling performance.

POWER IS KEY

When riding uphill the limiting performance factor is an individual's power-to-weight ratio. This is the watts of power they produce divided by their body weight. Increase power output, or reduce body weight while maintaining output, and power to weight increases. Essentially this means you will go uphill faster, and since climbing hills is a crucial part of road racing, the world's top professionals obsess about reducing their weight. They talk about being competitive at six per cent body fat and playing catch-up at seven per cent.

Top professionals train and race full time and have professional backup. Once they reach physical maturity the power they can produce when fully fit in a target race is pretty much all it's ever going to be, give or take a few watts. That means that when cycling uphill weight becomes the only variable. They can't reduce the weight of their bikes because cycling's governing body has a lowest-weight limit, so all top pros have to play with is reducing their body weight.

But for most cyclists increasing the power side of the equation is much more effective than reducing weight. For a start, the power-to-weight ratio isn't the limiting factor in riding on the flat. That's power divided by aerodynamic drag, and we discussed how to reduce that on pages 38–41.

Consider the mathematics of riding uphill. If a 70-kilogram (11-stone) rider puts out 250 watts when climbing a long hill, that's a power-to-weight ratio of 3.57 watts per kilogram. If that rider increases their power to 260 watts through training, which is easily possible, then their power-to-weight ratio increases to 3.71 watts per kilogram. Achieving the same increase through weight loss involves losing three kilograms (nearly half a stone), and that's quite hard.

Of course, it's even better if you can to do both, and as you train harder your weight, or at least your body fat percentage, will fall, so long as you pay attention to what and when you eat. Just don't get hung up on losing weight.

FAT LOSS

Despite adverts for wonder products claiming a shortcut to weight loss, the only way to reduce body fat is to burn it away as fuel. And the only way to do that is by creating a caloric deficit. You need to remove calories from your body's daily requirements so your body burns fat tissue instead. But a caloric deficit is difficult to create if you are training hard.

The best way to do it is by matching the amount of food you eat from each macro-nutrient food group to your activity.

To lose body fat you must look long and hard at your carbohydrate intake. If you consume carbohydrates in excess of your immediate need for glucose for energy, or to replenish glycogen stores, energy from the consumed carbohydrates is converted to body fat. You should match carbohydrate consumption to energy needs to maintain body weight, and consume fewer carbohydrates if you are trying to lose body fat. Restrict your carbohydrate consumption throughout the day and don't eat any carbohydrates an hour or so before bedtime.

Next, look at your protein intake. Your body tries to repair itself all day, but it can only use a certain amount of protein at once. If too much is consumed in one go it can't all be used, but will be stored as fat even though your muscles could still be crying out for protein. During times of calorie restriction and targeted body fat loss, increasing protein intake to 2–2.5 grams of protein per kilogram of body mass has been shown to preserve lean muscle mass. However, try to drip-feed the protein by eating it in 20–30-gram (0.7–1-ounce) portions.

Spread out your protein intake by having an omelette for breakfast, then protein with the next two meals, plus a protein recovery drink after a hard training session. Snack on protein too. And if you've trained really hard it's also a good idea to eat a protein source, such as yogurt, before bedtime.

Finally, control your fat intake, not because fat is inherently bad like it was once believed to be, but because fat contains lots of calories per gram. You need fats for a number of reasons, just be aware of how much you are eating.

WHAT TO CUT

Cut out cakes, biscuits, pies and pasties. There are always more calories, carbohydrates, fats and, often, trans fats in these foods than you think.

Cut out or cut down on alcohol consumption. Alcohol is converted to fats by the liver. The fats can be used for energy needs, but they are more likely to be stored. Carbohydrates in alcoholic drinks can also be used for energy, but they too might end up as stored fat.

It's not all bad news though. There are some vitamins and antioxidants in beer and wine. You don't have to stop drinking alcoholic drinks but beware of alcohol and carbohydrates as both could end up as stored fat.

2.8 FUELLING TRAINING

Training won't be effective unless you provide your body with the building blocks it needs, both to recover from each training session and to respond to the session's stimulus by growing fitter and stronger. To do that you need to eat things from the main three food groups in the correct proportions, as well as eating micro-nutrients to help you maintain the good health that helps you adapt to your training. You must also stay hydrated and replace the electrolyte minerals that are vital for performance but are lost during training and competition.

HYDRATION IN TRAINING

Water is crucial to your body, which won't function efficiently unless you are fully hydrated. The best way to check you are hydrated is by examining the colour of your urine. If it's clear then you are well hydrated. If it's darker than a pale straw colour you need to drink more water. A cyclist in training sweats and breathes out a lot of water, and it needs replacing as soon as possible to help you benefit from training.

Water is the key to good hydration because many other drinks – tea and coffee, for example – have a diuretic effect, so you pass more urine than you need to. Other drinks, such as fruit juices, have calories, so be careful with how much of them you consume. A combination of minerals – called electrolytes – and water is necessary for maintaining fluid balance within the body, especially around training. However, too heavy an emphasis on water can cause health issues, namely a condition called hyponatremia, which can be dangerous. Watch out for that when exercising in very hot weather, when you might be tempted to drink lots of water.

It's a good idea to start drinking water soon after you wake. Very diluted fruit juice is often more palatable than plain water and it contains small amounts of the electrolyte minerals that are essential to numerous processes, including the way nerve and muscle tissue works. Electrolytes are lost in sweat, so they need replacing during and after training, but the vast majority of your body's electrolyte needs are met by eating a wide variety of fresh foods, in particular fruit and vegetables.

DIETARY MANIPULATION

The most important way your diet can help you gain the most from your training is by eating a wide range of fresh food to support your health. However, there are other ways you can manipulate your diet to improve cycling performance. The first of those is by controlling the amount and type of carbohydrates you eat.

I've mentioned already that for anybody riding, and in particular competing over long distances, increasing the power output they can maintain while being predominantly fuelled by fats is a huge benefit. Even skinny people have large stores of fat which can be used to fuel activity, whereas glycogen stores are limited. However, even if your body is well adapted, only 60 per cent of maximum effort can be fuelled by using fat. At higher intensities carbohydrate utilization is preferable. Hill climbs, breakaways and putting in your turn at the front of a group will all be fuelled by carbohydrates.

You can increase your reliance on fats for fuel in several ways. Two simple methods are reducing the amount of carbohydrates you consume in some of your pre-training meals and by doing the occasional fasted ride. Both should only be done in conjunction with short easy rides. For harder training sessions you need more carbohydrates, particularly in your pre-ride meal.

You should also consume carbohydrates on longer rides through energy drinks, gels and normal food such as cakes and bananas. Nutrient absorption is a combination of passive diffusion and active transport. Passive diffusion is dependent upon concentration gradients and the solution in the gut being weaker than that of body fluids. Carbohydrates are absorbed via active transport and an isotonic solution, where the concentration of the ingested solution – for example, an energy gel – matches the concentration of the body fluids. If your energy drink mix is too strong it slows down absorption. That's why it's important to read the instructions when mixing your energy drinks. Isotonic gels do not need water and should be chosen over other hypertonic gels that do need water. Solid foods followed by plain water still have a place in fuelling while cycling.

CAREFUL WITH THE CARBS

Carbohydrates are still important after training, but be careful how much you consume. Always match your carbohydrate consumption to the amount and intensity of the work you've done. Carbohydrate replenishment after intense exercise would be 1 gram per kilogram of body mass within the first 30 minutes of finishing, and again every hour for the next four hours. For easier sessions, carbohydrate replenishment could be a carbohydrate-and-protein-mix recovery drink, followed by a normal meal two to three hours later.

During periods of hard training, daily protein consumption should be 20–30 grams (0.7–1 ounce) every 3–4 hours, including immediately after exercise. There is evidence that up to 40 grams (1.4 ounces) of protein can be utilized if exercise has incorporated a number of muscle groups.

Finally, on protein, it's worth repeating that while animal proteins contain all eight essential amino acids you need to repair body tissue, plant protein sources do not contain all eight in any one source. So, if you follow a vegan diet you need to combine sources at each meal to get all the eight essential amino acids you need. The best way for vegans to get all eight is to combine foods from the cereal and legume groups at each meal.

Fuelling your training is a constant balance between staying hydrated, replenishing vitamins and minerals, taking on enough food to recover from and adapt to your training but not eating any excess that could boost your fat stores and see you put on weight.

2.8 FUELLING COMPETITION

What you eat and drink in the 24 hours before and during any competition can make or break your performance. It's a time for great care, and not just physical care. You must factor in your emotional state, which can range from devil-may-care over-confidence to self-sabotaging nervousness. Over-confidence can cause you to make mistakes, and nervousness can affect your digestion and appetite.

THE DAY BEFORE

Eat what you would normally eat, and at the same times too, but cut down on the amount of protein in each meal, while slightly increasing the portions of lower GI carbohydrates. You will probably have tapered for an important race, so you will have been on a reduced carbohydrate intake. A slight increase in the number of carbohydrates you eat the day before a competition ensures your glycogen reserves are full.

Try to eat cooked vegetables rather than salads, especially during your evening meal. Limit the amount of fruit you eat because fruits and raw salads can upset your stomach, especially if you are nervous about the upcoming challenge.

Try not to eat a big meal late in the evening, but if you can't eat until late then still eat. Cut protein down to a minimum because it takes longer for your body to process.

Drink plenty of water the day before a competition. Drink little and often, and not too much in one go. Avoid drinks that have a diuretic effect, so limit coffee and tea to two or three cups in a day. Alcohol is diuretic too, so although a glass of wine or a beer might help you relax the evening before a race, any more than that could work against you.

THE DAY OF THE RACE

Drink a glass of water as soon as you wake on the morning of the event and keep sipping plain water until the start. Eat a light breakfast if your event is short. Porridge is great before any race, just adjust the portion to the duration of the event. If your challenge is a long one your breakfast has to be bigger. You might be nervous and find it difficult to focus on eating. You might not even want to eat, but you must. An omelette, poached or scrambled eggs, maybe with some cheese grated on them, with rice or pasta is a good breakfast before a long competition. Don't eat meat as it's difficult to digest. Eat at least two hours before a long race so digestion is well underway before you start. For shorter, more intense races, you should eat earlier.

IN COMPETITION

Your body loses fluid through sweating and breathing. A two per cent drop in body weight through fluid loss impairs temperature regulation. A three per cent drop reduces muscular endurance, while a four per cent drop reduces the force of muscle contractions. Once beyond a four per cent drop the core body temperature starts rising, and your body begins to shut down as safety mechanisms come into play.

You must keep drinking during a race, ideally enough to prevent any fluid loss, although some is inevitable when racing in hot conditions. One bottle of an electrolyte drink will be enough in a race of up to 1 hour. For anything in the 1–2-hour range an energy drink will meet your hydration needs and some of your on-the-bike fuelling needs too. In races of this length you should take one energy gel after the first hour, keeping another for close to the finish, or in case you feel you need it earlier.

For any competition over 2 hours you should carry one bottle of electrolyte drink and one of energy drink. Consider using energy bars and gels for longer races and try to use bars and gels that contain electrolytes. Cutting energy bars into thirds or quarters, depending on their size, makes them easier to eat. If you are riding an event that supplies energy bars and gels at feed stations, find out which brands they are and use them to fuel your longer training rides so you can get used to them.

Plain water can be useful in hot conditions: your body loses heat through the evaporation of sweat from your skin's surface. Pouring water over yourself conserves sweat by giving the body another liquid to evaporate and through which to lose heat.

Pouring water over yourself in hot conditions also helps maintain optimal power output. Your body loses heat by radiation as well as by evaporating sweat. Your blood carries heat to the skin's surface where it radiates away, but the blood diverted to the skin isn't taking oxygen and nutrients to your working muscles, so your power output drops. Pouring water over yourself cools your body, so more blood goes to your muscles instead of your skin, taking nutrients and oxygen with it, so you can keep powering the pedals.

IN-RACE NUTRITION

Here are some guidelines on how to manage what you eat and drink during a race.

Drink little and often, at least every 15–30 minutes depending on temperature.

In long cyclosportives take sachets of energy drink with you to mix with water from feed stations.

Eat something solid after the first hour and repeat at least every 30 minutes after that.

Take on a small mouthful of fluids every time you eat.

Resist the temptation to skip feed stations on your first cyclosportive. It's best to stop and make sure you've got enough fluid on board.

Start the race eating solid food. Then switch to gels later in the race.

If you feel your energy suddenly starts dropping, take a gel quickly. Then eat something solid as soon as possible.

Save something you really enjoy, a cake maybe, for when you need a bit of encouragement.

Eat only half an energy bar in one go, unless the bars are small.

2.8 **FUELLING RECOVERY**

Increasing your training volume will improve your overall fitness. However, no training programme can be effective unless you give your body the necessary time to recover. And the faster you recover, the sooner you can start training again. Recovery should be considered a fundamental part of your training and done as meticulously as any training session.

Recovery *is* training.

FIRST 30–60 MINUTES

You might not feel like eating straight after a hard session, but you will be thirsty. A protein drink will start addressing your body's repair requirements as well as providing some fluids.

The potential for glycogen replenishment in muscles is elevated straight after exercise, so this is an ideal time to have a carbohydrate serving. If you're in the middle of a block of lower-level training or targeted weight loss, you should reduce the amount of carbohydrate you eat with your evening meal.

It is advised that you should replace 150 per cent of fluid lost during exercise in the 4-hour post-exercise window in order to fully rehydrate. If you lose 1 kilogram (2 pounds) of body mass during exercise then drink 1.5 litres (2½ pints) of fluid in the 4-hour post-exercise window. Don't be tempted to drink too much beer and wine after a big effort to celebrate because it will set back your rehydration and interfere with all sorts of body processes you need to work optimally in order to get the maximum benefit from training.

METABOLIC & MUSCULAR RECOVERY

Metabolic recovery means rehydration and replenishing glycogen stores and lost minerals, such as electrolytes. Most of those needs can be met by drinking extra water, possibly some fruit juices too, and by eating.

For muscular recovery you need to eat protein that contains all eight essential amino acids, which means animal proteins, or by combining a cereal and a food from the legume group for plant protein sources. Be careful with protein drinks as they aren't all the same. Whey protein is absorbed very quickly and it stimulates protein synthesis, which is great straight after exercise when your body is in a catabolic condition and damaged muscle fibres need repairing.

Research has shown that a 20–30-gram (0.7–1-ounce) portion of protein is required to maximally stimulate muscle protein synthesis, and in some cases, say after very heavy weight training, this could be up to 40 grams (1.4 ounces). Any more than that is processed by the liver and used as fuel, or it could be stored as fat. Consuming 20–30 grams (0.7–1 ounce) of a quickly digested protein source is recommended post-exercise and whey protein is the most quickly digested. Protein drinks offer another source, while casein releases its protein much more slowly, and is ideal for consuming just before sleeping during bouts of heavy training.

METABOLIC STRESS & INFLAMMATION

Cycling puts your whole body under strain, and it either adapts to it or breaks down. Nutrition is one of the things that determines which one happens. Foods with antioxidants and anti-inflammatory properties will help you to recover.

Brightly coloured foods contain lots of antioxidants, while vegetables also help maintain gut health by helping to restore optimum pH. Vegetable juices can be excellent for gut health and contain lots of antioxidant vitamins and minerals. They can also remove some of the burden your gut has with processing and digesting lots of vegetables, which is a good thing after hard exercise because your gut already has enough to cope with, including inflammation.

Omega-3 oils, which are found in oily fish and other fats, aren't anti-inflammatories in the way that ibuprofen is, but omega-3 oils help your body to recover from inflammation. Modern diets tend to be low in omega-3 fish oils, which is why a supplement can be useful.

REST DAYS

It's a good idea to have a complete rest day following a race or a hard training session. Rest days help recovery really take hold, but they can be difficult from a nutritional point of view. You might do some gentle exercise – walking is good, or a very gentle recovery ride – but not enough to burn lots of calories. However, you still need fuel for repair and recovery.

The best plan to is follow a normal breakfast–lunch–dinner eating plan but cut back on the amount of carbohydrates you eat at each meal and have a smaller-than-normal evening meal. A couple of snacks are fine; in fact, rewarding yourself for the efforts you've made with a slice of your favourite cake as a mid-morning or mid-afternoon snack is a very good idea.

2.8 **SUPPLEMENTS**

The subject of supplements and their benefit to people in training is vast, but if you are eating a wide range of foods from all the food groups then most supplements are only necessary where there is a medically determined deficiency. That said, there are some supplements that can improve performance, support health and are convenient and time-saving to take in tablet or powder form. With all supplements it's important to read labels carefully before buying.

BETA-ALANINE & SODIUM PHOSPHATE

These two substances can be helpful to track racers, short distance time triallists and possibly some road racers. Beta-alanine is believed to increase levels of carnosine in muscles, and carnosine slows the build-up of hydrogen ions that occurs during intense exercise. Excess hydrogen ions increase acidity in muscles, which, as it builds, eventually reduces the force the muscles can apply. That is what slows a cyclist down toward the end of a one-kilometre time trial. So, if you can delay the build-up of hydrogen ions, you can ride harder for longer. There is evidence that sodium bicarbonate and sodium citrate have the potential to absorb excess hydrogen ions, so they could have the same effect.

Sodium phosphate is claimed to increase maximum oxygen uptake and enhance lactate tolerance. It is thought that sodium phosphate works on red blood cells, allowing them to off-load more oxygen to your muscles. Sodium phosphate is quite inconvenient to take because you have to go through a six-day loading period with four small doses spread over each day.

Beta-alanine is found in most meats, but especially in turkey. It's also easy to take as a supplement, but it can cause flushing in the face and hands, and tingling in the fingers, especially if you take too much. Sodium phosphate causes gastric distress in some people.

OMEGA-3 FISH OILS

Fish oils help reduce inflammation, so they can help you recover from training, and they are particularly helpful in maintaining gut health. Fish oils also promote vascular health, keeping all-important blood vessels in good working order. There is evidence that fish oils may be able to increase your training capacity, so you can train harder in order to give your body a bigger stimulus to get stronger and fitter. Fish oils also contain zinc and magnesium, which can increase the production of testosterone.

Not all fish oils are the same quality. Don't buy cheap stuff. It is worth noting that the microscopic krill on which fish feed has the greatest health benefits and some manufacturers sell krill oil capsules too.

PROTEIN SUPPLEMENTS

Whey protein powder mixed up as a shake is a quickly digested complete protein source, which kick-starts protein synthesis. Whey powder also reduces hunger, so it's useful if you are trying to lose weight. Timing when to take protein supplements is important. Whey protein is quickly digested, so it's best straight after hard training when you won't be eating much more in the following hour or so. Later in the day it's better to blend shakes from powders that are a mix of whey and the slower acting protein casein. This works well for recovery because whey switches on protein synthesis in your body, then casein provides a slower releasing shot of protein for your body to build with.

But inside that broad principle is the bio-availability of the protein, and its biological activity. Whey protein is the most common protein supplement used by sports people and research has revealed that the most bio-active whey protein is one prepared by low temperature pasteurization, so look out for that on the label.

There are also ingredients that can be added to or specially preserved in protein supplements that improve the way they work. Glutamine improves intestinal health and protein synthesis and supports the immune system. There are also protein fractions such as lactoferrin, which carries iron in the bloodstream so supports red blood cells in their oxygen-carrying capacity. These fractions are preserved during cold pasteurization, which requires great care and is reflected in the price of these protein supplements.

CONJUGATED LINOLEIC ACID (CLA)

This is a fatty acid found in meat and cheese that is thought to prevent weight gain. You can buy it in capsule form.

GLUTAMINE PEPTIDES

Glutamine is the most abundant amino acid in muscle tissue, but it can be stripped from the muscles during intense exercise and training, which potentially could cause muscle wasting and lower the immune function.

Those that participate in sports that require strength, speed and endurance may benefit from using glutamine peptide supplements to help increase and maintain lean muscle mass. This is because glutamine peptides play

a significant role in protein synthesis and in improving blood sugar levels.

Glutamine peptides potentially enhance the entire process by which protein is used by the muscles to repair and regrow, but also help control blood sugar levels, which can then prevent you feeling tired and lethargic or experiencing sugar cravings.

CREATINE

This is another supplement used by many sprinters. It helps when you are strength training and in sprints, by minimizing the rate of fatigue over a series of repetitions. The net result is maintaining intensity over the repetitions, so their training stimulus will potentially be greater. However, creatine tends to draw water into cells, so you could end up with a body mass increase. Not necessarily a problem for sprinters but it would be for road racers, so avoid creatine supplements if this applies to you.

VITAMIN D

Vitamin D acts as a vitamin and a hormone, helping to control levels of calcium and phosphate in the blood. It is also essential for the formation of bones and teeth. Sources of Vitamin D include oily fish and eggs, but it can be difficult to get enough through diet alone. Most people generate vitamin D by exposing their skin to ultraviolet rays in sunlight.

Previous studies suggest that vitamin D can lower levels of the stress hormone cortisol. High levels of cortisol may raise blood pressure by restricting arteries, narrowing blood vessels and stimulating the kidneys to retain water. As Vitamin D may reduce circulating levels of cortisol, it could theoretically improve exercise performance and lower cardiovascular risk factors.

In a study at Queen Margaret University in Edinburgh, scientists gave 13 healthy adults of the same age and weight 50µg of vitamin D per day or a placebo over a period of two weeks. Those taking vitamin D had lower blood pressure compared to those given a placebo, as well as having lower levels of the stress hormone cortisol in their urine. A fitness test found that the group taking vitamin D could cycle, on average, 6.5 kilometres (4 miles) in 20 minutes, compared to 5 kilometres (3 miles) at the start of the study – pretty compelling evidence for supplementing vitamin D.

The problem with getting enough natural vitamin D is our exposure to sunlight. People living in the northern and southern reaches of the planet probably don't get enough sun exposure to provide the vitamin D they need, and they certainly don't get it in winter. An increased awareness of the harmful effects of sunlight in causing skin cancer and the use of sunblock to combat that risk means that we are at increased risk of vitamin D deficiency. This not only has potential health consequences, but it could also have a detrimental effect on fitness and performance, so a supplement of vitamin D in the winter months is a good idea.

2.8 FUELLING THE TOUR DE FRANCE

This final section on nutrition covers its critical role in top-level performance, so let's look at how riders eat and drink to keep themselves competitive in the biggest bike race on the planet: the Tour de France.

Fuelling a Tour de France rider is a mammoth task, fraught with challenges. Competitors can burn up to 9,000 calories a day on the longest mountain stages. They will also be suffering from progressive fatigue, experiencing extreme hot and cold weather and the duration of each stage means that there is no time for a sit-down lunch.

In the past, some riders have under-fuelled during the competition and have run on empty during the final stages and finished the race feeling totally wrecked. However, advances in research into how athletes process food under extreme physical stress has enabled nutritionists to better advise on fuelling cyclists participating in gruelling challenges like the Tour.

HYDRATION

Pro racers are obsessive about staying hydrated and start drinking as soon as they wake. Staying hydrated is crucial to performance and is one of the key things you can do to support gut health, which is essential for recovery. Pros drink fruit juice with breakfast, often with added electrolytes which support muscle function and help your body to absorb water.

Tour de France riders often face a longish drive in their team buses before the start of each stage and they drink an electrolyte or highly diluted fruit juice throughout. They then maybe have an espresso just before the start, which not only gives them a lift, but also helps free up fatty acids to use as fuel.

Tour riders keep drinking throughout each stage; it is drilled into them. Each rider carries two bottles, one of plain water and one of an energy drink. More bottles are handed out in the feed zones, while designated riders drop back to their team support vehicles to collect additional bottles of water and energy drink in between. They stuff the bottles up the insides of their jerseys, distributing them around their teammates in the peloton. Riders can also take bottles from some official supporting motorcycles, which have special racks full of drinks.

Electrolyte drinks are consumed after very hot stages, then all riders start their recovery with a protein and carbohydrate shake mixed with water as soon as the stage ends. They'll continue drinking, maybe eat a protein flapjack or something similar, but dinner is the main refuelling opportunity.

All Tour de France teams have their own chefs, as well as nutritionists on the race. The Team Sky chef liquidizes vegetables and salad products to help the riders digest them and ensure that the bulk of it doesn't fill their stomachs. They still get the nutrients, which play a crucial part in recovery, but the fibre in vegetables is broken down by liquidizing, which

helps it pass freely along the gut. Riders eat protein and carbohydrates in the form of fat-free meat or fish with pasta or rice, then follow this with fruit.

IN-RACE FUELLING

Using carbohydrates to form glucose, which is then burned by the muscles to produce energy, is the body's fuel path when exercising. Until about 10-15 years ago riders ate sugary cakes and bread, and drank Coke or cold tea with glucose during stages. Now they use energy drinks, gels and bars, which do the same job but with more efficiency. More is understood about how the body processes and absorbs carbohydrates and converts them to sugar, so energy drinks and gels are also laced with minerals and other substances to help their uptake.

Carbohydrate fuelling in exercise is still best practice and riders will look to take on 30-60 grams per hour on a flat stage and 60-90 grams per hour on a mountain stage. Tactics to increase the efficiency of fat utilization during exercise are practised in training, but this is not relied on in a race.

PROTEIN

Protein is vital for recovery and performance in the Tour de France. Riders will consume 70-80 grams of protein in supplements every day, in the form of drinks and energy bars. It is possible that some Tour de France riders eat as much as 200 grams of protein a day in their meals. That's well in excess of the amount normally recommended for an athlete in heavy training, which is 2-2.5 grams per kilo of body weight (so an average sized Tour rider of 70 kilograms would normally be recommended to eat a maximum of 175 grams of protein). However, with the intense physical load

Tour riders are under, excess protein isn't stored as fat as it otherwise would be. Instead it is oxidized for use as fuel.

Protein needs to be eaten throughout the day. Riders often add whey powder to their breakfast porridge, but they also eat eggs at breakfast. Then, as well as post-race carbohydrate-and-protein-mix shakes and their normal food intake, they have a slow-release protein recovery drink before sleeping.

Taking attention to detail even further, sprinters and their support riders (the ones who get involved in the sprint lead-outs and who need a bit more muscle) might eat a protein bar about 90 minutes before the end of each stage. Yellow jersey contenders and climbers may eat protein bars on flat stages, but on mountain stages their bodies are working too hard to process protein.

FATS

Traditionally fats were avoided like the plague by pro bike riders. However, research into fat as a fuel and the benefits to health and recovery of "good" fats, such as those found in olive oil and oily fish, have prompted a rethink. Now, fats can form up to 20–30 per cent of a Tour rider's diet.

However, fat is prescribed at the end of each day for its anti-inflammatory benefits. Any earlier and the fats consumed could just be used as fuel along with everything else. This is fine, but if your goal is to use fats to prevent inflammation, and so assist recovery, then supplements and foods with concentrated amounts of fat are best eaten after the stage.

VITAMINS, MINERALS & OTHER SUPPLEMENTS

Tour de France riders have taken vitamin and mineral supplements to support their immune systems for quite some time. More recently teams have started supplementing their riders based on information from blood tests that flag up specific deficiencies. The discovery of low iron levels, for example, would likely be treated with an iron supplement. Left untreated, the iron deficiency would affect oxygen transportation by the blood, which would severely impact race performance.

Research on how supplements are absorbed, plus increased awareness of the importance of gut health, has changed the way vitamins and minerals are delivered. There used to be an acceptance in top-level professional road racing that the performance of the gut deteriorated during a race such as the Tour de France and so the gut would be bypassed during long stage races with vitamins and minerals delivered into a rider's body by injection. Now we know that deterioration of the gut is not inevitable in a race, nutritionists are focusing on supporting gut health. This has helped get rid of a needle culture in pro road racing and reduced the reliance on intramuscular or intravenous injections to deliver supplements.

A lot of riders use specific amino acid supplements. Things such as branched-chain amino acids to help recovery, plus specifics like Cystine, which helps form bacteria-attacking proteins. Argenine promotes new skin growth on cuts and grazes. Quercetin and thiamine support the immune system, while zinc helps in the production of natural testosterone. Zinc becomes more important as the race goes on, when testosterone production begins to dip, which can affect recovery.

Finally, sleep is crucial to the recovery of a Tour de France rider. During sleep the body produces human growth hormone. Products such as the night-time recovery drinks and camomile tea can really help to get good-quality sleep.

MENTAL

CHOOSING & MANAGING YOUR CYCLING GOALS

9

3.9 USING INSPIRATION

Let your long-term goal inspire you. There is nothing like setting a really big goal to get you out training. Shut your eyes and try to visualize something you would love to do, even if you think it might be a bit beyond you, and go for it. Of course, you have got to be a bit realistic. Olympic gold medals and winning the Tour de France are beyond a lot of people's reach, but if you are young enough they can be valid goals or dreams. Shoot for the stars, but be happy with the moon too.

For older cyclists, winning an age-group race, even an age-group National or World title, is possible if you have good health and the time and resources to train properly. Improving performances in time trials, or the time you achieved in a cyclosportive the previous year, are good goals.

Then there are big international cyclosportives to ride, such as l'Étape du Tour, which covers a mountain stage of each year's Tour de France. There are also big cyclosportives run on the routes of all the single-day Classics races. There is a whole world of inspiring goals you can go for.

THE MECHANICS OF INSPIRATION

Within your personal possibilities, what have you always wanted to do on your bike? Take a moment to imagine it. Does it give you goosebumps? Does it scare you a bit? If it does either of those, and it's better if it does both, it will inspire you. Now imagine what you will feel like when you have achieved you goal. Write down your objective, plan out a path to it, and go for it.

You might be scared about failing, but fear of failure can help you keep knocking out the training sessions. Your big, scary objective will also keep you on the right path nutritionally, and make it easier for you to turn your back on any temptation to slacken the healthy diet you need to support your ambition. Note, though, the occasional indulgence never hurts.

BE IN THE MOMENT

Use your inspiration to help you focus on each aspect of cycling as and when you are doing it. If you are planning, plan to the best of your ability. Focus on each training session, and only that training session as you do it, then move on to the next. In short, focus on only what you are doing at that moment and don't let everything get jumbled up, or you will end up simply going through the motions and not realizing your potential. Above all, regard everything – training, recovery, eating or looking after yourself and your bike – as essential steps toward your goal, because that's what they are.

Some coaches call living in the moment "being in the flow". Many consider "the flow" as the gateway to the perfect mindset for competition and they call that "being in the zone". The zone is a state beyond focus, where you feel in total control, where you are dictating what happens and everything around you slows down so you analyse it correctly and do the right thing. The flow is something you work on and practise, but once you have cracked it you can switch the flow on any time you need it. I'll talk more about "flow" later on pages 192–4.

VISUALIZATION

Visualization doesn't mean daydreaming and wishing you were out on your bike instead of in a boring meeting or at school. It means taking time to remember the good sensations of cycling and visualize yourself riding perfectly on the way to achieving your goals.

It doesn't mean seeing yourself dressed in yellow on the top step on the Champs Élysées with the Arc de Triomphe behind you, although that is a nice image to conjure up on a grey December day. It means thinking about particular aspects of your cycling challenge, your goal, and visualizing yourself doing them perfectly.

For example, a track pursuiter might visualize the perfect start and pick-up, then settling down into an aerodynamic position and fluidly pushing out the power into the pedals. A time triallist could visualize riding in a perfect aerodynamic tuck while cutting through bends on the perfect line. In fact, perfect should be a feature of all visualization: the perfect sprint, the perfect climbing performance or the perfect descent.

Try attaching a mantra to what you are visualizing, repeating it in your mind. It might be as simple as two words, "perfect start", for example, or "smooth as silk", when you visualize your pedalling style. Repeat the mantra in your mind when you visualize and when you practise. Every time you do this you are reinforcing the neuromuscular pathways that improve performance. I'll expand on mantras and visualization on pages 194 and 202–3 too.

3.9 WHY SET GOALS?

Scan this QR code to hear what to consider and how to go about setting your cycling goals.

It's important to set goals because they bring discipline to your training. Goals help you get out of the door and get on your turbo trainer or go to the gym. Goals centre you and give you specific objectives, from long-term major goals right down to what you want to achieve in a single training session.

Training goals are stepping stones to achieving bigger goals, and big goals spur you on. They help you strive, push yourself and do all of your training properly, including nutrition and recovery.

ANALYSIS

There is a system to effective goal setting. First, review your situation as it is now. If you are new to cycling, ask yourself what your fitness is like, how much time you have got in a week for training, what inspires you and what you would eventually like to achieve in cycling.

It doesn't matter how far you are from your inspiring goal when you set out, the key question is do you have the time, resources and physical capacity to achieve it? To answer this question you need to analyse the goal. What does it consist of, and what does it take to achieve it?

Look at the nature of the event you are training for. Break it down into its constituent parts and set specific goals for each of those components. As an example, for the one-kilometre time trial, I would be looking at my maximum strength and measuring my one-repetition max squat as a key performance indicator for my ability to generate force that would help me with my snap out the gate.

I would look at my standing start 65-metre times as a benchmark for my acceleration and set myself a series of performance goals for that exercise. I would do the same for my peak speed, my speed endurance and my lactate tolerance. I would also look at technical areas too – my technique out the gate, my line on the track, my aero position on the bike – and set goals of increasing difficulty along the way to challenge myself and ultimately improve the overall end result.

All these things need practice and training, and they determine the shape of your training plan, which should be task focused. You focus on one aspect of your goal, while maintaining other aspects you have focused on, then you move on to something else. It's like spinning plates; you get the next plate spinning then pop back and give another a little spin, and so on.

It's important to break down the demands of your goal and see if you have the resources, the time and the commitment to do the training to achieve it. In some cases, the money and desire to spend it on specialized equipment also needs careful consideration.

Then, whether you have a coach or not, sit down with a pen and paper to assess where you are now and specify where you want to go. Don't just think abstractly about your cycling, sit down, review and plan. That's how to get the best results.

MAKE BIG GOALS

Think big, something that excites you will keep you striving, training and moving in the right direction. Yes, you have to be realistic with where you are in life and what resources you have, but within those restrictions big goals work best.

Make your goals performance- and not outcome-oriented. That's one of the keys to good goal setting. If your goal is winning a race, don't focus on winning. Winning might be what you want, but it is an outcome. A lot of factors outside your control can prevent you achieving a specified outcome. Your best possible performance in the race is the only thing you can control. Of course, the outcome of your best possible performance might be winning the race. I would set my goals at the beginning of each four-year cycle, and while Olympic gold was my aim, the actual goal that I had control over was to arrive at the Olympics in the form of my life, and to be the best I could be.

By focusing on the process and not the outcome, you are in charge. "Controlling the controllables" is a well-used phrase, and for good reason. If you worry about things out of your control, such as your rivals' performances, then that will create stress. Only one gold medal is given out for each race, and not everyone can win, so if you can look yourself in the mirror on race day and truly say you have given your best in every training session up to that point, then you can go out and enjoy the race and accept the outcome. If you win, brilliant. If you don't, you shake the other person's hand and say well done, the better cyclist won. But if that happens then you make sure you come back next time even better prepared, and kick their backsides!

PLANNING FOR YOUR GOALS

Leave no stone unturned, that's a good way to think about writing out a plan. Your plan is your recipe for success. You should always have a detailed plan for what training you are about to do in the next four weeks, and a rough plan for the months beyond that. The rough plan then becomes more detailed in the light of the training you are currently doing. That way, at the end of each four-week period, you have another detailed four-week plan ready to go.

Above all, your plan should excite you. I remember talking to Chris Boardman early in my career, looking for advice. He said that his events were nothing like mine, but the one piece of guidance he could give me was that if I wasn't excited when I read through my plan I should tear it up and start again. When the plan you have written really excites you, that's when you will fully buy into it and fully commit to it.

3.9 PERFORMANCE REVIEWING

As you work toward your goal it is important to know where you are in relation to it, and to the interim goals you set along the way. Think of plotting a course on a map; you can have everything worked out, your eventual destination and the points you have to pass clearly marked, but once you set off you must keep track of where you are in relation to those points. If you don't know where you are, you are lost. The way to know where you are in relation to your interim and long-term cycling goals is to carry out regular performance reviews.

MAKING LISTS

The first thing to do in a performance review is make three lists under the following headings:

1   What are you doing now that's helping you move toward your goal?

2   What are you doing now that's working against your progress toward that goal?

3   What are you not doing now that could help you accelerate your progress toward that goal?

Your coach, if you have one, should be involved in reviewing. A coach is an objective third party and objectivity is what this exercise requires. But whether you have a coach or not, you should sit down with a pen and paper to do reviews.

Even if they don't keep diaries, most people have an intuitive idea of the training that worked for them in a particular race or challenge. Go back in your mind or diary to two or three weeks before a good performance and see what training you did in the three or four weeks before that. Whatever it was, it needs listing under list 1 or 3.

Go through as much as you can with a fine-tooth comb, asking the above three questions in respect of your goals and drawing conclusions before deciding on a plan of action. It might seem a lot of trouble, but if you really want to improve reviewing is key. The best professional teams always regularly use this process and coaches of the various British Cycling teams constantly review training and performance.

Once you have listed everything you can under the headings, work out a plan that preserves what you have listed under heading 1. Then resolve to stop doing the things you've listed under heading 2. Finally, work out how to fit the things listed under heading 3 into your training programme.

IDENTIFY AND CORRECT YOUR WEAKNESSES

Next, you should look a little deeper into your performance in training and in competition. If you are training for road races, do you keep getting out-sprinted or dropped on short, sharp hills? If that's happening, then plan in some specific training to address it, such as uphill interval training in which you ride as hard as you can up several hills of different lengths.

Most weaknesses are obvious, especially if you compete, but some are more difficult to identify. One way to identify weaknesses is to ask yourself if there is a type of training you really don't like doing. If so, the session you don't like doing is most likely the one that will help to improve your weaknesses. And even if you don't compete, weaknesses can reduce your enjoyment of cycling. It pays to address them.

STAY POSITIVE

No matter how far you appear to be from your goal, so long as you are going toward it, no matter how slowly, you are making progress. This is especially true if you set yourself a scary goal, which is often a good thing to do, so long as you have the time and resources to work toward it.

The thing to remember is that progress in fitness is rarely linear. You progress in distinct phases, and sometimes it can feel like you are taking a step back, especially if you're training hard. If that happens, don't let it put you off. Remember this table tennis ball analogy: the lower you push it under water, the higher the ball bounces back up. The water is your training and the ball is your fitness. Don't push too hard though, because like a table tennis ball in very deep water, you can get crushed.

It is always worth having a review of your goals and your plans. If you genuinely feel you are going backward, analyse why and address the reasons. And if there aren't any then just keep the faith, you'll soon be back on track. Above all, don't expect too much from yourself at once, practise realistic optimism instead.

WORK WITH WHAT YOU'VE GOT

Finally, when planning and reviewing, don't put things on hold until your perceived situation gets better. Even some extremely talented people do that and it's why they don't always reach their potential. You hear them saying things like, they did such and such a race for the experience of it, but next year, when "this" or "that" is in place, they will really go for it. The thing is, "this" or "that" might never be in place and they might already have missed their best chance. Top sports people don't put things off, they play the hand they've got. Their secret, though, is that they play it well.

SPORTS PSYCHOLOGY

3.10 THE MIND IN PERFORMANCE

The mind plays a huge part in sports performance. Its role invariably forms the most interesting aspect of watching elite athletes compete and often it's the decisive factor in victory. It is also the one thing that's universal across all sports and it hasn't changed over the years. The mind can be a help or a hindrance and, by paying attention to the mental side of your performance, you can greatly improve your chances of achieving your goals.

The biggest challenge most sportsmen and women face when competing is being able to deal with the perceived pressures they face so they can perform to their true potential. Do not expect to miraculously pull a performance out of thin air using the power of your mind. By working on controlling your thinking, however, you can greatly reduce the risk of underperforming when it comes to the crunch.

PRE-RACE NERVES

One of the most common questions I am asked by sports participants is: how can you overcome pre-competition nerves? Firstly, we need to understand the difference between "good" nerves and "bad" nerves. Good nerves can be described as a state of excitement prior to a competition, when you are fully adrenalized and ready to perform. You need to be in this state to be alert enough to get the best out of yourself physically, so these nerves have their uses. It is important to recognize this before you race and remind yourself it is a positive thing to feel the adrenaline and understand the role it plays in physiological activation.

Bad nerves are when your adrenaline state goes too far and anxiety sets in, with negative thoughts dominating and distracting you from what should be your objective: focusing entirely on the task at hand. This can be one of the greatest reasons for underperformance at any level in sport, from a kid's school sports day to an Olympic final.

DEALING WITH NERVES

We are all different, and therefore there is no single correct way to deal with pre-competition nerves. However, the following techniques served me well and I've heard many other athletes describe a similar approach.

Professor Steve Peters was British Cycling's psychologist for nearly a decade and his contribution to the team's success across the board cannot be overstated. He really helped me get the best out of myself and, while I didn't have any major issues with race-day nerves, I was always looking to optimize every area of my performance.

I learned to recognize the things I had control over and to focus only on those. I used visualization whenever I felt that "bad" nerves were starting to hijack my thoughts before

a race and, by focusing exactly on how I wanted to perform, I was able to push negative thoughts out of my head, a process known as cognitive displacement. It's very simple, but very effective.

In short, think about what you want to do, not what you don't want to do. Be aware that this will happen constantly throughout the lead-up to a big day; you will have negative thoughts popping up all the time and you will need to keep dismissing them. Visualization is a great way to do this.

PERSPECTIVE

Another thing that helped me was gaining perspective. I will discuss this more later on page 187 and explain techniques that can assist you, but essentially it is always good to remind yourself of a few simple things when you're getting stressed before a competition.

Firstly, you have chosen to be there. It may not feel like it at that moment, but you have chosen to be there because you love doing it, it's your passion. Nine times out of ten you will finish the race, look back and think, "That was brilliant, I can't believe I was so worried about it." Remind yourself of this before you start.

Secondly, it is not life and death. The world will not stop revolving if you don't win. I always found it helpful to remind myself that I was just riding a bike in anticlockwise circles, not going to war.

Thirdly, Steve Peters always told us the importance of smiling. It's weird, but even if you don't feel particularly confident, smiling can really help shift your mood. And even if it has no effect at all on you, it will always freak out your opponents, who assume you're totally relaxed and in control. Then they start worrying about you.

ADDRESS FEARS

Before you start your warm-up on race day, allow yourself to address your fears and negative thoughts. Use this time to answer the worries with logic, just knock them on the head with facts. Remind yourself of the weeks and months, and maybe years, of work you have put in as preparation. Remind yourself of past successes in training and competition. And remind yourself of the positive reasons why today will be another great day, just like those were.

Do the training, because being prepared is one of the biggest ways you can overcome pre-race stress. Knowing there is nothing more that you could have done to be ready for the big day is very powerful.

Once you have faced these fears and addressed them all with a logic based on facts, you can then start to visualize a positive outcome to keep your focus solely on positivity and the process of performance.

Finally, go out there and express yourself on the bike. Show people the passion you have for this wonderful sport and give it your all. Focus on the process of what you are doing and how you want to do it, and the results will follow.

LUCKY SOCKS?

I used to get asked all the time about whether I had any superstitions or lucky charms, and my answer was always no. If I began to rely on an external object to provide me with confidence, then what if I forgot to bring it to the track? Or worse, lost it forever?

Everybody is different, and I totally understand that we all need luck on our side, regardless of how well prepared we are. However, I feel that superstitions can create unnecessary stress. And also, when you win your race, you can take full credit for all the hard work and not just put it down to your lucky socks!

3.10 CENTRAL GOVERNOR THEORY

The mind, or at least the brain, might play a role in the actual mechanics of performance, not just the way we think or frame things in competitive situations. Classical exercise theory holds that muscles fatigue because they run out of fuel or they are swamped by the by-products of exercise. Central governor theory holds that the brain limits the amount of muscle fibres being contracted at any one time in order to protect the body from damage and ensure our continued wellbeing. And it's very likely that they both play a part in the fatigue processes that serve to limit performance.

EVIDENCE FOR THE EXISTENCE OF CENTRAL GOVERNOR THEORY

One of the proponents of central governor theory, Professor Tim Noakes, has carried out several studies into it, including one where he asked seven experienced cyclists to complete two 100-kilometre (62 miles) time trials on static bikes. On several occasions during each trial the subjects were asked to ride as hard as they could for between 1 and 4 kilometres (0.6 and 2.5 miles). Electrical sensors recorded how many individual muscle fibres were recruited during the whole of this exercise.

In any given muscle contraction, the brain will never fire all the muscle fibres at the same time. It spreads the load between fibres, resting some that have worked hard and recruiting fresh ones all the time. If fatigue was due to fibres hitting a limit you would expect the total number recruited to increase as the body tires. However, Noakes found that as fatigue set in, the number of fibres recruited dropped, even during sprints.

CLASSICAL THEORY

Classical exercise theory holds that increased acidosis (excessive acid) within muscles causes fatigue, and the onset on acidosis occurs when there are high levels of lactate present. However, experiments simulating exercise at high altitudes revealed that fatigue can also set in without any significant changes in lactate levels, providing evidence of a central governor at work, protecting the body from damage. Researchers claim that when exercising in conditions of low oxygen pressure, the brain limits muscle-fibre recruitment to prevent the heart from pumping blood with a low oxygen concentration around the body.

However, the fact that there might be some sort of central governor activity going on during exercise doesn't mean that what happens *inside* the muscles is irrelevant. What the supporters of this theory claim is that the governor constantly monitors what's going on in the muscles on a chemical level and takes that into consideration, along with other signals coming from the muscles.

The theory goes that the central governor is there to protect vital organs, especially the heart. Recruiting more and more muscle fibres would require more and more oxygen to be pumped by the heart. But since the amount of oxygen we can take in is finite, the heart itself would become starved of oxygen. The result could be a heart attack. This is especially true if exercising at high altitude: studies revealed that mountaineers not using oxygen at very high altitude are so weak they have to crawl on all fours, despite there being very little lactic acid in their muscles.

INTERVAL THEORY

So how do Noakes and other believers explain that central governor theory works in respect of the undoubted improvements that can be gained from tough interval training? Classical exercise theory says that intervals increase the efficiency with which your muscles work. However, Noakes claims that going hard in training may also re-educate your central governor to the possibility that doing so doesn't necessarily do damage to your body.

It would appear that repeated high-intensity efforts can re-set the central governor to allow your body to work harder. The natural progression from that thought, though, is that very hard intervals will allow you to go very hard indeed. This may be why the VO_2 max intervals on pages 125–6 and the shorter, even harder training sessions on pages 128–9, if used sparingly, are so effective at improving your fitness.

The role the central governor plays in the changes these intervals can make to your athletic performance is still not totally clear. But the evidence that the brain limits muscle-fibre recruitment in the light of what it knows is compelling. So high-intensity training may not only result in beneficial metabolic adaptions, but also play a crucial role in assisting the re-education of the brain. There is more work to be done on central governor theory, and much to learn.

3.10 MANAGING EMOTIONAL THOUGHT

Many have heard about Professor Steve Peters and the chimp. He has written a fascinating book called *The Chimp Paradox* (2012), which explains his mind management model and how it works in all aspects of life, not just in sport. I consider myself very lucky that I was able to benefit from Steve's expertise during his time working with the British Cycling team. He played a key role in our success and was often referred to as the glue that held the British Cycling team together.

MIND MODEL

Steve is a consultant psychiatrist who holds degrees in mathematics and medicine. He has worked in many different fields and began working with the British Cycling team in 2001. His mind management techniques are part of the success that our elite cyclists have had ever since.

The best way to get a full understanding of Steve's mind management model is to read his book, but in a nutshell, when I first met with him he explained it as follows. The brain can be viewed as a machine of three main parts. Firstly, a logical "human" part, responsible for rational behaviour and calm and sensible choices. Secondly, an emotional part – the "chimp" – responsible for the "fight/flight/freeze" reactions that we experience during times of extreme stress or fear. The decisions made by this part of the brain are fast and can be very unpredictable, sometimes the right choice, sometimes the wrong choice. Finally, there is the "computer", which carries out automatic functions and doesn't require conscious thought to operate. Of course, it's a bit more complex than that, but it helps to simplify it in this context.

The aim of all the work I did with Steve was to improve my ability to control my emotional thoughts (the "chimp") during competitions and, wherever possible, to use the logical part of my brain or, even better go on autopilot and let the "computer" take over.

That may sound odd, and it didn't mean that I walked around like a robot for four years leading up to each Olympic Games. It was all about learning the skills to recognize when I had allowed the chimp to sabotage my thoughts and then doing something about it. After years of working with Steve, he helped me develop the skills to be able to enter a highly pressurized situation and perform as calmly as if it was any other day. Like any skill it took time to develop and also required maintenance – very much a case of use it or lose it.

Before meeting Steve, I was a bit reluctant to engage with any psychologist. I didn't really know what the process would involve and there was definitely a stigma attached to it, as if I was admitting I didn't have sufficient mental strength and this was a chink in my armour. Ridiculous really, because if I had a broken bike I'd take it to a mechanic, if I had an injury I'd go to the physio and if I was ill I'd go to the doctor. So why not speak to the psychologist to see if I could improve my ability to focus and perform when it came to the big stage?

Steve kept things simple but effective. "Life's Not Fair!" – if you expect it to be, you'll be sorely disappointed. "Accept it, move on!" – when things happen outside of your control, put it to bed and get on with the things you can control. "Focus on the process, not the outcome" – essentially, focus on your performance and not the end result, to minimize stress, something that I will discuss in more detail on page 188.

He helped me to gain perspective on what it was I was doing: I wasn't saving people's lives, I was riding a bike in anticlockwise circles. That didn't mean I shouldn't care about what I was doing, far from it, it meant that I needed to enjoy doing it, be passionate about it, give my best, but realize that the world wouldn't stop revolving if I lost a race.

A big part of dealing with the chimp was listening to it and addressing its fears. By letting it "out of the cage" now and again, hearing what was making it anxious, I was able to cage it with logic. It would still try and get out on competition day, fear of failure causing it to get edgy, but by then I had a strategy for dealing with emotional thoughts and would begin my mental warm-up at the same time as I began my physical one. I would arrive on the start line ready in body and mind.

GET HELP

If you've ever felt you've underperformed in a competition due to nerves or allowing negative thoughts to creep in, I would definitely recommend trying to address the problem. You may be putting in hundreds of hours of training, getting yourself in the best possible physical shape, but then coming up short on race day all because you can't deal with the pressure. You don't necessarily need to see a sport psychologist, *The Chimp Paradox* (I'm not on commission, I promise!) or many other mind management books could be a great way to start improving the way you perceive things under pressure. You will find that you can apply it to all aspects of your life – public speaking, fear of flying, anger management, the list goes on.

3.10 OVERCOMING FEARS & SETBACKS

There is a degree of fear involved in cycling – fear of failing, of underperforming or of letting yourself or the team down. There can also be fear of particular situations – a rough corner, a steep descent or a particular hill. Or fear of other riders. A certain level of fear might even be good; it can keep you training hard and make you stick to a good diet. It's when fears prevent you from doing things and hold you back that they become a problem.

But there are rational ways to overcome fears, and you can also use them to reframe setbacks and stress. Because you *will* have setbacks in your cycling journey. It's easy to let stress creep in, particularly if you are very competitive (which is probably essential if you want to succeed at top level). It just has to be kept in check.

NATURE'S WAY

Fear and stress aren't necessarily unhealthy things. They are a way of telling you something is wrong and that you should take action to put it right. You could do without setbacks, of course but, along with fear and stress, they are a part of life. The key thing is to deal with them constructively.

When a fear takes hold or a setback happens, or you are stressed, you will react irrationally at first. That's Professor Peters' chimp response, and it can be okay as an initial reaction, it's the way our minds are wired to react. Your emotional side has three responses when confronted with a stressful situation, a threat or a setback. It will urge you to fight, freeze or flee, any of which could be crucial to your survival.

So it's okay to feel angry at a setback in normal life, just try not to overreact. When Mark Cavendish was young and was in almost constant contact with his coach Rod Ellingworth, Ellingworth says that nearly every phone call started with who had pissed Mark off that day. Ellingworth was fine with it, he recognized it was how Mark was wired, so he would listen to a short rant, then ask, "Are you better now?" and they would carry on a rational, useful conversation.

I'm not saying that Mark's way is best, but it works for him. Also, Rod Ellingworth is a caring, talented coach who understood that it was part of how Mark Cavendish was then (he's mellowed a lot now). Feeling angry is okay, telling somebody you trust how you feel is healthy, but if you get angry too often or for too long you will irritate and upset other people, including cycling coaches, even if you are as talented as Mark Cavendish.

Anger is better than freezing as a first response to a setback, because freezing solves nothing, it's just denying there is a problem. While taking flight is simply an avoidance tactic and the problem or setback will still be there.

RECOGNIZE, REACT & CONTROL

So, say something goes wrong or you are confronted with a fear. Recognize that you will react emotionally at first, and that is your trigger to hit the pause button, slow down your thinking and give the logical side of your brain time to catch up and take over.

Next you need to stand back. This might be mentally standing back or physically doing so. Physically is better, because distancing yourself from a problem gives you time to pull yourself together and think things through. Say you are in an argument, some physical space allows you time to think logically and return with a well-thought-out answer.

PLAN A WAY FORWARD

Ask what you could have done differently to avoid whatever is bothering you. Look at the events and circumstances that led up to the situation. Can any of those be changed? Change what you can, ignore what you can't, but don't just do nothing. If you do nothing the problem stays or, if it's an injury, a fear or similar stress, it persists. Never allow yourself to become a victim of circumstances. Ask for help if you need it. Plan and move forward.

HELICOPTER THINKING

So now you are in control and you are emotionally, if not physically, distanced from the problem, use the following technique to put the problem in perspective. Imagine rising from where you are in a helicopter. What would you see? For me, if I was in a velodrome, I'd see a city below me full of people going through all kinds of things. Most of it far more stressful than what I'm facing.

Maybe I had a little niggle or a full-blown injury, but there would be people in the city below me fighting for their lives in hospital or going through all kinds of other traumatic events. It puts things into perspective, and when people are really immersed in something, as athletes tend to be in their sport, they often have it out of perspective. Occasionally they have to make a conscious effort to put it back into perspective.

Another helicopter technique is to imagine your whole life laid out below you. How important is what you are going through now in comparison with the rest of your life? Imagine the things that are really important in it. Does this problem change them? Most likely the answer is no, and that also helps bring perspective to the problem.

Keep your racing and training in perspective. There's always somebody going through something much more stressful, however hard that might be to believe at the time.

3.10 PROCESS VS. OUTCOME THINKING

Thinking about what you are doing and thinking about the outcome of what you are doing are two different things, and it's important not to confuse them. However, there are times when either way of thinking comes into its own when training and in competition.

FOCUSING ON THE PROCESS

In competition the desired outcome would be whatever you had defined as success when you set your goal for that competition. However, to give yourself the best chance of achieving that successful outcome, you need to think only of the *process* of what you are doing.

To a certain extent, you make your own luck by being proactive, minimizing the variables and taking control wherever possible. However, you cannot control the outcome of a competition as there are too many uncontrollable factors. Your rivals might be fitter than you and, since you had no control over their preparation, there is no point in thinking about it. They might have better tactics in a road race, which you can counter but not control. The weather could stand in the way of achieving your target in a time trial. And it's always possible that you could simply have a bit of bad luck.

The only thing you can control is your performance, which is determined by doing everything you need to do to the best of your ability. Doing everything you can do is a process, and there is more than enough in the process of racing to keep you occupied. If you focus on what you have to do to be the best you can be on that day, you won't have time to think about the outcome.

It often helps to look at the process chronologically. I would plan the whole day of a competition from waking up to going to bed. There needs to be flexibility in any plan, but from the moment my alarm went off in the morning, I was following a plan. Wake up, shower, breakfast, pick up kitbag (pre-packed the night before), meet in reception five minutes before leaving so there was no rush and I didn't hold up my teammates, head to the track, commence pre-planned mental and physical warm-up at a specific time, towel down, kit on, numbers pinned, race!

It was like being on a conveyor belt and all I had to do was follow the plan I had laid out. I knew exactly what I needed to do to get to the start line and be ready to go. Once I got there, I had visualized the perfect race in my mind over and over, running through different permutations if it was a sprint or keirin, or that one perfectly executed ride if it was a kilo or team sprint. Your mind is kept occupied by always having something to actively focus on, which stops you drifting into thoughts of what it might feel like to win the gold or to fail miserably. It minimizes the chances of emotional thought creeping in. It keeps you focused on the task at hand. Process thinking is unemotional; it is logical thinking done by the human side of your brain. Professor Peters' chimp must have no say in the process.

PROCESS THINKING IN ACTION

The best example of focusing on the process not the outcome that I experienced in my career was in Athens 2004. I was competing in the kilo time trial and, as World Champion, I would start last. I sat and watched three different riders break the Olympic record (and sea-level World record) before I stepped up onto the track for my ride.

Steve had predicted this might happen and helped me to prepare for this eventuality. Rather than "try not to think about it", he told me I would need to actively choose something else to think about to displace the negative thoughts. So I simply focused on every single part of my dream performance, from start to finish.

I visualized over and over in detail exactly what I needed to do to give my best performance out on track. To hell with everyone else. I didn't care what amazing times they were setting, I was going to do my own personal best performance and nothing would distract me from doing it.

Would that be enough for gold? I had no idea. That wasn't in my control, so I didn't worry about it. I just rode my own race, genuinely did my best and thankfully the outcome that followed was a gold medal.

TRAINING THOUGHT & OUTCOME THINKING

In competition, I have no doubt that staying focused on the process is the best way to perform optimally. In training too, it can help on a daily basis to get you through a particularly tough phase. However, there is a time when focusing on the outcome can be really helpful. When motivation is down, the end goal is months or even years away, and it feels like just "another" session, you can do well to remind yourself of that pot of gold waiting at the end of the rainbow.

Imagine the feeling of achieving your dream – how that perfect race will unfold, the roar of the crowd, the feeling of crossing the line, the elation, the celebrations. This reminds you what you're striving for and that can have a very powerful effect on your morale and your commitment when things otherwise might feel a bit flat.

3.10 MOTIVATION

There's an old saying in cycling that summer medals are won in the winter. Meaning, although the race is important, the foundations for success are laid months, sometimes even years, in advance. There's another saying, this time a military one: "Train hard, fight easy." Applied to sport it means that if you do all the training and preparation you can and you commit fully in every effort of every session, then the race will look after itself. Although I'd add, and I'm sure combat soldiers would agree, you need the right state of mind in the race too.

MOTIVATION FROM WITHIN

There are techniques you can use to engender the correct mindset to go into a training session and complete it to the best of your ability. To get you through tough sessions or a tough training phase, you've got to establish *why* you are doing it. Then, while keeping that thought in your mind, focus on the *process* of doing it. The reasons why you want to train hard depend on your motivation, and motivation falls into three categories, depending on what type of person you are.

1 TASK MOTIVATION

You are motivated by the thought of a job well done. You want to master something, and you are interested in the process of doing so. You focus on showing improvement on your previous performances in racing and in training.

2 OUTCOME MOTIVATION

You compare yourself with others. You need to win or finish high in your category to feel that you are making progress in your sport. Outcome motivation is when you focus on beating others.

3 SOCIAL APPROVAL MOTIVATION

You want to gain recognition and praise from others for performing well and trying hard in your sport. You need to fit in and doing well in sport will help you do that.

If you think hard enough about these three categories of motivation you will identify one that best describes why you are doing a sport. Once your personal motivation for hard training is established, you should try to be robotic about the process of doing the training you have set yourself, or your coach has set for you. Carry out each training session to the letter, without getting carried away or doing too much, and also without being at all lethargic or lax about it.

RACE MINDSET

My training sessions were the foundation of my confidence. They helped me keep my emotions under wraps and think logically when I was competing. I'd reflect on how hard I had trained, what I'd gone through to get to that point and the fact that I was fully prepared and ready. Now was the time to reap the rewards and enjoy the moment.

That reminder of enjoyment is something that I feel can be lost sometimes when athletes compete, particularly at elite level. No matter what sport you do, or the level at which you participate, I think it always helps to keep at the front of your mind the main reason why you took up the sport in the first place. Because it gives you a buzz and you love it.

TOUGHING IT OUT

I always wanted to arrive at the big day knowing I'd done everything within my powers to be the best I could. A big part of that was committing 100 per cent in every effort I did, even if it was the middle of the off-season, so that I knew I hadn't taken any shortcuts. The most painful but effective sessions took place on the static bike in the lab for the lactate tolerance intervals. With no crowds to cheer me on and no medals at stake, it required a serious internal drive to push right to the limits of my pain threshold.

Sprint athletes have a high percentage of fast-twitch muscle fibres, predetermined by genetics, and these fibres have the potential to contract quickly and with great force. Athletes with this make-up can produce explosive efforts that create massive fatigue in a short space of time. The by-products of this anaerobic effort result in acidosis within the muscles, and it hurts.

The lactate tolerance intervals hurt a lot. That was the point of them. We measured the lactate levels throughout the sessions and the aim was to get them as high as possible, training the body to become as efficient as possible at processing lactic acid.

I did the sessions as hard as I could because I knew they were the one area where some athletes would hold back a fraction, even if it was subconsciously, for self-preservation. They stung like hell and the pain didn't stop when you got off the bike. It kept getting worse, with nausea building as the searing pain in your legs made them feel like balloons ready to pop.

I used my competitive streak in training to get the most out of myself, imagining all my rivals doing this session but with them backing off a tenth of a per cent when they really began to suffer, while I pushed on until I was ready to collapse. I've no idea if that was actually the case but it helped me squeeze the last drops of energy out myself.

The worst thing about them, of course, is that the "fitter" you get, the more power output you produce and therefore the more damage and pain you could cause.

Hard training also helped me banish any self-doubt before competition. I didn't want to stand on a podium in second or third place thinking, "what if I'd just committed that fraction more in my daily routine?" You get out what you put in and I couldn't have put in any more or pushed any harder.

Pushing yourself is about focus, and about finding the thoughts that inspire you and using those thoughts to commit and really drive yourself. Sometimes it's the carrot, sometimes the stick.

3.10 **FLOW**

Flow is a state of mind that can be entered while doing any activity, although it is most likely to occur when you are doing something you really want to do. It's also known in sport as "being in the zone" and is a state of mind where you are in control. You are dictating what happens to you, and not reacting to others all the time. It's the perfect state of mind for taking part in sport.

FLOW CONDITIONS

Flow is a valuable state of mind for doing any task and there are seven conditions that are generally accepted as prerequisites for it to occur:

1 You should know what you are doing.
2 You should know how to do it.
3 You should know how well you are doing.
4 You should know where you are going.
5 You should see the task you are involved in as a testing one.
6 You should see the skills involved as being high and warranting attention.
7 You should be free from distraction.

Bike races, and any form of competition really, meet all of these conditions.

FLOW & PERFORMANCE

Feeling the flow or being in the zone means that you feel a certain mastery of what you are doing. There's also evidence that being in the zone influences movement patterns, because it integrates conscious movement with subconscious reflexes. This improves coordination and many athletes describe how their movements feel freer and more fluid when they are performing at their best

But you can take things further. When top athletes talk about being in the zone they refer to what is an almost altered state of consciousness: a state of mind where things around them seem to slow down, giving them time to analyse, plan and choose the right moment to play the right tactics.

Many top cyclists, especially sprinters, say the seconds in a race seem a lot longer to them, they see things in slow motion and because of that they have time to make the right decisions.

I experienced this many times in races, particularly in keirin races, where it felt like everything slowed down and I was able to see things unfold at a reduced pace, giving me more time to react. It also felt like I could predict moves before they happened when I was in this mental state.

USING FLOW & TRUSTING YOUR INSTINCTS

In Melbourne at the 2012 World Championships I was in fourth place with 80 metres (87.5 yards) to go in the keirin final – totally out of contention and the chance of winning all but gone. I instinctively felt, however, like the New Zealand rider, Simon van Velthooven, was going to flick out and move up the track on the final bend. I dropped down, went straight up the inside and rushed at a gap that didn't yet exist. Almost miraculously it opened just in the nick of time, I went straight through and, with that momentum, passed Maximilian Levy to snatch the gold right on the line. There was certainly an element of luck involved, but by not panicking and being able to assess the situation in what felt like slow motion, I'd given myself the best opportunity to get out of a bad situation.

Of course, experience does help when faced with decision-making in the midst of competition, but flow is often not as conscious a process as the one described above. It can sometimes feel like you are observing the whole moment in an out-of-body way, as though it is all happening automatically and you are merely a passenger. There are times when you get to the end of the race and have no memory of what happened.

It's hard to work out where experience ends and flow starts, but it has to be said that top racers have an uncanny knack of making good tactical decisions. And it's not just cyclists who speak about flow. It's mentioned a lot in motor sport, where really great drivers are said to be able to slow down the action going on around them. People involved in balls sports report the same sensations. It's a valuable tool across the board.

GETTING IN THE ZONE

Your ambitions might not include making good split-second decisions in track sprints, but being in control, making good decisions in a race, choosing the best line through a corner in a time trial, and knowing the safest and quickest way down a hill are all things that improve cycling performance. Being in the zone makes those things simple and clear, but what you practise in order to get there helps your training and preparation too.

Giving yourself ample time to get ready before an event and having confidence in your training and your bike will help your mind move toward being in the zone. So does having a clear objective for the challenge you are taking on. Professional road race teams never race without a plan, and everybody in the race will know his or her part in that plan.

Once the race is underway you must stay in the moment, focus on what's happening around you and do not think too

far ahead. Races must be broken down into manageable chunks. If you are suffering on lap one of a 50-lap criterium, the worst thing you can think is, "how am I going to manage 49 laps more at this pace?" Just focus on yourself, pedal fluidly, relax your upper body as much as possible, breathe deeply and rhythmically. Deal with the present moment.

Have courage that you have done the training and hold onto the fact that the current pace won't continue. It can't continue. You have two legs, a heart and lungs. So do the other competitors. They might have trained hard and prepared well, but so have you.

Professional road racers never go into a Grand Tour thinking about it being three weeks long. They take it stage by stage, only focusing on what they are doing, not what is coming up. Doing that when you take on your cycling challenges helps to get you in the zone.

GATEWAY

Flow is the gateway to being in the zone. Work on establishing it by living in the moment and concentrating completely on what you are doing, then you can switch it on any time you need. Once the right neural pathways are opened, it's a short step into the zone.

Consider flow as being another word for focus, and you should focus on every training session you do. By doing that you are opening yourself up to being in the zone. It means thinking about *what* you are doing *when* you are doing it. And doing it perfectly. One way to evoke this state of mind in training is to use evocative words to make up a mantra. Then keep the mantra running through your mind during important parts of your training, such as when you climb a hill or make a big effort.

The mantra should be just three words long, starting with a power word such as "strong" or "drive". Next use a descriptive word, such as "smooth", to focus on your technique, because doing that helps hardwire the neuromuscular connections you need to pedal efficiently. The third word should be what you are looking for, so "speed" or "fast" would be good for riding on the flat, and "light" could work when going uphill. You might end up with a mantra such as "strong, smooth, fast". Work on yours, write it down and use it while you are training, or get it running through your mind before and during a race.

TAKING IT FURTHER

You can also get in the zone by understanding and getting a feel for the efforts involved in high performance. That comes with experience. The best time triallists have a natural feel for pace judgment on any given course, no matter what length or terrain it is. A downhill mountain biker will have the course mapped out in their head and visualize it in real time over and over before the race, so they are always ready for the next section approaching. A track sprinter will start their match sprint at walking pace, crawling around the bottom of the velodrome, eyeing up their opponent, but they are mentally and physically primed, ready for the attack when it comes. You should be too.

MENTAL TECHNIQUES

11

3.11 **PINK ELEPHANTS**

By 2003 I had won an Olympic silver medal, two gold medals in the Track Cycling World Championships and a Commonwealth Games gold. I was 27, coming to my peak, and my cycling future looked great with just over a year to go until the 2004 Olympic Games in Athens. Then, out of nowhere, things started to go wrong. I went from being the one-kilometre time trial World Champion to not even making the podium in the space of 12 months. To cap off a disastrous season, I could only manage a bronze in the British National Championships.

A number of things caused this dip in my progress and one of them was a mistake I made in my pre-race thinking. I managed to get that back on course with the help of a pink elephant, and it helped me win my first Olympic gold medal in Athens.

PANIC THINKING

After a solid foundation of winter training I actually started the 2003 season well. I won the first round of the Track Cycling World Cup in Cape Town, but then things began to go less well. It happened gradually at first; the odd session was below par, but nothing to worry about. Then my training performances became a little hit or miss and the consistency that I'd always enjoyed seemed to be slipping away. I started putting pressure on myself, each morning waking up and thinking that today would be the day to get things back on track.

I tried to push even harder in training, reacting the way that most athletes do when they are faced with a dip in their form. But when you're trying to get out of a hole, digging even deeper is rarely the answer. My form on the bike was becoming ragged. I was trying to force things rather than let them flow, and was increasing my training volume to make up for the fact that I was behind where I wanted to be at that stage of the season. Soon I started having muscle spasms, physical symptoms of the fatigue that kept me awake at night and compounded my tiredness.

As defending World Champion, I was the favourite going into the one-kilometre time trial in the 2003 Track Cycling World Championships in Stuttgart and, as defending champion, I would be the last man to ride. It was very hot inside the velodrome, so times were fast. My training had actually gone a little bit better just before the Worlds, so I decided to increase the gear ratio I'd use in the race. Not by much, but enough to take advantage of the fast conditions. Well, that was my thinking. It was derailed soon after the event started.

Germany's Stefan Nimke was among the early starters and he flew around the track, going half a second faster than anyone had ever achieved at sea level. I reacted emotionally. Instead of sticking to my game plan – reminding myself that conditions were fast, focusing on myself and my own pacing strategy for the race – I decided I had better up my game, attack the start with everything I had and try to hang on. It was a bad idea.

I ended up going as quickly as I'd ever gone, but that was primarily down to the fast conditions. I started far too fast, tied up badly toward the end and finished fourth. To make matters worse, I had to race the British National Championships a couple of weeks later and, with low morale, I only finished third in the one-kilometre time trial. The chance of representing Great Britain at the 2004 Olympic Games was now in jeopardy.

TURNAROUND

With help from a number of people, I began to turn things around. I went back to basics, closely analysed the year I'd had and tried to find out not only what went wrong, but also what I could do to improve in the future. I was no longer the current World Champion, so I wasn't afraid to make changes to my programme. Often when you're winning you don't want to change a thing, but if you want to keep on improving you need to tweak what you do, even if it's only in subtle ways. I laid the foundations for the year ahead with a great training camp through the winter in Australia. Confidence grew and I went on to win the 2004 World Cup Classics in Sydney and regain my World Champion title in Melbourne a couple of weeks later, securing my place in the event at the Olympic Games. Also, as World Champion, I qualified the British team for an additional place in the race, which was a nice plus.

Things looked good, but in Athens I would face the same scenario I'd had in Stuttgart. I would be the last rider to start in the kilometre time trial – could my thinking in that situation let me down again? Steve Peters thought it was probably a good idea to talk about my chimp.

I had spoken to him a few times before. He was working closely with the British team by 2004 and, in his casual style, he sought me out at the pre-Olympic training camp in Newport, Wales. We sat down together and after chatting in general about how I was feeling going into the Olympics, Steve asked me how I was going to react if someone posted a really amazing time, which I'd then have to beat, as had happened in Stuttgart.

I said I'd be fine, because this time I would just ignore it and carry on. But then he asked, what if someone set a new World record, how could I ignore that? It would be there, a new World record, a massive thing. I said I wouldn't think about it. His response was simple but effective. He said, "You need to have a plan for what you want to think about. If I say to you right now, 'DO NOT THINK ABOUT A PINK ELEPHANT!' What's the first thing that pops into your head?"

"A pink elephant," I replied.

That's when Steve told me I can't say I'm not going to think about something, but I *could* say I'm going to think about something else. I could prevent the negative thoughts from creeping in by displacing them with a positive one that I had chosen. That would prevent my emotional side, my chimp, from making the decision on how I'd react to a new World record, which I would then have to beat to win gold. Thinking about something else meant that it would be my logical side making the decision as to what to think about, and by doing that I would be in control.

The technique Steve encouraged me to use to displace any negative thoughts was visualization. Very simply, whenever I had any thought pop into my head that wasn't constructive in the run up to the Olympics, I would visualize my perfect performance, in real time, imagining exactly how it would feel, all 1000 metres of it, from the snap out the gate, right to the finish line. By the time the 60 seconds of visualization were done, the negative thought had gone. Magic! And to top it off, it was reinforcing the perfect performance in my mind, like a dress rehearsal in my head, many times a day.

DO NOT THINK ABOUT A PINK ELEPHANT!

Almost inevitably, as though Steve had a crystal ball, the Olympic record did fall before I stepped up for my ride. Not once though, but three times. The last rider to raise the bar before I took to the track was Arnaud Tournant of France, going inside the magical 61-second barrier for the first time ever.

I'm not saying it was easy, because it wasn't, but I managed to switch my thoughts to logical ones. You feel terrible just before riding a one-kilometre time trial. The pressure to get it right, and the pain that's waiting for you out on the track, they can all combine to make you dread the thought of riding. But if you think logically you can overcome the dread. You just focus on your rehearsed routine; it's the only logical thing you can do, the only thing you can control. I had visualized the perfect ride in my head so many times and physically I was ready. I was focused on the process of executing this performance, I wasn't thinking about the gold medal and I certainly wasn't thinking about Arnaud's new sea level World record.

As well as Arnaud's magnificent ride, several other things happened in Athens that I could have reacted emotionally to, but I didn't react emotionally. I used the logical side of my brain, and I won my first Olympic gold medal.

NEW TRICKS

Becoming Olympic Champion was something I'd dreamed about and worked toward for so many years. It's impossible to explain the feeling I got from achieving that goal, I kept the medal close by me for weeks afterward, as if to remind myself that it wasn't a dream and it had really happened. There were seemingly endless receptions and parties to celebrate on our return home from Athens, and I enjoyed every minute of them, but it wasn't long before I was itching to get back to the daily grind and begin the long journey toward the defence of my Olympic kilo title in Beijing 2008. Unfortunately, I had a shock coming.

Halfway through 2005 it was announced that, to make room for new events in the Olympic cycling programme, the one-kilometre time trial for men, and the 500-metre time trial for women, were to be dropped from the 2008 Olympic Games. That was a real body blow. I had the team sprint, but the only individual event I had any chance of being successful in was the kilo. Or so I thought.

There were two other individual sprint-based events: the keirin and the sprint. They were both far more chaotic than the one-kilometre time trial, a simple race against the clock, and they required tactical and technical nous, as well as power and speed. I liked the controllability of the kilo. To me, the keirin and the sprint were events full of variables outside of my control.

Tackling those variables would be my biggest challenge but, as ever with British Cycling, help was on hand. Jan van Eijden, a former World Champion in the sprint and team sprint events for Germany, was enlisted as Team GB's new sprint coach. He helped to break down the events for me, to simplify them, take away the chaos and encourage me to play to my strengths.

Learning the timing of when to unleash my effort was the toughest part of the sprint but, like anything, practice makes perfect: race after race, making mistakes, but learning along the way. I analysed videos of every ride, going over them with a fine-tooth comb, looking at the best sprinters in the world and picking apart their performances to learn from them, over and over until the penny dropped.

In the keirin, the number of variables is even greater due to the increased number of riders in each race. I decided my best chance of success was to control the race from the front, out of danger and dictating the pace. The downside to this approach was that from the perspective of physical effort it was by far the toughest way to do it. But I figured that with my background as a kilo rider I could train to manage two and a half laps flat out. Easier said than done.

Steve Peters was also able to help in the build-up to Beijing, but on a more generic level, helping to keep things in perspective. When your life revolves around trying to win Olympic and World titles you can sometimes get a bit too wrapped up in their importance. Steve would remind me of the fact that it wasn't life and death, to enjoy the process of what I did and to work on using logic during the stressful moments of a competition.

Beijing went as well as it could have. I won three gold medals and set one World record and two Olympic records, alongside my teammates Jason Kenny and Jamie Staff (see opposite). I have continued to use Steve's mental techniques, not only for the next four years leading up to London 2012, but also beyond, applying them to my everyday life to help deal with all sorts of things. It's amazing how useful they can be. Whether you've just been cut up by someone out on the road or your two-year-old son won't eat his greens, being able to stay calm is almost always the best approach!

3.11 VISUALIZATION

Visualization is a very useful mental technique in sport. You can use it to mentally rehearse races, visualizing yourself doing what you have to do perfectly. You can also use mental images to help you during a race. Visualization can even help build confidence and increase your awareness of what is going on around you.

MIND VIDEO

Visualization is the process of creating a mental image of what you want to happen, or how you want to feel, in a competition. It can take the form of daydreaming, where you see yourself riding an upcoming event, or even a training session, and everything is going perfectly. Or it could extend right up to a full-blown mental film, covering every bit of an upcoming race.

The former Olympic and time trial World Champion Fabian Cancellara would ride time trial courses as a recce, remembering every detail of them, then play back the route in his mind like a video. "While I think about what I've seen I add the sounds and the feel in my legs of going fast. I even add the pain you feel in a time trial, but never bad pain, just the good pain, the good sensation you feel in your legs when you

are trying really hard and going very fast," he said a few years ago when talking about his preparation for road time trials.

This is named by sport psychologists as to "intend" an outcome of a race. By imagining a scene, complete with images of previous good performances mixed with a desired outcome, a cyclist can almost step into the feeling he or she needs to have in the race.

Depending on what level an individual thinks and operates best – visual, auditory or feel – they can create images of an upcoming race. It might be an image of them mastering a climb in the race, hearing cheers from the crowd or even feeling their legs working perfectly.

It looks like Fabian Cancellara used three senses in his visualization practice and, in doing so, amplified the images

Fabian Cancellara winning gold in the road time trial at the 2016 Olympics.

in his mind, and that is an important point. When using imagery like this, try to brighten the picture that you see, make colours vivid and sounds clear and positive. The same goes for physical feelings: make them good, joyful and enjoyable.

As Cancellara said, he tried to feel the pain in his legs, but it was always a good pain, a manageable pain. And most cyclists would agree, that feeling of slight strain in the muscles when you are really bombing along, breathing deeply but very much on top of things, is a really positive sensation.

Visualize the times when everything went well on a bike ride, when you were flying along. Try to re-create that feeling in your mind, even down to the birdsong you heard, the smells, and how warm or cool it was. Then, when you've created a picture of the sights, sounds and feeling, dwell on it so your brain can create a pathway to access the same thoughts when you need them.

HOLDING BACK THE TIDE

Visualization can also be useful during a competition. The Irish rider Dan Martin has said he uses a visualization technique to control pain when he's climbing mountains, and Dan is a very good climber. He says he imagines the pain is water and its level is rising up his legs, and he uses his mind to force the level of water downward.

A few easy-to-remember mantras can help you gain confidence and persevere through tough sections of a race. Things such as, "I've trained for this, I can do it," or "I am strong." Don't use a negative mantra like "Push through the pain" or "Don't give up." You don't need "nots" in your mantra, and you really don't want to go anywhere near the word "pain". They both have negative connotations, which you don't need.

You can also use words as mental cues to remind yourself to focus on proper form when going up a hill or when you start to get tired. "Relax" is good, "stay loose" is too, and "wind it up" is especially helpful when you want to put pressure on opponents on a hill. And while I'm talking cues, the words "eat and drink" stuck onto your handlebar stem is a very practical cue to have.

MAKE TIME

It can be a good idea to set aside some time to really focus on visualization and practise it, at least until you become good at bringing to mind the positive words, feelings, sounds or images you require.

It's best to do this exercise alone. Close your eyes and imagine a good place, a place you like, a warm sunny beach or a garden in the summertime. Then, bring the images you want into your mind. See yourself in the situation you want to be in during a race and let your mind go.

It's good to throw different race scenarios into your visualization too, but always be the master of them. The outcome you want to see is your success. So that no matter what you imagine, say it's a rival attacking you, you control it quickly and easily. It's good fun actually, because you always win.

Dan Martin on the Col de Portet d'Aspet climb in the 2013 Tour de France.

3.11 **MENTAL TOOLBOX**

We've covered the major areas in which the way you think can affect your performance in sport. The following are important too, but they involve smaller shifts in thinking. You should see them as being mental tools that you can use in different aspects of training and competition.

CHANGE YOUR PERSPECTIVE

This is a very powerful mental tool that helps in cycling. It is possible to change how certain things feel by reframing them in your mind. Take riding in the wet. When you get down to it, unless it's lashing it down and/or really cold, riding in wet conditions isn't too bad once you get going. However, what we tend to remember and have imprinted in our brains are the first few minutes in the wet, when a spray of cold water is squirted up our backs, onto our legs and into our faces.

Think about when that's happened to you; it's unpleasant, isn't it? Try this though – while keeping the feeling of that horrible first splash of rainwater in your mind, create a picture of it, then diminish it. Fade the picture and the feeling it created down into the bottom left-hand corner of your mind, while at the same time bringing up a picture and a good feeling of bowling along, nicely warmed up, in the rain. Make the second picture, the good one, bigger and brighter; try to feel it more intensely too. Keep practising this. It's a tough tool to master, but it's worth it. You can use it for all sorts of aspects of cycling.

You can change perspective at all levels of cycling, even in the biggest competitions and challenges. When you get down to it, the Olympic Games cycling programme and Tour de France are really only races.

BE DOGGED

See things through. Stick to your training plan. Keep pushing until the end of each interval. In a sprint, keep going right until you cross the line, even when you get beaten. Carry on climbing hard, even if you are dropped from a group. If top cyclists share one thing, it's doggedness. Some of the best simply cannot accept defeat. They keep coming back until they win. Some win by simply refusing to be beaten.

Of course, you've got to look after yourself. You can't stick to a training plan when you are sick or injured. And you shouldn't stick to one that's obviously not working, perhaps because it's too demanding for the level of fitness you are at right now. Maybe dial it back a bit, but at the same time, give your training a chance to take hold.

Don't just give in because it hurts. Lifting weights can make you feel like that, leg exercises in particular. If you are just starting a weights programme your legs can really hurt after the first few sessions. Give the training a chance to take hold and let your body adapt to it. Then, if the pain continues, dial the sessions back a bit, reduce the load you are lifting and make sure your form is correct.

Many experts believe that it takes 10,000 hours of doing something before you reach your potential. That's a lot of riding. Stick at it, grit your teeth and see it through.

WHY ARE YOU CYCLING?

Understanding *why* you ride and why you want to do the things you want to do is very important. Once you are sure of the reasons why you ride a bike and what you want from it, it can help you to explain your desires to others. That can be invaluable in any relationship, from those with your boss or teachers to those with your loved ones.

DON'T MAKE EXCUSES

Make the best of what you have now and don't put things on hold until your perceived situation gets better. At the same time, there is no point in making too many excuses if you underperform. Okay, it's all right to have a bit of a grumble straight after something hasn't gone well for you, but park it afterward. Analyse why you didn't perform as well as you had hoped to and address what you need to do to improve. Excuses, although possibly comforting at first, won't help you to move on. "Could have" and "what if" never win races.

RACE HARD BUT UNDERSTAND TACTICS

Be wholehearted with your effort in a competitive situation. If you do that, win or lose, you know did your best. And doing your best is the only way to guarantee a satisfactory outcome from competition, because it's the only thing that you can control.

However, pay attention to tactics. It's a rare competitor who just rides away from everybody else. Races are more often than not decided by who uses the best tactics. Study races, but most of all study the races you've been in rather than the top professional ones you see on TV. The way big professional road races develop is quite unique because of all the teamwork going on. However, there are still a few things you can learn from watching big races, such as how breakaway groups form, and how riders work within them and win from small breakaway groups.

LIVE IN THE MOMENT WHILE HOLDING ONTO YOUR DREAMS

Focus on each aspect of your cycling as you do it. When you're planning, plan to the best of your ability. Focus on every single training session, and only that training session, as you do it. Then move on to the next. Focus even down to every repetition you do in a training session, focus on that one, then on the next, and so on.

In short, focus on what you are doing and don't let everything get jumbled up, or you'll end up going through the motions of training and not realizing your potential. And regard everything – training, recovery, eating or looking after yourself and your bike – as an essential step toward your goal. Because that's what it is.

3.11 **GETTING A GRIP ON PAIN**

Cycling very hard and really pushing yourself can hurt. Some of the training sessions I did hurt so much that I really dreaded them. I would ride so hard in each effort that I had to lie down after it, writhing in agony to recover. Then I had to do another, and another. Those were terrible days. I dreaded them.

Maybe you won't push that hard (although if you have big ambitions you will have to) but you will encounter discomfort quite regularly in cycling. It helps to know how pain works, because knowing the mechanisms of pain and discomfort can help you to cope with them, and to master them.

GATE THEORY

Pain is an essential mechanism for survival. It draws your attention to the fact that something could be wrong with your body. It's a signal that you should take action by removing the pain stimulus or otherwise stop what's causing it.

The best working explanation for the mechanics of pain is gate theory, which holds that the degree of pain felt can be influenced by independent factors. The use of the word "gate" in explaining pain helps to understand that pain is more acute when the gate is open, and less so when it's closed. The brain plays the pivotal role in opening and closing the "gate".

Professor Lorimer Moseley is a world-renowned expert on pain. He describes the working of the pain "gate" as a "gate cycle", where the brain processes messages it receives from the nervous system then interprets them in the light of its (your) experiences, amplifying or reducing the pain felt in accordance with those experiences.

In lectures he cites his personal experience of being bitten by an eastern brown snake, considered the second deadliest land snake in the world, while walking in the Australian bush. Moseley didn't see the snake bite him. He was next to some bushes and thought his leg had brushed against a twig, because he'd been scratched by a twig in similar circumstances. Within minutes however, Moseley was unconscious and fighting for his life.

Months later, after he'd recovered, Moseley was walking through the bush again, and this time his leg did brush against a twig. He collapsed in agony. The huge pain he felt was the result of messages from his brain sent in accordance with its snakebite experience, when he had only been lightly scratched by a twig.

Professor Moseley says, "Pain is not based on what is happening in the tissue, it's based on what the brain thinks is happening in the tissue." Appreciating that fact can help you reframe the pain you might feel when riding very hard on your bike. Yes, something is happening in your tissue – high muscle-fibre acidosis during really hard intervals, for example, but the pain is your mind's construction. Knowing that can help you to control it.

CONTROLLING PAIN

Most elite athletes have a high pain threshold; it's one of the reasons they can perform like they do. Their gates don't allow as much pain through as other people's might. Your brain can help you to establish a higher pain threshold too.

Training probably helps. Gate theory holds that pain is felt in the light of experience, so pushing hard and feeling the pain often, helps sportspeople grow more comfortable with it. The act of exercising itself helps you control pain as well, because of the release of endorphins, which are natural painkillers that work, like some manufactured painkillers, by closing the pain gate.

Rationalizing a situation also helps. Rationally, if you are suffering in a race, then so are your competitors. The thing is, it's very hard to think rationally when you are suffering. This closing anecdote might help you.

Sir Bradley Wiggins says that some advice given by a very experienced former teammate, Christian Vande Velde, helped him when he was making the transition from a world-class track cyclist to a world-class road racer. He says, "Christian told me that on a mountain stage of a Grand Tour every rider in the front group is just one kilometre from letting go, they are all suffering. So just do that one kilometre, then if you are still there at the end of it you hang on for another, and another, and so on. And eventually you get to the top, and you are still there."

It's good advice, and something I've repeated throughout this book – focus on what you are doing then move on to the next thing. Don't think about what you must do in a race or in training sessions as a whole. It's nice to know it works at the front of the Tour de France too.

PUTTING IT ALL TOGETHER

3.12 **PERFECT PERFORMANCE**

I get asked a lot if I ever achieved my own "perfect performance", a race that couldn't be improved upon. I don't think I ever got to where I could honestly say I didn't have any area that could have been better, even after winning a World title or an Olympic gold. I always reviewed my races and picked them apart with my coaches to try to find ways to go faster in the future. For the keirin or the sprint it was usually based on tactics, areas where I could have dictated the race better or left myself less vulnerable to attack. In the one-kilometre time trial it was more about aero position, pace judgment and line on the track. Sometimes it was all about my state of mind and how I had handled stressful points in the week of the competition.

YOUR BEST PERFORMANCE

Achieving your own best performance within the parameters you face in your life is what pushes most of us on in sport. For the vast majority of people, the parameters they have to work within involve family commitments, age, employment hours and/or studying, access to adequate facilities, financial support, coaching support and their genetic make-up. As an elite-level athlete, most of these barriers are removed to allow you to truly see where your physical potential lies. I was incredibly lucky to be one of those people who had the chance to live my dream and chase that elusive "perfect performance".

For the 99 per cent of the population who have to deal with all the other factors that limit their ability to commit fully to their sport, but still want to do the best they can within those parameters, striving to be the best you can be can still be an incredibly exciting and rewarding journey. It's easy to focus on the things holding you back instead of highlighting what you can do, but if you really plan your programme well and use your initiative you will surprise yourself how far you can go with limited time and resources.

In the early years, I wasn't lucky enough to have funding, coaching, indoor facilities or a great bike, and I was studying full time. But, along with a small group of club mates who were equally committed and determined, we found ways to make the most of what we had to get to the level where we could receive more support.

It's easy to listen to people who tell you that you can't do something. If you let their negativity creep in, then it will limit what you can achieve. Surround yourself with positive people and the chances of reaching your goal will improve dramatically. And you'll have a lot more fun too.

PITFALLS & TRAPS

So how do you go about achieving your own personal best? Well, of course it all starts with setting a goal, working back from there, creating a plan and committing to it. Treat each day as an opportunity to improve yourself and commit fully in every effort of every session, even if it's "just" another turbo session in your garage in the middle of winter and the big day seems a long way off. As my hero Graeme Obree used to say, "Gold medals are won on wet Tuesday afternoons." It's the hard yards you put in away from the big stage that set you up for success.

Take care of yourself, look after your diet, try to get the best recovery you can and don't worry too much if life gets in the way. Just do the best you can within the parameters you face.

So, to race day. What can you do there to help achieve your best? Well, it's often more a case of what you should not do. The biggest pitfall before a competition is suddenly to start thinking emotionally. Competition is stressful and unless we are careful our minds can react emotionally to stress. There have been competitors who ruin their chances just before their target race by listing to their emotional thoughts, which will inevitably pop up during stressful moments.

They start noticing the strengths of their opponents and they suddenly notice weaknesses in themselves. Often these observations are skewed. The other big thing that can derail people before an event is worrying about things that are out of their control. It's a classic mistake and there's no point to it. If something is out of your control you have no say over it, so leave it there. I know it's easier said than done but there it is. Focus on what you can directly affect, namely your own performance.

I suppose you could say the road to success has plenty of pitfalls and just before the event it's particularly littered with them. Focusing on the outcome – the medal, the victory or whatever you perceive is a successful outcome – can overtake you immediately before an event. The outcome depends on what your rivals do, so that's outside of your control. Focus on the process of what you need to do to be your best. If you do that then you give yourself the best possible chance of achieving what you want. The look of surprise on a lot of athletes' faces immediately after a race as they realize they have won is often down to this. They have focused so intently on themselves and their performance that they haven't considered the outcome until it happens. If you want to see the best example of this, check out Kelly Holmes' reaction to winning both of her races in the Athens Olympics.

Never change your game plan at the last minute based on emotional reactions. There might be grounds for changes if it's raining or the wind is blowing in an unexpected direction, but changing something just because of last-minute doubts or worries that your emotional thoughts have come up with will most likely have a negative effect on performance.

SAVING OUR BEST TOYS FOR RACING

One of the big things that other nations noticed was how the performance of British riders really stepped up at each Olympic Games. One of the big reasons that happened, aside from the periodization of our training to arrive in the best possible physical and mental state on the day that counted, was because we had a whole team of people working to create the optimal bikes and clothing for the big event. However, unlike other nations who were doing the same thing, we waited until the Games to bring the whole package out in one go. Our rivals would use any new piece of kit as soon as it was designed, incrementally improving over the four-year cycle, but not feeling the full benefit when it mattered most.

It wasn't just a physical matter of more speed for the same effort, taking the gains all at once was a huge mental boost. I loved the feeling when I won World titles on fairly standard equipment and clothing; it gave me confidence knowing that there was more to come. Using new kit was something you really looked forward to and anticipated with relish through the long hours, days and months of training between Olympics and it helped spur you on. Then, once on the track at each Olympic Games, the new kit felt so fast, which was very good for boosting positive thinking right before going into action. Sometimes I look back and wonder how much of the improvement we found was actually down to the psychological boost.

YOU TOO

Gaining a mental as well as a physical advantage by saving your best kit for racing is something everybody can do. Riding a great bike with all the performance bells and whistles on it is a fantastic feeling and there's no reason not to ride your best kit all the time if you're just riding for the pleasure of it. But when preparing for races there is a competitive advantage to be had by training on heavier, less aerodynamic kit. If you want a competitive edge, think about buying some ordinary non-aero wheels to train on and fit them with heavier tyres. There are other things you can try too. Save your race clothing for races so that it always feels special when you put it on. And if you race in an aerodynamic helmet, use a standard one for training. You can even add extra weight to yourself or your bike (for example, a brick in a saddlebag), 0.5 kilogram (1 pound) extra on a long climb will significantly increase your workload and you will notice it when you take it off.

I promise that when you put your best wheels on your race bike, dress in your race kit and put on your aerodynamic helmet, you will feel a lot better about the race. It's part of the routine of getting into the right frame of mind to compete. Give it a go and see what you think.

3.12 FULFILMENT – WHAT WINNING FEELS LIKE

In writing this book I've relived parts of my cycling career by having to reflect on what I did in various situations and how I trained and thought about cycling. It's interesting, looking back, to see how I'm able to use some things I did then in my everyday life now, even if it's as simple as trying in vain to react calmly and logically when the autosave failed while working on this book.

I'm often asked what it feels like to win an Olympic gold medal: is the first thing you feel a rush of joy? To be honest, personally my immediate emotions after winning were always disbelief and relief in equal measure. Particularly after winning at the Olympic Games.

The four-year build-up, with every race along the way merely a stepping stone, makes the Olympics feel different. The tension accumulates toward it, so the initial feeling after winning is often relief that it's all gone well. And the first time you become an Olympic Champion, after dreaming about it for so long? Well, the initial reaction to winning then is total disbelief. The joy comes shortly after.

ENJOYMENT

The reaction to winning might be relief or disbelief, but nonetheless it's an incredibly enjoyable experience. My cycling victories are among the best moments of my life so far. They have provided me with some amazing things to look back on with great satisfaction.

Winning means that everything you and those involved with you have done, what we've all worked for, has come together at the right time. The effort you've invested, the disciplined lifestyle, and the work and discipline of others, have all enabled you to produce a performance that reflects all the hard work you and your support team put in. That's an incredible feeling. It's something you feel together as well, something you share.

So relief is the first thing you feel, then satisfaction, then you have the medal ceremony. You stand on the podium, the national anthem plays and the flags are raised. For me, that was always emotional. I know I've talked about keeping emotion under wraps when you are competing, but I invested a lot of emotion into my daily routine and it came out during victory ceremonies.

It reflects that difference between process and outcome thinking I wrote about on page 188. Just because I was able to contain the emotion right before and during the race itself, doesn't mean that I was constantly in a controlled state, relaxed and thinking logically. Far from it. The fear of failure, the thought of not doing my best on the big day, and all the other doubts, were never far away, and it took a huge amount of work to contain these thoughts. It was often a case of the swan gliding along on the surface while below there was frantic action. So that moment when you could let it out was simply amazing, and sometimes it really did all come flooding out.

However, when I think about enjoyment in my cycling career, it most certainly isn't just confined to the races and podiums. It's more often related to the random fun moments that happened in all sorts of places. Airports, restaurants, hotels, gyms and cafés, all over the world, sometimes in countries that I would never have visited had it not been for cycling. Sharing these happy memories with your teammates and family is, without doubt, one of the best parts of having been an elite athlete for nearly 20 years. Sometimes the media can paint an image that elite sport is all suffering and misery. From my experience it was hard work, no doubt about that, but it was also fun.

REFLECTIONS

Looking back, would I change anything about my cycling career? I don't think I could have asked for any more from my time, even the disappointments, crashes and defeats (of which there were many) only served to shape my career and teach me lessons.

In terms of technical things I could have improved upon, I would definitely have paid more attention to my position on the bike, especially when I was younger. My sprint position wasn't the best, I struggled to keep my elbows in and they acted like an air brake. It's only when I got a bit further down the line

that I realized just how important riding position is, particularly for sprinters hitting peaks speeds just shy of 80kmph (50mph). I would have done so if I had taken the aero side of things more seriously from a young age. It's very hard to change something as fundamental as your riding position once you get older and have it set in stone. Like any skill, when you start to fatigue the bad habits tend to creep in, and I would always end each sprint or keirin with my elbows out catching the air. If you can develop good habits at a young age it will definitely pay dividends further down the line.

I also look back and see how far cycling has come in the UK. Both from a participation perspective and a performance one, the first two decades of the twenty-first century have been truly remarkable. To have witnessed it, and to have played a very small role in this transformation of our sport, gives me huge satisfaction. Cycling for the sake of it is still the joy it always has been, only now there are so many more people than ever before benefitting from it.

MOVING ON

I retired from competitive cycling in April 2013, although I still love riding my bike. It's what I do to keep fit. I still go to the gym too, doing some of the lifts I did in my strength and conditioning programme when I raced. And now and again I get competitive with myself, trying to see what I can still do, which is fun.

I've become a dad, which is absolutely fantastic. I have launched my own cycling brand, which takes up a lot of time and energy but is hugely enjoyable too. I'm an ambassador for UNICEF, Laureus Sport for Good Foundation and the Scottish Association for Mental Health. I do a spot of track cycling TV punditry with the BBC and I've also started writing kids' books, the *Flying Fergus* series. I've become an ambassador for Pure Gym and Science in Sport and run my own sportive, the "HOY100" since 2014, trying to encourage people to get out and enjoy riding their bikes. You'll still see me down at the velodrome every now and again, catching up with the team.

I also took up motor racing, which is great fun. It's another reason to train and keep fit, and it satisfies the desire to compete. At the same time, though, it's a sport where the training you do fits within a normal life and doesn't encroach too much on family time. I've done quite a few motor races now and I've even completed the Le Mans 24-Hour race, the first summer Olympian ever to do that.

There are other objectives I want to go for. I'd love to break the World record for cycling to the South Pole, and I'm working on a project aimed at trying to do that over the coming years. I've also always fancied having a go at setting a new human-powered land-speed record to follow in the footsteps of my hero and good friend Graeme Obree. And who knows, I might think up some more yet!

INDEX

ACKNOWLEDGEMENTS

This book has been a huge amount of fun to write and has reminded me just how much I still love discussing, analysing and thinking about cycling as well, of course, as actually doing it.

The first person I have to thank for making it possible is my agent and good friend Rob Woodhouse, who pitched the idea initially. Thanks also to the team at The Blair Partnership for their work in securing the publishing deal and to everyone at Octopus Books, in particular Pauline Bache and Yasia Williams, for their tireless work in getting the book edited, formatted and published, and Trevor Davies, for getting it all started.

A huge thanks to Chris Sidwells for his massive amount of work and support in helping me get it all down on paper. It was great to get to know you and we'll have to get out on the bikes for a spin sometime to carry on with our chats!

Thanks to Chris Terry and his crew for the fun photoshoots and for braving the weather up in the Peak District on that wet miserable day!

To all those people who contributed whether they realised or not, those who passed on their knowledge and experience to me over the years and helped me on my way. To Ray Harris and the Dunedin CC, Brian Annable and everyone at City of Edinburgh RC, all the coaching staff at British Cycling and Scottish Cycling, in particular Shane Sutton, Jan van Eijden and Iain Dyer, thank you.

Thanks to Steve Peters for everything I learned from you, which not only helped me get the best out of myself on the bike, but also in everyday life. This book's section on the mental side of cycling would have been pretty thin without having met you!

To everyone at Science In Sport for the assistance on the nutrition section and to Andy Jones for the use of some fantastic archive shots.

To Craig Maclean and Jason Queally, my former teammates, thank you for all your patience and inspiration, and for making me think about my training from different perspectives.

Finally, to my family; my Mum, Dad and sister Carrie for the love and support that allowed me to follow my dreams and turn a hobby into a professional career, and to my beautiful wife Sarra and kids Callum and Chloe.

PICTURE CREDITS

Special photography by Chris Terry

Additional photographic acknowledgements:
Alamy Stock Photo Ed Endicott 136; Evan Sklar 199; Roussel Images 187
Andy Jones 50, 51 above left & above right
Anthony Pepera Senior Graphic Designer at Science in Sport 167
@chrishoy1/Instagram 215
Dreamstime.com Imelda Kiss 43 above right; Oleg Zabielin 45 above right
Evans Cycles evanscycles.com 12-13
Getty Images 179; Artur Debat 27; Bettmann 81; Bryn Lennon 18 right, 35, 137, 147, 149, 183, 189, 213; David Stockman/AFP 26 left; Dean Mouhtaropoulos 193; Doug Pensinger 203; Godong/UIG via Getty Images 26 right; Harry How 214; Ian MacNicol 206; Jamie Squire 194; Kate Peters/Contour by Getty Images 98; Mark Dadswell 117; Michael Steele 211; Nathan Stirk 164; Odd Andersen/AFP 177; Phil Walter 41; Popperfoto 37, 175; Ryan Pierse 40; Simon Gill/Action Plus via Getty Images 169; Tim de Waele/Getty Images 127; Tommy Hindley/Professional Sport/Popperfoto 80
Mike King 191 above & below
Offside L'Equipe 32
REX Shutterstock Colorsport 17 above; Dave Shopland/BPI 202; John Pierce Owner PhotoSport Int 25; Oliver Weiken/EPA 200; Simon Kadula 51 below
Science Photo Library Martin Oeggerli 95
HOY bikes can be purchased at Evans Cycles. For more information on these, and all of the products available at Evans Cycles, please visit www.evanscycles.com